Design and Implementation of 3D Graphics Systems

Design and Implementation of 3D Graphics Systems

Jonas Gomes
Luiz Velho
Mario Costa Sousa

CRC Press
Taylor & Francis Group
Boca Raton London New York

CRC Press is an imprint of the
Taylor & Francis Group, an **informa** business

AN A K PETERS BOOK

CRC Press
Taylor & Francis Group
6000 Broken Sound Parkway NW, Suite 300
Boca Raton, FL 33487-2742

© 2013 by Taylor & Francis Group, LLC
CRC Press is an imprint of Taylor & Francis Group, an Informa business

No claim to original U.S. Government works

Printed in the United States of America on acid-free paper
Version Date: 20120621

International Standard Book Number: 978-1-4665-7121-1 (Paperback)

Visit the Taylor & Francis Web site at
http://www.taylorandfrancis.com

and the CRC Press Web site at
http://www.crcpress.com

To my family
—J.G.

To my father, Luiz Carlos
—L.V.

To my family
—M.C.S.

Contents

About the Cover

"The Liquid Dark Side of the Moon"

Simplicity itself, a jet black $12'' \times 12''$ square with a line drawing of a luminous white prism at its center. A thin beam of white light penetrates the left side of the prism at an angle and exits on the right, split into a fanned spectrum of glowing color.

My name is Dan Abbott and I work as part of a compact but busy design collective StormStudios, based in London, England. You may or may not be familiar with our work, but chances are you've stumbled across the image I describe above as the 1973 cover graphic to Pink Floyd's gazillion-selling "The Dark Side of the Moon" album. Of course the same graphic elements were already well rooted in the collective conscious well before 1973, thanks to the work of our old friend Isaac Newton, and reproduced in a thousand and one school science textbooks.

That the prism landed on the cover of Pink Floyd's seventh album was due to the efforts of my esteemed colleague and tormentor Storm Thorgerson, who at that time co-helmed influential sleeve design company Hipgnosis with Aubrey 'Po' Powell. Hitherto, Storm and Po's designs for Pink Floyd had been exclusively photographic in nature, but the band requested something graphic by way of a change. Hipgnosis rustled up seven exciting new designs and much to their surprise the band voted unanimously for the one with the prism. Storm claims he tried to talk them out of it, but their minds were all made up. Thus ends the fable of "How the Prism Got Its Album" and magically leapt from textbook to record racks worldwide.

Two decades later in 1993 history started to repeat itself—traditional practice in the rock 'n' roll universe. The Dark Side of the Moon was re-released in shiny, all new digitally remastered, twentieth anniversary CD form. So Storm decided to "remaster" the cover too, replacing the 1973 drawing with a photo of real light being refracted through a real-life glass prism. What could be more honest than that? Funnily enough, few fans seemed to notice the switcheroo, which I think might tell you something about the power of the basic setup of the image.

Ten years later still and it was suggested that the design be tweaked once again for the thirtieth anniversary re-release on SACD (which we were reliably informed was the absolutely definitive audio format of the future). Thirtieth anniversaries are very significant for all triangular life forms, so how could we refuse? So we built a four-foot square stained glass window to the exact proportions of the original design, and photographed it. "Hmm, maybe this idea's got legs after all" we thought. In the following years we created several further homages to the original design: a prism made of words for a book cover, a prism painted a-la Claude Monet, a Lichtenstein-esque pop art number, and rather curiously, a prism created entirely with fruit for a calendar (this probably came about after someone joked about calendars being made from "dates").

To execute the above-mentioned "Fruity Side of the Moon," we built a large wooden tray with each line of the design being a walled-off section, keeping all the dates, raisins, cranberries, apricots, oranges, and baby lemons in their right and proper positions. It was then photographed from above. I can't remember if we ate the contents afterwards, but shoots are hungry work so it's very likely. Later, one of us (might've been Pete, might've been Storm) inspected the empty tray and had the bright idea that colored paint or ink poured into the various sections might make yet another cool photo. The tray was quickly modified with any leaky corners made watertight, and the relevant hue of paint was poured into each section. The effect was smooth, glossy, and rather pleasing to the eye.

Then, the unplanned started to occur. The separate areas of paint began slowly but surely to bleed into each other. But rather than becoming a hideous mess the experiment began to take on a whole new dimension, and we experienced something of a eureka moment. We started helping the migrating paint go its own sweet way. A swish here, a couple of drips there, and soon the previously rather rigid composition began to unravel into a wild psychedelic jungle. Areas of leaking paint expanded into impressive swirling whorls and delicate curlicues of color, stark and vibrant against their black backdrop. Fine and feathery veins of pigment unfurled like close-ups of a peacock's plumage or like NASA photos of the gigantic swirls in Jupiter's atmosphere. Blobs and bubbles emerged organically bringing to mind Pink Floyd's early liquid light shows. Detail was crisp and went on and on, a feast for the eyes and seriously entertaining for us. All the time, our intrepid photographer Rupert was poised a few feet above, dangling with his camera from a gantry, snapping frame after frame. Our magic tray had done most of our work for us, and we christened the process "controlled random." All that remained was for us to select a couple of shots for use—a nigh-on-impossible task given the multitude of beautiful frames we'd captured.

And so we come to the most recent stop on our prismatic journey. A few months ago we received an email from Mario Costa Sousa. He had spied "Liquid DSoM" (as we came to call it) on our website and politely enquired as to whether he and his fellow authors might use it as the cover for their new computer graphics textbook. Our first response was a friendly "yes" followed by fairly patronizing words to the effect of, "But Mario dear, do you realize that we created this for real, that it's not computer generated in any way?" Mario, clearly a man with his head screwed on the right way round, calmly explained that it was just what was needed.

First off, the basic image of the prism diffracting a beam of light is central to light and color theory and a truly crucial element in computer graphics. Second, the controlled randomness of the paint as it flows in specific, distinct directions reflects algorithmic modeling techniques often used in computer graphics, particularly in procedural image synthesis. Third, they enjoyed the idea of featuring a hand-created real life image on the front of a computer graphics textbook, implying that a technical reader might gain valuable insights into the theory and practice of computer graphics by observing real-world phenomena. And fourth, I suspect the authors may also be Pink Floyd fans, but we'll leave that for another day.

How appropriate then, that our design, an image that some might say was cribbed from a school textbook, should wind up through a variety of fairly exotic twists and turns, back on the cover of a textbook. Nothing random about that, eh?

— Dan Abbott, StormStudios
London, December 2011

Preface

This book grew out of a course, Design and Implementation of 3D Graphics Systems, taught by the authors at the Institute of Pure and Applied Mathematics (IMPA), Rio de Janeiro, beginning in 1997. The course is part of the joint graduate program with the Catholic University of Rio de Janeiro (PUC-Rio) in computer graphics. These materials have also been used in recent years in a course for senior undergraduates and first year graduate students in the Department of Computer Science at the University of Calgary. Many students of mathematics, engineering, and computer science have attended these courses at IMPA, PUC-Rio, and the University of Calgary.

This book covers computational aspects of geometric modeling and rendering three-dimensional scenes. Special emphasis is given to the architectural aspects of 3D graphics systems. The text contains a description of basic 3D computer graphics algorithms, all implemented in the C language. This didactic material is complemented by library routines for constructing graphics systems. The routine libraries, examples, and other supplemental materials can be downloaded from the book's website:

http://www.crcpress.com/product/isbn/9781568815800

This book is the companion volume to *Computer Graphics: Theory and Practice* [Gomes et al. 12], which focuses on the conceptual aspects of computer graphics, the fundamental mathematical theories and models, as well as an abstraction paradigm for computational applied mathematics used to encapsulate problems in different areas of computer graphics.

Acknowledgments

Various colleagues collaborated on the initial volume from 1998 that gave origin to this book. Paulo Roma Cavalcanti gave us a great incentive for materializing this project. Paulo not only taught the course and created a set of initial notes, but also provided the very early preliminary reviews. Luiz Henrique de Figueiredo did a detailed and thorough review of some of the chapters and produced some of the illustrations that appear in the text, all properly credited. Many thanks to Margareth Prevot (IMPA, VisGraf Lab) who collaborated in the production of various images used in the text. We also thank everyone who allowed us to use figures from their works, all properly acknowledged in this book.

Various other colleagues read the preliminary versions of various chapters, saved us from some pitfalls, and gave us valuable suggestions. Among them, we can highlight Antonio Elias Fabris, Romildo José da Silva, Cícero Cavalcanti, Moacyr A. Silva, Fernando W. da Silva, Marcos V. Rayol Sobreiro, Silvio Levy, and Emilio Vital Brazil. We thank all sincerely. We also thank Jamie McInnis, Sarah Chow, and Patricia Rebolo Medici for their reviews and suggestions and for carefully editing and proofreading the book.

We sincerely thank Alice Peters for her dedication to this book project. We are honored to have the foreword in this book by Eugene Fiume and thank him for his inspiring words.

We are very grateful to Storm Thorgerson and Dan Abbott from StormStudios for giving us permission to use their original art photography "The Liquid Dark Side of the Moon" as our book cover. Many thanks to everyone else from StormStudios who helped to produce this art piece: Peter Curzon, Rupert Truman, Lee Baker, Laura Truman, Jerry Sweet, Charlotte Barnes, and Nick Baker. We would like to thank Dan Abbott very much for also describing "How the Prism Got Its Cover" as part of this book. Many thanks to Kara Ebrahim for working in the final cover layout design and production and to Dan Abbott for his valuable design suggestions.

The project of writing this book has been facilitated by the fruitful teaching and research environments of the computer graphics laboratory at IMPA (Visgraf Lab), and both the Department of Computer Science and the Interactive Reservoir Modeling and Visualization Group (*Illustra*Res/iRMV)/Computer Graphics Research Lab at the University of Calgary. Our sincere thanks go to all their members for their constant support. Finally, we sincerely appreciate the support from NSERC/Alberta Innovates Technology Futures (AITF)/Foundation CMG Industrial Research Chair program in Scalable Reservoir Visualization.

— Jonas Gomes, Luiz Velho, and Mario Costa Sousa
Rio de Janeiro and Calgary, December 2011

1 Introduction

This book covers practical aspects of computer graphics at an introductory level. The material presented focuses primarily on the fundamental algorithms of the area, the implementation problems associated with them, and the relationship between the various components of a graphics system.

1.1 Computer Graphics

Computer graphics is the study of computational processes involving *geometric models* and *digital images*. The relations between data and processes in computer graphics are illustrated in Figure 1.1.

From a computational point of view, we have two distinct types of *data*: models and images. The *processes* that can be applied to these data either modify a single tyep of data or convert the data from one type into another: Creating or modifying models is done by *geometric modeling*; manipulating images is called *image processing*. *Image synthesis*, used in the field of computer vision, is the transformation of geometric models into digital images.

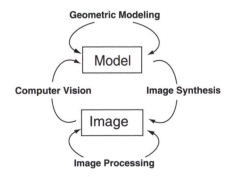

Figure 1.1. Data and processes in computer graphics.

The inverse transformation, from digital images to geometric models, is *image analysis*, used in the field of computer graphics, or visualization.

In this book, we will focus on geometric modeling and image synthesis. We will touch lightly on image processing, which is necessary in almost every type of image manipulation. This book will cover codification and quantization of images, but other important image processing techniques such as sampling, reconstruction, and deformations, which are used in texture mapping, are outside the scope of this book. Computer vision is also outside the scope of this book.

1.2   Scope and Applications

More specifically, we will study 3D computer graphics, treating the problem of modeling and images synthesis of 3D scenes. This may be the most complex and important part of computer graphics, and has many practical applications, including

☐ **Scientific visualization.** In this area, computer graphics is used for visualizing simulations and complex structures found in various scientific disciplines such as mathematics, medicine, and biology.

☐ **CAD / CAM.** In this area, computer graphics is used as a planning and design tool in engineering, architecture, and design applications.

☐ **Entertainment.** In this area, computer graphics is used for the creation of special effects and interactive programs in movies and television, as well as applications in thematic parks and games.

There are also applications of geometric modeling and image syntheses in 2D computer graphics and graphical interfaces. Both are quite important and have a significant intersection with 3D computer graphics; for example, 2D computer graphics is closely related to the graphics devices used for both visualization of images and construction of 2D elements, such as planar curves, used in the modeling of 3D objects. Despite the importance of these applications, due to their particularities they should be studied separately and so will not be covered in this book.

Human-computer interaction is part of any computational system, and in a graphics system, interface issues are very important. In this book, we will restrict discussion of graphical interfaces to a minimum and assume the reader has some familiarity with the existing interaction resources of a generic windows system.

1.3   Methodology

We have adopted a minimalist methodology in this book, meaning that the presented material will be restricted to the minimum necessary for understanding the basic computer graphics processes. Our goals with this method are to demystify the complexity of a graphics system and reveal the essential processes in computer graphics.

Overall, the material presented covers all the basic techniques of a 3D graphics system. For each problem, we will discuss the possible solution strategies, including their advantages and disadvantages. All will be presented in an algorithmic form. Finally, we will show the implementation of the most appropriate techniques for the construction of a simple graphics system.

1.4   System Architecture

In terms of systems, the processes we identified above appear in three basic modules of a graphics system, implementing the functions of modeling, image synthesis, and imaging.

The modeling module creates a geometric representation from the specifications of objects in a scene. The image synthesis module transforms this geometric description of the scene into a "virtual image" called a coloring (or shading) function. The imaging module creates a digital image from the shading function.

By combining the processes described above, we obtain the basic structure of a graphics system. This is illustrated in Figure 1.2. In this book, we will study how these modules are implemented.

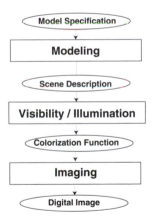

Figure 1.2. Structure of a graphics system.

1.5   Implementation and Extensions

We will develop three complete graphics systems, corresponding to the main architecture alternatives of a graphics system.

As we said, these systems were created for teaching purposes, and therefore their code is developed to be simple and clear, without much concern for efficiency or completeness. Despite this, they have all the essential functionality of a real graphics system and can be used as the embryo of a complete system. To do so, one would need to increase their efficiency, which would require some local changes to the algorithms implemented in the book, and their functionality, which would require introducing new, complementary algorithms.

We will try to guide this extension work by indicating existing options and suggesting what should be done in the implementation exercises of each chapter.

1.6   Implementation Paradigm

In this book we follow the implementation paradigm used in the UNIX-like GNU system development environment. Besides the C language, we will use the programs make for system compiling and yacc for generating interpreters, among other tools. This environment can be reproduced in the Windows system using the public domain utilities developed by GNU.

Communication between programs will be made using the C standard input and output mechanisms (*stdin* and *stdout*). This will allow to explore the UNIX pipeline resources that are quite appropriate for the architecture of our systems.

1.7   Graphic Standards

Given that this book is intended as an introduction, we do not use any programming resource besides the GNU development environment. This means we will not adopt specific libraries or graphics standards for the development of the systems studied in the book. We recognize the importance of graphics standards, but they are best used for the developing sophisticated programs in professional applications. But our choice to not use external programming resources in this book makes the material self-contained and independent.

The methods and algorithms we will study constitute the basis for the majority of important graphic standards, such as OpenGL, the VRML language, and Renderman. Therefore, their study will allow a better understanding and mastery of these standards. At the end of each chapter, we will explicitly describe how the studied algorithms fit in with the existing standards.

1.8   Advanced Applications and Future Studies

As previously stated, this book approaches 3D computing graphics in an elementary way. We explore the basic principles of this discipline with the goal of establishing a solid basis for advanced studies.

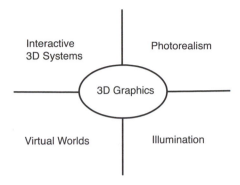

Figure 1.3. Advanced applications.

Starting from this basic kernel, future research can be developed in several directions. To position the reader, we contextualize those specializations, placing them in relation to the object of our study.

Computer graphics establishes the foundations of at least four main areas for more advanced studies: interactive graphic systems; graphics databases; photorealism; and physical illumination simulation. The relation between these areas and 3D computer graphics is shown in Figure 1.3.

In the area of interactive graphic systems, the OpenGL and Inventor standards are very important. In the area of multimedia and distributed graphics applications, we have the VRML language. In the photorealism area, we have the Renderman standard. In the area of physical illumination simulation we have radiance.

1.9   Content

The structure of the book reflects the structure of a graphics system. The book is organized in the following way:

- □ **Part 1.** Foundations

  - graphics devices
  - geometry
  - color
  - digital images

- □ **Part 2.** Modeling

  - description of scenes
  - geometric representation

- – construction of forms

- – composed objects and hierarchies

□ **Part 3.** Viewing

- – camera

- – clipping

- – rasterization

- – visibility

□ **Part 4.** Illumination

- – light and material

- – shading (colorization)

- – illumination models

- – mappings

Image synthesis, which involves visualization and illumination, is organized in two parts for didactic reasons. We therefore have four main parts naturally corresponding to the processes in computer graphics. In each part, we have individual chapters treating the various components of these processes.

As previously stated, our goal is to discuss computer graphics from a practical point of view. Therefore, this book uses three approaches in parallel:

□ analysis of the computational problem, presented in text form;

□ basic algorithms, presented in pseudocode form;

□ system implementation, presented in the C language;

What is more, each chapter includes a section with comments on references and implementation exercises.

1.10   Supplemental Material

Support material, which complements the book, is available at the http://www.visgraf.impa.br/cgtp. On this website the reader will find the source code with the implementation of all the algorithms presented in the book.

2 Objects and Graphics Devices

In this chapter we give a general conceptualization for graphics objects and show how they relate to graphics devices. From these concepts, we will present the 2D graphics library that will be used in the implementation of interactive programs discussed in this book.

2.1 Graphics Objects

To study computer graphics processes, ideally we would have an inclusive conceptualization that would allow us to understand the area as a whole. This conceptualization should be based on a mathematical model including the relevant objects in the area, such as geometric models and images.

The concept of a *graphics object* will be the starting point for constructing our analysis. From there we can define computer graphics as the area where graphics objects are studied. The processes in computer graphics include operations with graphics objects of a certain type, as well as conversions between different types of graphics objects.

A graphics object, $\mathcal{O} = (S, f)$, consists of a subset $S \subset \mathbb{R}^m$, and a function $f \colon S \to \mathbb{R}^n$; S is called the *geometric support* of $\mathcal{O}$ and determines the geometry and topology of the graphics object. Function f specifies the properties of $\mathcal{O}$ at each point $p \in S$ and is called the *attribute function* of the object (see Figure 2.1).

The dimension of object $\mathcal{O}$ is given by the dimension of its geometric support S. The several attributes of $\mathcal{O}$ correspond to 1D subspaces in the Euclidean space $\mathbb{R}^n$. For

Figure 2.1. Generic graphics object.

more information on graphics objects, see [Gomes et al. 96]. This definition is sufficiently general to include all of the relevant objects for computer graphics, such as points, curves, surfaces, solids, images, and volumes.

A family of graphics objects of great importance is constituted by the "planar graphics objects," for which $m = 2$; that is, the geometric support is contained on the Euclidean plane $\mathbb{R}^2$. Its relevance is due to the fact that the class of objects can be mapped directly into the usual graphics devices. These objects have dimension $\text{Dim}(S) \leq 2$ and correspond to points, curves, and planar regions (we exclude the set of fractals).

Two important examples of planar graphics objects are curves and polygonal regions. In general, these objects are used to represent, in an approximate way, curves and arbitrary regions on the plane. Another important example of graphics objects is a digital image. For more details on these graphics objects, see [Gomes and Velho 98].

2.1.1   Description of Graphics Objects

Two general forms exist to mathematically describe the geometric support of a graphics object: the parametric and the implicit forms.

In the *parametric* description, the set of points $p \in S$ is directly specified by function $g : \mathbb{R}^k \to \mathbb{R}^m$, where $k = \text{Dim}(S)$

$$S = \{(x_1, \ldots, x_m) \quad | \quad (x_1, \ldots, x_m) = g(u_1, \ldots, u_k)\}$$

In the *implicit* description, the points of S are indirectly determined by function $h : \mathbb{R}^m \to \mathbb{R}^{m-k}$

$$S = h^{-1}(c) = \{(x_1, \ldots, x_m) \quad | \quad h(x_1, \ldots, x_m) = c\}$$

Example 2.1 (Circle). To compare these two descriptions, we will use as example the unit circle (see Figure 2.2).

□ Parametric description: $(x, y) = (\sin(u), \cos(u))$, where $u \in [0, 2\pi]$.

□ Implicit description: $h^{-1}(1)$, with $h(x, y) = x^2 + y^2 = 1$.   □

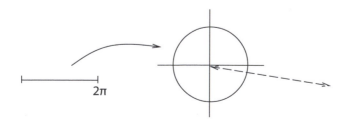

Figure 2.2. Parametric and implicit descriptions of a circle.

Notice the above descriptions constitute a continuous mathematical model of the geometry of a graphics object. Therefore, we have to obtain a finite representation of these models to work with them in the computer, which is a discrete machine.

2.1.2 Discretization and Reconstruction of Graphics Objects

The passage from a continuous to a discrete object is called *discretization*, or *representation* of the object. The inverse process, of recovering the continuous model from its discrete representation, is called *reconstruction*. Reconstruction can be exact or approximate, depending on the process as a whole.

For this end a simple form, widely used in practice, consists of discretization by point sampling and reconstruction by linear interpolation, as represented in Figure 2.3.

Consider a continuous function $f : \mathbb{R} \to \mathbb{R}$. Representation by uniform point sampling is given by the sequence of samples $(y_i)_{i \in \mathbb{Z}}$, where $y_i = f(x_i)$ corresponds to the value of f at the sampled points $x_i = x + i\Delta x$. The reconstruction is obtained from the samples (y_i) by linear interpolation $\overline{f}(x) = ty_i + (1-t)y_{i+1}$, where $t = x \bmod \Delta x$ e $i = \lfloor x/\Delta x \rfloor$. Notice in this case the representation provides only an approximate reconstruction; that is, $\overline{f} \approx f$ (see Figure 2.3).

Example 2.2 (Representation of Implicit and Parametric Objects). To construct a discrete representation of a circle starting from its parametric description, we discretize the parameter $u \in [0, 2\pi]$, making $u_i = i/2\pi$, $i = 0, \ldots, N - 1$, and evaluate $(x_i, y_i) = g(u_i)$, obtaining the coordinates of these N points on the circle. The circle representation is therefore given by this list of points (see Figure 2.4).

To construct a discrete representation of a unit disk starting from its implicit description, we discretize the environment space $\mathbb{R}^2$ and evaluate the implicit function $f(x_i, y_j)$ from a given regular grid $N \times M$. The representation will be given by the matrix A of dimensions $N \times M$. If $f(x_i, y_j) < 1$, we then make $a_{ij} = 1$, otherwise $a_{ij} = 0$. This representation corresponds to a discretization of the characteristic function of the disk (see Figure 2.4). □

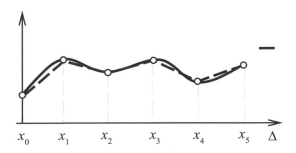

Figure 2.3. Sampling and reconstruction.

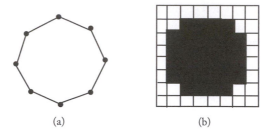

Figure 2.4. Formats of (a) vector and (b) raster (matrix) data.

2.2 Graphic Devices and Representation

A graphics device has a representation space in which we should map the object to be manipulated by the device. To visualize a graphics object $\mathcal{O} = (U, f)$, we need to obtain a representation of the object so that the discretized object can be mapped in the representation space of the device. Once mapped in this space, the device performs the reconstruction of the object, allowing its visualization.

2.2.1 Vector Devices

In vector devices, the representation space consists of points and straight line segments. More precisely, the representation space is a subset of the plane where we can assign coordinates to points; besides, given two points A and B, the device performs the reconstruction of the segment AB. These devices can be used to visualize polygonal curves and surfaces or polyhedral regions. In this case, we draw only the polygon edges of the representation, as shown in Figure 2.5(a).

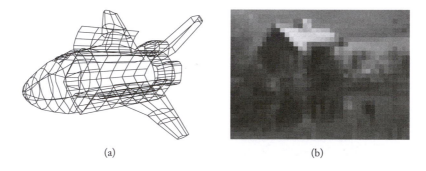

Figure 2.5. Visualization on a (a) vector and (b) raster (matrix) device.

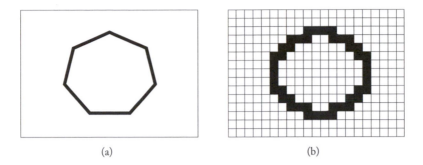

(a)   (b)

Figure 2.6. (a) Vector and (b) raster (matrix) representations.

2.2.2 Raster (Matrix) Devices

The representation space of these devices allows us to visualize a $m \times n$ matrix in which each point has a color attribute. Therefore, to visualize a graphics object in these devices we need to obtain a matrix representation of the object. For more details on raster representation of planar graphics objects, see [Gomes and Velho 98]. Raster devices are appropriate for visualizing digital images (see Figure 2.5(b)).

Example 2.3 (Rendering a Circle). We should have the appropriate representation to visualize (render) a graphics object in either a vector or raster device. For example, the visualization of a circle can be performed by representing the circle by a polygonal curve (see Figure 2.6(a)). To visualize the circle in a raster device, it must be *rasterized* (i.e., scan converted) to obtain its matrix representation (see Figure 2.6(b)). Notice the polygonal approximation of a circle can be displayed in a raster device; for this, the straight line segments constituting the sides of the polygon must be rasterized.   □

Some graphics objects are difficult, or even impossible, to appropriately visualize in vector devices. The visualization of a polygonal region can be obtained by placing hatch marks in the reconstruction, while in a raster device its visualization is immediate. The visualization of a digital image is very difficult in vector devices. Consequently, we generally use the vector format to represent geometric models and the raster (matrix) format to represent digital images.

Even so, both geometric models and digital images can be represented in any of these two formats. In fact, the concept of a graphics object allows a unified treatment of these two elements. On the one hand, we can consider an image as a Monk's surface and use differential geometry techniques in its processing. On the other hand, we can consider the coordinates (x, y, z) in the parametric space (u, v) of a surface as values of an image and in this way use image processing techniques for modeling purposes (see Figure 2.7).

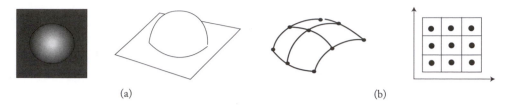

Figure 2.7. (a) An image as a model and (b) a model as an image.

2.3 Classification of Graphics Devices

User-computer interaction with graphics objects takes place through graphics devices.

2.3.1 Conceptualization

To classify graphics devices, we approach them from a paradigm of four universes: the physical world, mathematical models, their representations, and implementations. Thus graphics devices can be analyzed according to their use, functionality, graphics format, and implementation structure (see Figure 2.8).

Usage mode. The *usage mode* relates to the application for which the graphics device is intended. According to this criterion, graphics devices can be interactive and noninteractive.

Functional characteristics. The *functional characteristic* relates to the role of the device in the computational model. According to this criterion, graphics devices can be for input, processing, and output.

Data format. Devices can be classified as *vector* and *raster (matrix)*, according to the geometric nature of their representation space.

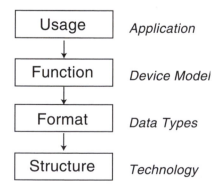

Figure 2.8. Abstraction levels of graphics devices.

Implementation structure. The *implementation structure* is determined by the technology used to construct the graphics device, as well as the usage, functionality, and format modes of the device. An example of different implementation structures for a device with the same function can be given by the calligraphic and matrix display devices: both are noninteractive graphics output devices, but the former adopts the vector format while the latter adopts the raster format.

2.3.2   Classification

Using the conceptualization above, we can classify graphics devices according to their functionality, and for each type, according to the graphics data format. In this way, we have graphics devices for input, processing, and output, in the vector and raster (matrix) formats.

Examples of vector input devices include mouse, Trackball and Joystick, operating with relative coordinates; and tablet, touch screen, and data glove, operating with absolute coordinates. Notice that all of them are 2D, except the date glove, which has six degrees of freedom. Examples of raster input devices include frame grabber, scanners, and range devices.

Examples of vector graphics processing devices are the graphics pipelines, such as the geometry subsystem of SGI. Examples of raster graphics processing devices are the parallel machines from Pixar and the Pixel Machine.

Examples of vector graphics output devices are plotter and vector displays. Examples raster graphics output devices are laser or inkjet printers, and CRT or LCD monitors. Vector graphics output devices were very common in the '60s and '70s. Raster devices became more prevalent in the '80s. Today, a good combination consists of using input vector graphics devices (mouse and tablet for instance) and raster output devices (CRT or LCD monitors and laser printers or inkjet).

2.4   Graphics Workstations

Above we saw examples of individual graphics devices. In practice, graphics devices are used in conjunction. For interactive applications, we combine input, processing, and output graphics devices into a complete graphics system.

Interactive graphics workstations are the most common class of graphics system. In fact, most current computers can be considered a graphics system.

In this book, we will assume that graphics implementation is aimed at a standard graphics system, formed by a raster output device, a vector input device, and a general purpose processor (see Figure 2.9). Vector graphics input descriptions are converted to raster descriptions by the windowing system of the graphics workstation.

Figure 2.9. Interactive graphics workstation.

2.4.1 Windowing System

A modern interactive graphics workstation is controlled by a graphics subsystem known as a *windowing system*. This subsystem is usually incorporated into the operational system of the machine and controls the graphics input, processing, and output functions. Windowing systems are based in the paradigm of the "desktop"; in other words, they implement the view of a work table with multiple documents. In this type of system, each window corresponds to a separate computational process. Examples of windowing systems are X-Windows for UNIX platforms, MS-Windows for PC platform, and the Desktop for Macintosh platforms.

2.4.2 Viewing Transformations

To visualize a planar graphics object, we define a window in the coordinate system of the object (*world coordinate system*, WC). This window should be mapped into a viewport in the display space of the device. To increase the degree of device independence, a system of normalized coordinates is used (*normalized device coordinates*, NDC). This system is defined in the rectangle $[0, 1] \times [0, 1]$ (see Figure 2.10).

In this case, the viewport is defined in normalized coordinates, and it is in this viewport that we map the window defined in the object space. The transformation that maps the points of the window into points of the viewport in normalized coordinates is called a *2D viewing transformation*. If the window is defined by the coordinates $(x_{\min}, y_{\min})$ and

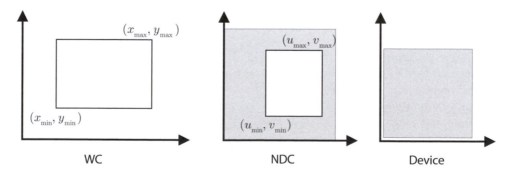

Figure 2.10. Viewing transformations.

$(x_{\max}, y_{\max})$ and the viewport is defined by $(u_{\min}, v_{\min})$ and $(u_{\max}, v_{\max})$, the viewing transformation is given by

$$u = \frac{u_{\max} - u_{\min}}{x_{\max} - x_{\min}}(x - x_{\min}) + u_{\min}, \qquad (2.1)$$

$$v = \frac{v_{\max} - v_{\min}}{y_{\max} - y_{\min}}(y - y_{\min}) + v_{\min}. \qquad (2.2)$$

For the final stage of the viewing process, the viewport (in normalized coordinates) is mapped into the graphics device.

The transformations between the window (in space coordinates), the viewport (in normalized coordinates), and the graphics device are obtained by a simple change of scaling in the coordinates, which alters the window dimensions (see [Gomes and Velho 98]).

2.5   The GP Graphics Package

A key problem related to the implementation of interactive graphics programs is *portability*. Ideally, graphics programs would indiscriminately work in any platform. At least, it would be desirable that the same code could be used for graphics devices of each basic type.

The solution to this problem the concept of *device independence*, which involves creating a programming layer to isolate implementation differences from the several devices. This layer is the *graphics package*. As in our conceptual schema of the four universes, this allows a common representation for different implementations.

2.5.1   GP Characteristics

In this book, we will adopt the GP (graphics package), originally developed by Luiz Henrique Figueiredo. The current version of GP was updated to work with OpenGL and SDL.

GP uses a representation space that allows only vector specifications. Starting from the vector specifications, GP performs the appropriate conversion to reconstruct the graphics object in the device being used. Because of this, we say that GP uses a vector metaphor to manipulate the graphics objects in both the input and output.

In general, GP assumes the existence of a graphics workstation composed of a 2D raster output device and a vector input device (besides the keyboard). The graphics subsystem of the workstation should be based on the windows paradigm.

The following characteristics of GP make it ideal for use in this book:

□ **Minimality.** GP implements an API (application programmer interface) that is minimal but enough for simple graphics programs.

□ **Portability.** GP is a device-independent package based on the paradigm of windows.

☐ **Separability.** The architecture of GP isolates the implementation details of the graphics API.

☐ **Availability.** The package supports most existing platforms.

To create these characteristics, the architecture of GP was divided in two separate layers: gp and dv.

The *gp* layer is responsible for 2D viewing transformations. The routines at this level are device independent and they have the purpose of mapping application coordinates into device coordinates.

The *dv* layer is responsible for controlling graphics devices. The routines of this layer are called by the routines of the gp layer. Routines at this level perform the conversion from vector description to a raster (matrix) representation of the device (rasterization). In other words, this layer implements the vector metaphor in the which GP is based. The dv layer should be implemented for each platform supported by GP. Implementation of this layer will not be discussed in this book.

The current implementation of the dv layer uses OpenGL for 2D vector graphics output and SDL for window creation and event handling. This is because OpenGL and SDL are two mature standards that are platform independent and fit well with the API model of GP. OpenGL uses the same 2D viewing paradigm of GP and is supported in hardware in most modern workstations. SDL (simple direct media layer) is a cross-platform multimedia library designed to provide low-level access to keyboard, mouse, and 3D hardware via OpenGL. It is very popular in the game community and has an event model very similar to GP.

2.5.2 Attributing Color in GP

Color is an important attribute of any graphics object. In GP, the attributes of graphics objects consist basically of the color of the vector primitives.

The color attribution process adopted in GP is based on the concept of a color map. This allows an indirect definition of colors in the GP representation space. A *color map* is the discretization of a curve in the color space. This discretization is represented by a table associating a numerical index $i \in \{0, \ldots 255\}$ to the color values of the device $c = (r, g, b)$, with $r, g, b \in [0, 1]$. This table is called *look up table* (LUT) (see Figure 2.11).

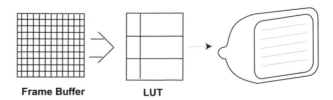

Frame Buffer   **LUT**

Figure 2.11. Color map.

This model is implemented in the majority of raster display devices. In these devices, the matrix representation is stored in the graphics board (frame-buffer), and the color of each representation cell (pixel) is obtained by performing an addressing in the LUT.

The routine gprgb allows us to associate a color to an index of the color map. The color is specified by the intensity values of the R, G, and B components. This routine returns the value 1 if the attribution can be performed, and 0 otherwise. In case the color index has the value -1, the color attribute is set for immediate usage. To support a full color device, it is convenient to use the immediate mode of gprgb that is implemented in the display with 24 bit RGB values.

```
int gprgb(int c, Real r, Real g, Real b);
#define gprgb dvrgb
```

Color attribution in gp is performed through the current color. This color is set in the immediate mode of gprgb or selected through the routine gpcolor. The parameter of this routine is an integer, indicating the table input containing the target color. This routine returns the index of the previous current color. When the specified index is not valid, it returns a negative number indicating the size of the color map.

```
int gpcolor(int c);
#define gpcolor dvcolor
```

2.5.3   Data Structure and Objects in GP

Given that GP is based on the windows model, the fundamental graphics object in GP is a *box*. This object consists of a rectangle on the plane whose sides are parallel to the coordinate axes. The geometry of this rectangle is given by the coordinates of its main diagonal $(xmin, ymin)$, $(xmax, ymax)$. Besides, we associate to this object a scaling attribute defined by the linear transformation $T(x, y) = (x \cdot xu, y \cdot yu)$. These scaling attributes are used to allow a change on the aspect ratio of the box, without requiring us to redefine the entire box.

The basic data structure of this object is the structure Box, given by

17   ⟨*Box data structure* 17⟩≡
```
   typedef struct {
     Real xmin, xmax;
     Real ymin, ymax;
     Real xu, yu;
   } Box;
```
Defines:
  Box, used in chunk 18a.

The box has therefore the dimensions xu (xmax - xmin) and yu (ymax - ymin). Notice that xu and yu are separate scale factors for each of the directions.

The internal state of GP is stored in the following data structure:

18a   ⟨*internal state* 18a⟩≡
```
static struct {
  Box w, v, d;
  real ax ,bx, ay, by;
} gp = {
  {0.0, 1.0, 0.0, 1.0, 1.0, 1.0},
  {0.0, 1.0, 0.0, 1.0, 1.0, 1.0},
  {0.0, 1.0, 0.0, 1.0, 1.0, 1.0},
   1.0, 0.0, 1.0, 0.0,
};
```
Defines:
   gp, used in chunks 18–21.
Uses Box 17 and real 46 46.

This structure consists of three boxes, w, v, and d, representing, respectively, the window in the 2D space of the scene to be visualized, the viewport in normalized coordinates, and the window of the graphics device.

The coefficients ax, bx, ay, and by will be used as scale factors to implement the 2D viewing transformations. Notice the initial state corresponds to the standard configuration, where all of the boxes are unitary (and consequently, the viewing mapping is the identity function).

A window in GP has a color attribute called *background color*. However, this color is not stored in the Box data structure. The background color is given by the color at the index $i = 0$ of the look up table. This color is attributed using one of the routines gppallete or gprgb (as previously seen).

The API of GP. The API of GP can be divided into four classes of routines according to function: control; viewing; drawing and text; and graphics input and interaction. We will next study in detail the routines of each of these classes.

2.5.4   Control Routines

We can deduce from GP's internal state that it supports only one window. The control routines in GP are for manipulating this window on the screen of the graphics workstation. The routine gpopen initializes GP and opens a window with its name passed as a parameter.

18b   ⟨*initialization* 18b⟩≡
```
real gpopen(char* name, int width, int height)
{
 real aspect;
 gp.d=*dvopen(name, width, height);
 calculate_aspect();
 gpwindow(0.0,1.0,0.0,1.0);
 gpviewport(0.0,1.0,0.0,1.0);
```

```
gprgb(0,1.,1.,1.);
gprgb(1,0.,0.,0.);
gpcolor(1);
return (gp.d.xu/gp.d.yu);
}
```
Uses calculate_aspect 19, dvopen, gp 18a, gpcolor, gprgb, and real 46 46.

This routine calls the dv layer to initialize the device. In this call, the box parameters of device d, structure gp are defined. The routine also creates a standardized window and viewport $[0, 1] \times [0, 1]$ by calling the routines gpwindow and gpviewport, respectively. These two routines will be studied next in the section on viewing routines. The routine calculate_aspect calculates the box scaling parameters of the device, so we can map a square window of maximum dimensions in the device:

19   ⟨*window aspect* 19⟩≡
```
static void calculate_aspect (void)
{
  if (gp.d.xu > gp.d.yu) {
    gp.d.xu /= gp.d.yu;
    gp.d.yu =  1.0;
  } else {
    gp.d.yu /= gp.d.xu;
    gp.d.xu  = 1.0;
  }
}
```
Defines:
    calculate_aspect, used in chunk 18b.
Uses gp 18a.

Notice the routine gpopen initializes the background color of the window as being white. The routine also attributes black to the index 1 of the color map, and the call to the routine gpcolor(1) attributes this color to the current color of the package.

The routine gpclose shuts down GP, eventually waiting for a certain time in case the parameter wait is positive, or for an action from the user in case wait is negative. This routine is implemented in the layer *dv*, which is why it is defined as a macro.

```
void gpclose(int wait);
#define gpclose dvclose
```

The routine gpclear clears the window by painting the background color. The parameter wait follows the convention described above.

```
void gpclear(int wait);
#define gpclear dvclear
```

The routine gpflush immediately executes all the pending operations for any graphics output. The routine gpwait pauses according to the parameter value t: $t > 0$ waits for t milliseconds; $t < 0$ waits for the user's input.

```
void gpflush(void);
#define gpflush dvflush

void  gpwait(int t);
#define gpwait           dvwait
```

2.5.5   Viewing Routines

The routines `gpwindow` and `gpviewport` are used to specify the 2D viewing transformation, as we saw in the previous section.

20a   ⟨*window* 20a⟩≡

```
real gpwindow(real xmin, real xmax, real ymin, real ymax)
{
  gp.w.xmin=xmin;
  gp.w.xmax=xmax;
  gp.w.ymin=ymin;
  gp.w.ymax=ymax;
  gpmake();
  dvwindow(xmin, xmax, ymin, ymax);
  return (xmax-xmin)/(ymax-ymin);
}
```

Uses gp 18a, **gpmake** 20c, and **real** 46 46.

20b   ⟨*viewport* 20b⟩≡

```
real gpviewport(real xmin, real xmax, real ymin, real ymax)
{
  gp.v.xmin=xmin;
  gp.v.xmax=xmax;
  gp.v.ymin=ymin;
  gp.v.ymax=ymax;
  gpmake();
  dvviewport(xmin, xmax, ymin, ymax);
  return (xmax-xmin)/(ymax-ymin);
}
```

Uses gp 18a, **gpmake** 20c, and **real** 46 46.

To calculate the viewing transformation coefficients between the window (in the space of the scene) and the viewport (in normalized coordinates), the routines `gpwindow` and `gpviewport` call the routine `gpmake`.

20c   ⟨*transformation* 20c⟩≡

```
void gpmake(void)
{
real Ax=(gp.d.xmax-gp.d.xmin);
real Ay=(gp.d.ymax-gp.d.ymin);
gp.ax = (gp.v.xmax-gp.v.xmin)/(gp.w.xmax-gp.w.xmin); /* map wc to ndc */
gp.ay = (gp.v.ymax-gp.v.ymin)/(gp.w.ymax-gp.w.ymin);
```

```
    gp.bx =  gp.v.xmin-gp.ax*gp.w.xmin;
    gp.by =  gp.v.ymin-gp.ay*gp.w.ymin;
    gp.ax = Ax*gp.ax;                              /* map ndc to dc */
    gp.ay = Ay*gp.ay;
    gp.bx = Ax*gp.bx+gp.d.xmin;
    gp.by = Ay*gp.by+gp.d.ymin;
    }
```

Defines:
  gpmake, used in chunk 20.
Uses gp 18a and real 46 46.

The viewing transformations are effectively realized by the routines gpview and gpunview, which map points from the application space to the graphics device space and vice versa.

21a   ⟨*view* 21a⟩≡

```
    void gpview(real* x, real* y)
    {
     *x=gp.ax*(*x)+gp.bx;
     *y=gp.ay*(*y)+gp.by;
    }
```

Defines:
  gpview, used in chunk 24.
Uses gp 18a and real 46 46.

21b   ⟨*unview* 21b⟩≡

```
    void gpunview(real* x, real* y)
    {
     *x=(*x-gp.bx)/gp.ax;
     *y=(*y-gp.by)/gp.ay;
    }
```

Defines:
  gpunview, used in chunks 23 and 24.
Uses gp 18a and real 46 46.

2.5.6   Drawing Routines

The drawing routines in GP specify the objects displayed in the device. In GP, polygonal curves (open or closed) and polygonal regions are called *polygonal primitives*. These primitives can be drawn using a combination of the routines gpbegin, gppoint, and gpend. The primitive is defined by the sequence of coordinates given by calls to gppoint, delimited by gpbegin and gpend. Notice this schema is similar to the one in OpenGL.

```
void gpbegin(int c);
#define gpbegin dvbegin

void gpend(void);
#define gpend dvend
```

```
int gppoint(Real x, Real y)
{
 gpview(&x,&y);
 return dvpoint(x,y);
}
```

The type of primitive polygonal is specified by the parameter c of the routine gpbegin.

- ☐ l   open polygonal curve

- ☐ p   closed polygonal curve

- ☐ f   filled polygon

An example of using this schema is in the implementation of routine gptri, which draws a triangular region given by

22   ⟨triangle example 22⟩≡

```
    void draw_triangle(real x1, real y1, real x2, real y2, real x3, real y3)
    {
      gpbegin('f');
       gppoint(x1,y1);
       gppoint(x2,y2);
       gppoint(x3,y3);
      gpend();
    }
```

Defines:
    draw_triangle, never used.
Uses gpbegin, gpend, gppoint, and real 46 46.

Text routines. A text is a sequence of alphanumerical characters. The most common attributes of a text are the color of the characters, the family type of the fonts (Helvetica, Times, etc.), and the variations of the font in each family (bold, italic, etc.). GP uses a fixed-size vector font.

The routine gptext draws a sequence of characters s at the position (x, y)

```
void gptext(Real x, Real y, char* s, char* mode)
#define gptext dvtext
```

2.5.7   Routines for Graphics Input and Interaction

In general, several input devices exist in a workstation. The most common devices are the keyboard and the mouse. The keyboard is used for alphanumerical data entry, and the mouse is used as a locator; that is, a device allowing the user to specify positions on the screen. The mouse also has buttons allowing the user to define different states of the device.

The user's actions with the devices are captured by the system in a process called *pooling*: the devices are continuously verified by the system, and a queue is created, where each queue input contains the identification of the device and the data related to the user interaction with the device. This queue is called the *event queue* of the system.

The gp, in general, supports the mouse and keyboard as input devices. In this way, it allows access to a queue of events where we have actions from the keyboard, buttons, and relative mouse position (locator). There are also other events allowing to verify the state of the device (e.g., an event to inform there was a change in the size of a window).

The access to events queue is performed by a single data input routine gpevent, allowing the user to interact with the system. This routine is used to retrieve the first event from the event queue associated to the window in GP. The parameter wait determines the behavior of the routine.

□ wait!=0   waits until the next event.

□ wait == 0   returns if the queue is empty.

23   ⟨*event* 23⟩≡

```
char* gpevent(int wait, real* x, real* y)
{
  int ix,iy;
  char* r=dvevent(wait,&ix,&iy);
  *x=ix; *y=iy;
  gpunview(x,y);
  return r;
}
```

Defines:
  gpevent, never used.
Uses dvevent, gpunview 21b, and real 46 46.

The routine returns events according to the code below:

bi+	button i is pressed
bi-	button i is released
kt+	key t is pressed
ii+	cursor not moving with button i pressed
mi+	cursor moving with button i pressed
q+	window closed by the windowing manager
r+	request for redrawing
s+	window has new size (x, y)

Button events. In a standard hardware configuration used by GP, the button devices correspond to the mouse buttons. The sequence of data of this event begins with the character b, followed by a digit, 1, 2, or 3, identifying the button, and finally the + sign to indicate that the button was pressed or − to indicate it was released. In short, the sequence of button events has the format bi+ or bi −.

Locator events. The mouse, besides being a button device, is also the standard locator used in a workstation. Mouse motion events begin with the character m. In this case, the position of the mouse is stored in the parameter (x, y) of the routine gpevent. Note that simultaneous mouse motion events using buttons are also preceded by the character m. For example, the mouse motion with the button i pressed is indicated by the sequence mi+.

Keyboard events. When the keyboard key k is pressed, it returns the string "kt+", indicating the event, where t is the ASCII code of the key.

2.6   Comments and References

The reader can find more information on planar graphics objects and representation in [Gomes and Velho 98]. Further information on graphics devices can be found in [Gomes and Velho 95].

The external API of GP is composed of the following routines:

24   ⟨*API* 24⟩≡

```
    real    gpopen          (char* name);
    void    gpclose         (int wait);
    void    gpclear         (int wait);
    void    gpflush         (void);
    void    gpwait          (int t);

    real    gpwindow        (real xmin, real xmax, real ymin, real ymax);
    real    gpviewport      (real xmin, real xmax, real ymin, real ymax);
    void    gpview          (real* x, real* y);
    void    gpunview        (real* x, real* y);

    int     gppalette       (int c, char* name);
    int     gprgb           (int c, real r, real g, real b);
    int     gpcolor         (int c);
    int     gpfont          (char* name);

    void    gpbegin         (int c);
    int     gppoint         (real x, real y);
    void    gpend           (void);

    void    gptext          (real x, real y, char* s, char* mode);

    char*   gpevent         (int wait, real* x, real* y);
```

Defines:
    gpevent, never used.
Uses **gpbegin**, **gpclear**, **gpclose**, **gpcolor**, **gpend**, **gpflush**, **gppoint**, **gprgb**, **gptext**,
    gpunview 21b, **gpview** 21a, **gpwait**, and **real** 46 46.

2.6.1   Programming Layer

The GP graphic library implements the lowest layer of an interactive graphics program. It is restricted to the 2D component and corresponds to the 2D functionality of the OpenGL library.

Exercises

1.   Compile and install the GP library.

2.   Using the GP library, write an interactive program to model polygonal curves. The program should write the curve as a list of points.

3.   Using the GP library, write a program to read files with polygonal curves and to draw them.

4.   Design and implement a toolkit interface consisting of the following 2D widgets: button, valuator, choice, text area, and canvas.

5.   Using the toolkit of the previous exercise, write a program showing a menu composed of several buttons. When a button is pressed, the program should print the text on the button.

6.   Using the toolkit of the previous interface, write a program showing a valuator. When the valuator is modified, the program should print the corresponding value.

7.   Combine the programs of the previous exercises to implement a complete editor for polygonal curves. It should contain a menu for the different functions (to read a file, to write a file, to clean the screen, etc.), valuators for window scaling and translations, and editing functions associated to the mouse buttons (to insert a vertex, to move a vertex, to delete a vertex).

8.   Modify the editor for polygonal curves to also work with Bézier curves. Use a subdivision algorithm for the visualization by curve refinement. Figure 2.12 shows the example of a curve editor.

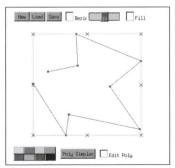

Figure 2.12. Curve editor.

3 Interaction and Graphical Interfaces

This chapter is devoted to the development of interactive programs and the design of user interfaces. It builds on the the infrastructure of the **gp** 2D graphics package introduced in the previous chapter. This chapter covers event treatment, interface actions with callbacks, interaction objects with multiple views, interface managers, toolkits, and widget design, and concludes with an example of an actual graphics interactive program: a polygonal line editor.

3.1 Creating Interactive Programs

Using the simplicity of the function `gpevent`, it is possible to develop graphical interfaces that possess great complexity and a high degree of interactivity. The interaction will be *event driven*, which makes the implementation easier.

In developing a good interface, we need to take into account two main elements. The first is graphical input/output. We need to decide how the user is going to specify the various graphical objects of the program and their behavior. For example, one can create a line segment in a drawing program by simply marking two distinct points on the screen. Or one could use a rubber banding technique, which involves first defining the initial point of the line segment as an anchor, and subsequently dragging the cursor to the line endpoint, as an elastic string. Note that both techniques can be used to produce the same result: creating a line segment. But the rubber band method gives more control and visual feedback to the user.

The other element to take into consideration is the interface design. We must create a global architecture of interactive objects that reflects the internal state of the program and allows the user to interact with its parameters. This is done through widgets and an interface manager. Continuing with the previous example, the whole interface could be made of a set of buttons for creating, deleting, and modifying line segments. They would be associated with various interactive methods, such as rubber-banding and others.

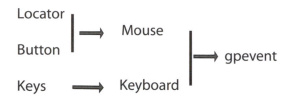

Figure 3.1. Logical input devices.

3.2   Interaction Fundamentals

Graphics interaction is basically a process by which the user manipulates objects though various logical commands. Usually this process involves the combination of graphics output devices, such as a graphics display, and graphics input devices, such as a mouse. At the core of the interaction we have a feedback loop such that user actions are depicted on the screen, reflecting changes of state caused by these actions.

3.2.1   Graphical Feedback

Graphical feedback essentially couples input and output, such that the graphics objects involved behave like real and active entities to the user. An *event*, which is caused by an input action of the user, such as moving the mouse, should trigger a corresponding reaction in terms of graphics output. For example, when the mouse moves, the image of the cursor on the screen changes accordingly. In that way, the user knows that the system understood the gesture and also can see the current state of the parameters (in this case the mouse location relative to the screen).

3.2.2   Logical Input Elements

We have already seen in the previous chapter the main abstractions for device-independent graphics *output*, and the basic mechanisms for events.

The next step is to develop the concept of *logical input elements*, which provide graphics *input* functions. Logical input elements include locators, buttons, and keys. As can be seen in Figure 3.1, these logical input elements are usually associated with the mouse and keyboard. They interface with the gp graphics package through the function gpevent.

The locator provides input for 2D coordinates relative to the window coordinate system. The buttons provide binary state values (i.e., pressed or released), while the key are associated with the ASCII character set.

3.2.3   Overview

The process of interface design entails the coupling of graphical input and output through some feedback implementation model and the construction of an architecture for an interface manager that coordinates interaction objects.

Feedback implementation models. The most common feedback implementation models are pooling, direct event handling, callbacks, and boxed callbacks. In the next sections, we study these models in more detail.

Interface manager architectures. The architecture for interface design consists of a package that includes several elements for the construction of interactive programs. The main components of an interface package are

- **Toolkit.** Contains a set of prepackaged *widgets* (i.e., interface objects) for the various common interaction tasks, such as selecting an option from a menu or entering a text string. Section 3.5 presents the architecture and implementation of a simple toolkit.

- **Interface builder.** Allows the user to graphically create the interface layout.

- **Runtime manager.** Implements the feedback model during program execution.

3.3 Interaction Mechanisms

In order to discuss and compare interaction mechanisms, we are going to show the pseudocode of simple programs exemplifying their usage and implementation.

3.3.1 Noninteractive

The simplest graphics program is noninteractive. Its structure consists of an initialization to create a window and a sequence of drawing commands to display something on the screen.

```
main()
{
  gpopen();
  gpwindow();
  gpviewport();
  // set gpattributes
  // execute drawing primitives
    .
    .
  gpclose();
}
```

3.3.2 Event Driven

The basic event-driven interactive program uses the function gpevent to explicitly handle all graphics input and to perform the associated output action.

```
main()
{
  gpopen();
  gpwindow();
  gpviewport();
  draw_initial_state();
  while (!quit) {
        e = gpevent();
        parse_exec_event(e) ;
  }
  gpclose();
}
```

Notice that the major implementation burden fall on the function `parse_exec_event`, which is responsible for explicitly handling all interaction.

```
parse_exec_event(e)
{
  switch (e) {
  case k:  // key pressed
      .

      .
      .
  case m: // mouse movement
      .

      .
      .
 }
}
```

As the program gets more complex and the interface more involved, this model becomes very difficult to extend and maintain. The reason is that each input event must be handled explicitly, taking into account the affected objects and the state of the program. For example, when a key is pressed, it may have different meanings depending on where the mouse is located or which object is selected.

3.3.3   Callback Model

The callback model comes to the rescue of the difficulty presented by direct handling of input events. It uses events but associates particular events to specific graphical objects or interface conditions.

For example, a particular function can be associated with the action of pressing the left mouse button. Under this model, that function is called whenever the mouse button is pressed; thus, it is referred as *callback* function.

```
main()
{
  gpopen();
```

```
gpwindow();
gpregister("b1+", f1, d1);
gpregister("b2+", f2, d2);
     .
     .
     .
gpmain_loop ()
gpclose()
}
```

So, in the initialization phase, the user defines all callback actions through the function gpregister. Subsequently, the interaction loop is implemented by the function gpmain_loop, which handles the events automatically by calling the desired actions at the appropriate times. In this way, the behavior of the interaction can be changed by simply replacing the implementation of callbacks.

3.3.4   Callback with Multiple Views

The callback model can be greatly improved by establishing a link between events and graphical objects. Note that in the general callback model, the event association is global, i.e., the same callback is activated for a particular class of event, such as a mouse button press.

The callback with multiple views model associates a local event to an action. For example, a different callback is activated depending on where the mouse button is pressed.

This model is implemented with the help of *multiple views*. The screen is tiled with different areas and they different local actions.

For example, the function

```
mvreg(1,"b1+",displ1,id1);
```

specifies that the callback displ1(id1) will be activated if mouse button 1 is pressed in the screen area v1. The function

```
mvreg(2,"b1+",displ2,id2);
```

specifies a similar action displ2 for screen area v2.

Of course, in this model it is possible to maintain global events. This is done by a special identifier (-1) for the whole screen.

```
mvreg(-1,"=q",exit,0);  //  call exit(0) if key 'k' is pressed in any area
```

The callback with multiple views is the model we are going to adopt to build our toolkit infrastructure. Under this model the structure of an interactive program is as follows:

```
main()
{
 gpopen()
 mvopen()
```

```
interface_setup()
mvmain_loop ()
gpclose(0)
}
```

The configuration of the interface is done by the function `interface_setup`, which defines each view area and the corresponding callbacks, as well as the initial state of the interface.

```
interface_setup()
{
  mvviewport(1, x, x, y, y)
  .
  mvregister (1, , x, 0)
  .
  draw_initial_state()
}
```

In the next section we will describe the implementation of the for the multiple view callback model.

3.4   Interface Objects

Graphical interface objects can be created using the multiple view callback model discussed in the previous section. The multiple viewport framework allows interface objects to be associated with areas of the screen, while the callback framework makes these objects active by an event-driven graphical feedback.

The `mvcb` package provides an integrated implementation of these frameworks.

3.4.1   Multiple Viewports

The multiple viewport framework essentially provides a tiled screen manager on top of gp. This is done by implementing the abstraction of *multiple views*. Each view behaves exactly like the gp package, but is confined to a particular screen area.

The internal state of mv consists of a set of views, each defined by a window and viewport. There is also the notion of a *current view*, to which all the gp commands apply.

32   ⟨*mv internal state* 32⟩≡
```
        static int      nv;                /* number of views */
        static Box*     w;       /* windows */
        static Box*     v;       /* viewports */
        static int      current;    /* current view */
```
Defines:
  current, used in chunks 33–35.
  nv, used in chunks 33, 35b, and 36a.
  v, used in chunks 33, 35–39, 41c, and 44.
  w, used in chunks 33–35 and 42–44.

The main control functions of gp are replicated in the mv package to encapsulate the corresponding functionality.

33a ⟨ *mv open* 33a⟩≡

```
int mvopen(int n)
{
if (n<=0) return 0;
v=(Box*) emalloc(n*sizeof(Box)); if (v==0) return 0;
w=(Box*) emalloc(n*sizeof(Box)); if (w==0) return 0;
nv=n;
current=0;
for (n=0; n<nv; n++) {
  w[n].xu =  w[n].yu = 1.0;
  mvwindow(n,0.0,1.0,0.0,1.0);
  mvviewport(n,0.0,1.0,0.0,1.0);
}
return 1;
}
```

Defines:
  mvopen, used in chunk 40b.
Uses current 32, mvviewport 33d, mvwindow 33c, nv 32, v 32, and w 32.

33b ⟨*mv close* 33b⟩≡

```
void mvclose(void)
{
efree(w);
efree(v);
}
```

Defines:
  mvclose, used in chunk 41a.
Uses v 32 and w 32.

33c ⟨*mv window* 33c⟩≡

```
void mvwindow(int n, real xmin, real xmax, real ymin, real ymax)
{
if (n<0|| n>=nv) return;
w[n].xmin=xmin;
w[n].xmax=xmax;
w[n].ymin=ymin;
w[n].ymax=ymax;
}
```

Defines:
  mvwindow, used in chunks 33a and 42a.
Uses nv 32, real 46 46, and w 32.

33d ⟨*mv viewport* 33d⟩≡

```
void mvviewport(int n, real xmin, real xmax, real ymin, real ymax)
{
```

```
        if (n<0|| n>=nv) return;
        v[n].xmin=xmin;
        v[n].xmax=xmax;
        v[n].ymin=ymin;
        v[n].ymax=ymax;
    }
```
Defines:
  mvviewport, used in chunks 33a, 34c, and 42a.
Uses nv 32, real 46 46, and v 32.

34a   ⟨*mv clear* 34a⟩≡
```
    void mvclear(int c)
    {
      int old=gpcolor(c);
      int n=current;
      gpbox(w[n].xmin,w[n].xmax,w[n].ymin,w[n].ymax);
      gpcolor(old);
    }
```
Defines:
  mvclear, never used.
Uses current 32 and w 32.

The auxiliary function mvframe draws an outline around the view, making it easier to see its area on the screen.

34b   ⟨*mv frame* 34b⟩≡
```
    void mvframe(void)
    {
      int n = current;
      gpline(w[n].xmin,w[n].ymin,w[n].xmax,w[n].ymin);
      gpline(w[n].xmax,w[n].ymin,w[n].xmax,w[n].ymax);
      gpline(w[n].xmax,w[n].ymax,w[n].xmin,w[n].ymax);
      gpline(w[n].xmin,w[n].ymax,w[n].xmin,w[n].ymin);
    }
```
Defines:
  mvframe, used in chunk 43b.
Uses current 32 and w 32.

The function mvdiv divides a rectangular area of the screen into a tiling of nx by ny views.

34c   ⟨*mv divide* 34c⟩≡
```
    void mvdiv(int nx, int ny, real xvmin, real xvmax, real yvmin, real yvmax)
    {
      int i,n;
      real dx=(xvmax-xvmin)/nx;
      real dy=(yvmax-yvmin)/ny;
      for (n=0,i=0; i<ny; i++)
      {
```

```
      int j;
      real ymax=yvmax-i*dy;
      real ymin=ymax-dy;
      for (j=0; j<nx; j++,n++) {
        real xmin=xvmin+j*dx;
        real xmax=xmin+dx;
        mvviewport(n,xmin,xmax,ymin,ymax);
      }
    }
  }
```

Defines:
  mvdiv, used in chunk 35a.
Uses mvviewport 33d and real 46 46.

The function mvmake applies mvdiv to the whole screen area.

35a   ⟨*mv make* 35a⟩≡

```
    void mvmake(int nx, int ny)
    {
      real x,y;
      if (nx>ny) {
        x=1.0;
        y=((real)ny)/nx;
      } else {
        x=((real)nx)/ny;
        y=1.0;
      }
      mvdiv(nx,ny,0.0,x,0.0,y);
      gpviewport(0.0,x,0.0,y);
    }
```

Defines:
  mvmake, never used.
Uses mvdiv 34c and real 46 46.

The function mvact makes the specified view active, i.e., it becomes the current view.

35b   ⟨*mv activate* 35b⟩≡

```
    int mvact(int n)
    {
      int old=current;
      if (n<0|| n>=nv) return old;
      gpwindow(w[n].xmin,w[n].xmax,w[n].ymin,w[n].ymax);
      gpviewport(v[n].xmin,v[n].xmax,v[n].ymin,v[n].ymax);
      current=n;
      return old;
    }
```

Defines:
  mvact, used in chunks 36a and 43b.
Uses current 32, nv 32, v 32, and w 32.

3.4.2   Callback with Views

The callback model is implemented for multiple views by creating a mechanism that associates events with views. For this purpose the function mvevent is defined.

36a   ⟨*mv event* 36a⟩≡

```
char* mvevent(int wait, real* x, real* y, int* view)
{
 int n; real gx,gy, tx,ty;
 char* r=gpevent(wait,&gx,&gy);
 if (r==NULL) return r;
 gpview(&gx,&gy); tx=gx; ty=gy;
 gpwindow(0.0,1.0,0.0,1.0);
 gpviewport(0.0,1.0,0.0,1.0);
 gpunview(&gx,&gy);
 *view=-1;
 for (n=0; n<nv; n++) {
  if (gx>=v[n].xmin && gx<=v[n].xmax && gy>=v[n].ymin && gy<=v[n].ymax) {
   int old=mvact(n);
   gpunview(&tx,&ty);
   *x=tx;
   *y=ty;
   *view=n;
   mvact(old);
   break;
  }
 }
 return r;
}
```

Defines:
   mvevent, used in chunk 38a.
Uses mvact 35b, nv 32, real 46 46, and v 32.

The callback abstraction is implemented through a list of events patterns that are matched to views.

36b   ⟨*mv callbacks state* 36b⟩≡

```
typedef struct event    Event;

struct event {
 int v;
 char* s;
 MvCallback* f;
 void* d;
 Event* next;
};

static Event*   firstevent=NULL;
static int      gp_wait=1;
```

Defines:
  firstevent, used in chunk 37.
  gp_wait, used in chunks 37b and 38a.
Uses **next** 37a 46 and **v** 32.

For convenience we define the following macros:

37a ⟨*mvcb macros* 37a⟩≡

```
#define new(t)                ( (t*) emalloc(sizeof(t)) )
#define streq(x,y)            (strcmp(x,y)==0)
#define V(_)                  ((_)->v)
#define S(_)                  ((_)->s)
#define F(_)                  ((_)->f)
#define D(_)                  ((_)->d)
#define next(_)               ((_)->next)
#define foreachevent(e)       for (e=firstevent; e!=NULL; e=next(e))

static Event*   findevent     (int v, char* s);
static Event*   matchevent    (int v, char* s);
static int      match         (char *s, char *pat);
```

Defines:
  D, used in chunks 37b and 38a.
  F, used in chunks 37b and 38a.
  findevent, used in chunk 37b.
  foreachevent, used in chunks 38b and 39a.
  matchevent, used in chunk 38a.
  new, used in chunks 37b and 47.
  next, used in chunks 36b, 37b, and 47.
  S, used in chunks 37–39.
  streq, used in chunk 38b.
  V, used in chunks 37–39.
Uses **firstevent** 36b, **match** 39b, and **v** 32.

The function **mvregister** associates a callback action to a particular event and view.

37b ⟨*mv register function* 37b⟩≡

```
MvCallback* mvregister(int v, char* s, MvCallback* f, void* d)
{
 MvCallback* old;
 Event* e=findevent(v,s);
 if (e==NULL) {
  static Event* lastevent=NULL;
  e=new(Event);                          /* watch out for NULL! */
  V(e)=v;
  S(e)=s;
  F(e)=NULL;
  next(e)=NULL;
  if (firstevent==NULL) firstevent=e; else next(lastevent)=e;
  lastevent=e;
 }
```

```
old=F(e);
F(e)=f;
D(e)=d;
if (s[0]=='i' && f!=NULL) gp_wait=0;
return old;
}
```

Defines:
    mvregister, used in chunks 40b and 43a.
Uses D 37a, F 37a, findevent 37a 38b, firstevent 36b, gp_wait 36b, new 37a 46, next 37a 46,
    S 37a, V 37a, and v 32.

The mvmainloop is the function that actually implements the runtime callback model
matching events to views.

38a   ⟨*mv mainloop* 38a⟩≡
```
void mvmainloop(void)
{
  for (;;) {
  real x,y;
  int v;
  char* s=mvevent(gp_wait,&x,&y,&v);
  Event*e=matchevent(v,s);
  if (e!=NULL && F(e)(D(e),v,x,y,s))
     break;
  }
}
```

Defines:
    mvmainloop, used in chunk 41b.
Uses D 37a, F 37a, gp_wait 36b, matchevent 37a 39a, mvevent 36a, real 46 46, and v 32.

The functions findevent and matchevent are used to query the list of event patterns
when an event is processed.

38b   ⟨*find event* 38b⟩≡
```
static Event* findevent(int v, char* s)
{
  Event* e;
  foreachevent(e) {
  if (V(e)!=v) continue;
  if (s==NULL && S(e)==NULL) break;
  if (s==NULL|| S(e)==NULL) continue;
  if (streq(S(e),s)) break;
  }
  return e;
}
```

Defines:
    findevent, used in chunk 37b.
Uses foreachevent 37a, S 37a, streq 37a, V 37a, and v 32.

39a   ⟨*match event* 39a⟩≡
```
static Event* matchevent(int v, char* s)
{
 Event* e;
 foreachevent(e) {
   if (V(e)<0|| V(e)==v)
     if (match(S(e),s)) break;
 }
 return e;
}
```
Defines:
  matchevent, used in chunk 38a.
Uses foreachevent 37a, match 39b, S 37a, V 37a, and v 32.

The actual pattern matching of strings is done by the auxiliary function match.

39b   ⟨*match string* 39b⟩≡
```
static int match(char *s, char *pat)
{
 if (s==NULL) return pat==NULL;
 if (pat==NULL) return s==NULL;
 for (; *s!=0; s++, pat++) {
   if (*s!=*pat) return 0;
 }
 return 1;
}
```
Defines:
  match, used in chunks 37a and 39a.

3.5   Toolkits

The tk toolkit package builds on top of the mvcb package to create interface objects (i.e., widgets). Rectangular areas of the screen are associated with such objects, and the tk library implements the proper feedback for each type of widget. This is done by registering specific callbacks for each active widget.

For example, a *pushbutton* widget will have as a state a binary value (on / off), and it will be materialized as a box on the screen with text over a black or white background, depending on the current value. Every time the user clicks on the button, it changes state and the callback function informs the user program that the value has changed. Notice that the graphical feedback is handled automatically by the widget.

In summary, the toolkit creates a layer of abstraction that implements basic interface objects to be used by the application program.

Figure 3.2. Essential widgets: (a) button, (b) slider, (c) selection, and (d) text area.

3.5.1   Basic Elements

The central issue in the design of an interface toolkit is the definition of the set of widgets to be implemented and the mechanisms for creating new widgets.

Here we are going to suggest a minimum set of widgets that implement the essential functionality of a general user interface. The minimum toolkit is composed of the following widgets: button, slider, selection, text area, and graphics canvas. A simple graphical depiction of each widget is shown in Figure 3.2.

3.5.2   The TK Package

The widget API consists of functions for creating and destroying widget instances, mapping and unmapping them on the screen. These functions are

```
w = create_widget (pos, par, fun)
destroy_widget (w)
map_widget (w)
unmap_widget (w)
```

The internal state of the package has a vector of widget pointers, the size of the vector, and the last available entry in the vector.

40a   ⟨tk local state 40a⟩≡
```
Widget **wa = NULL;
int wn = 0;
int wi = 0;
```
Defines:
   wa, used in chunks 40–42.
   wi, used in chunks 40–42.
   wn, used in chunks 40–42.
Uses Widget 44c.

The basic functionality of the runtime interface manager is implemented through the functions tk_open, which initializes the interface; tk_close which terminates the interface, and tk_mainloop, which handles the interaction loop.

40b   ⟨tk initialization 40b⟩≡
```
void tk_open(int n)
{
```

```
    int i;
    mvopen(n);
    wa = NEWARRAY(n, Widget *);
    for (i=0; i<n; i++)
      wa[i] = NULL;
    wn = n;
    wi = 0;
    mvregister(-1,"r",tk_redraw,NULL);
    gpflush();
  }
```

Defines:
  tk_open, never used.
Uses mvopen 33a, mvregister 37b, tk_redraw 41c, wa 40a, wi 40a, Widget 44c, and wn 40a.

41a ⟨*tk close* 41a⟩≡

```
  void tk_close()
  {
    efree(wa);
    wa = NULL; wn = wi = 0;
    mvclose();
  }
```

Defines:
  tk_close, never used.
Uses mvclose 33b, wa 40a, wi 40a, and wn 40a.

41b ⟨*tk main loop* 41b⟩≡

```
  void tk_mainloop()
  {
    mvmainloop();
  }
```

Defines:
  tk_mainloop, never used.
Uses mvmainloop 38a.

The function tk_redraw is used to display all the current active widgets on screen.

41c ⟨*tk redraw* 41c⟩≡

```
  int  tk_redraw(void* p, int v, real x, real y, char* e)
  {
    int i;
    fprintf(stderr, "redraw\n"); fflush(stderr);
    for (i=0; i<wi; i++) {
      switch (wa[i]->type) {
      case TK_BUTTON:
        button_draw(wa[i], 1); break;
      default:
        error("tk"); break;
      }
```

```
    }
    gpflush();
    return 0;
}
```
Defines:
  tk_redraw, used in chunk 40b.
Uses button_draw 43b, real 46 46, redraw 47, TK_BUTTON, v 32, wa 40a, and wi 40a.

A new widget is instantiated by calling the function tk_widget and specifying its type and parameters.

42a   ⟨*tk widget* 42a⟩≡
```
    Widget* tk_widget(int type, real x, real y, int (*f)(), void *d)
    {
      Widget *w = widget_new(type, x, y, 0.2, f);
      if (wi >= wn)
        error("tk");
      w->id = wi++;
      wa[w->id] = w;
      mvwindow(w->id, 0, 1, 0, 1);
      mvviewport(w->id, w->xo, w->xo + w->xs, w->yo, w->yo + w->ys);
      switch (type) {
      case TK_BUTTON:
        button_make(w, d); break;
      default:
        error("tk"); break;
      }
      return w;
    }
```
Defines:
  tk_widget, never used.
Uses button_make 43a, mvviewport 33d, mvwindow 33c, real 46 46, TK_BUTTON, w 32, wa 40a,
  wi 40a, Widget 44c, widget_new 42b, and wn 40a.

The internal function widget_new creates a generic widget object that should subsequently be bound to a specific widget class.

42b   ⟨*new widget* 42b⟩≡
```
    Widget* widget_new(int type, real x, real y, real s, int (*f)())
    {
      Widget *w = NEWSTRUCT(Widget);
      w->id = -1;
      w->type = type;
      w->xo = x; w->yo = y;
      w->xs = w->ys = s;
      w->f = f;
      w->d = NULL;
      return w;
    }
```

Defines:
  widget_new, used in chunk 42a.
Uses real 46 46, w 32, and Widget 44c.

A new widget class is defined in the tk framework by specifying functions for creation and drawing, as well as the interaction mechanism, which is handled through callbacks under the mvcb package.

As an example of creation of a new widget class, we show how to define a button widget. This is done through the functions button_make and button_draw.

43a ⟨*make button* 43a⟩≡
```
void button_make(Widget *w, char *s)
{
  mvregister(w->id,"b1+",button_pressed,w);
  mvregister(w->id,"b1-",button_released,w);
  w->d = s;
  button_draw(w, 1);
}
```
Defines:
  button_make, used in chunk 42a.
Uses button_draw 43b, button_pressed 44a, button_released 44b, mvregister 37b, w 32,
  and Widget 44c.

43b ⟨*draw button* 43b⟩≡
```
void button_draw(Widget *w, int posneg)
{
  char *label = w->d;
  int fg, bg;
  if (posneg) {
    fg = 1; bg = 0;
  } else {
    fg = 0; bg = 1;
  }
  mvact(w->id);
  gpcolor(fg);
  gpbox(0., 1., 0., 1.);
  gpcolor(bg);
  gptext(.2, .2, label, NULL);
  mvframe();
  gpflush();
}
```
Defines:
  button_draw, used in chunks 41c, 43, and 44.
Uses mvact 35b, mvframe 34b, w 32, and Widget 44c.

The button behavior is defined through the callbacks button_pressed and button_released which handle respectively the events button press and release.

44a   ⟨*press action* 44a⟩≡

```
int  button_pressed(void* p, int v, real x, real y, char* e)
{
  button_draw(p, 0);
  return 0;
}
```

Defines:
   button_pressed, used in chunk 43a.
Uses button_draw 43b, real 46 46, and v 32.

44b   ⟨*release action* 44b⟩≡

```
int  button_released(void* p, int v, real x, real y, char* e)
{
  Widget *w = p;
  button_draw(w, 1);
  return w->f();
}
```

Defines:
   button_released, used in chunk 43a.
Uses button_draw 43b, real 46 46, v 32, w 32, and Widget 44c.

A widget object is defined by a data structure that contains its ID, type, position, and size on screen, as well as local data and an application callback function.

44c   ⟨*widget data structure* 44c⟩≡

```
typedef struct Widget {
  int id;
  int type;
  real xo, yo;
  real xs, ys;
  void* d;
  int (*f)();
} Widget;
```

Defines:
   Widget, used in chunks 40 and 42–44.
Uses real 46 46.

3.5.3   Example

As an example of a graphics interactive program that uses the tk toolkit to generate its interface, we show below a simple application that creates two buttons on screen: one for printing a value and the another for quitting the program. Figure 3.3 shows the interface layout of the program.

```
int main(int argc, char* argv[])
{
  Widget *w0;
  gpopen("tk test", 512, 512);
```

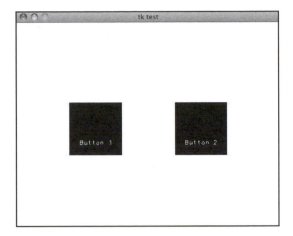

Figure 3.3. Example of interactive program using TK.

```
    tk_open(10);
    tk_widget(TK_BUTTON, .2, .5, but1, "Button 1");
    tk_widget(TK_BUTTON, .6, .5, but2, "Button 2");
    tk_mainloop();
    tk_close();
    gpclose(0);
}

int but1()
{
    fprintf(stderr, "Button 1 pressed\n"); fflush(stderr);
    return 0;
}

int but2()
{
    fprintf(stderr, "Button 2 pressed - quitting\n"); fflush(stderr);
    return 1;        // exits the main loop when 1 is returned.
}
```

3.6   Polygon Line Editor

As an example of the use of a graphics canvas, we show in this section the implementation of a polygon line editor application. Note that the program implements a rubber banding method for line input, as discussed in the introduction of this chapter. The screen of the program is depicted in Figure 3.4.

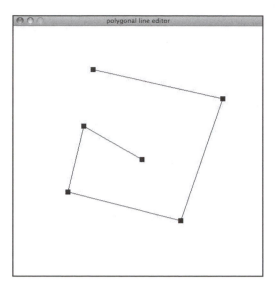

Figure 3.4. Polygon line editor.

46   ⟨*ple state* 46⟩ ≡

```
#define TOL       tol

typedef struct point     Point;

struct point {
 real   x,y;
 Point* next;
 Point* prev;
};

void    redraw          (int clear);
void    delpoints            (void);
void    showpolygon     (void);
void    showspline      (void);
void    showpoints      (void);
void    addpoint             (real x, real y);
void    movepoint       (real x, real y);
void    delpoint             (real x, real y);
void    startmove       (real x, real y);
void    endmove         (real x, real y);
void    showchange      (Point* p, int c);
void    showpoint       (Point* p);
void    showside             (Point* p, Point *q);
Point* findpoint        (real x, real y);
```

```
Callback
 do_polygon,
 do_quit,
 do_redraw,
 do_addpoint,
 do_startmove,
 do_endmove,
 do_delpoint,
 do_movepoint;

#define X(p)            ((p)->x)
#define Y(p)            ((p)->y)
#define new(t)  ((t*)emalloc(sizeof(t)))
#define next(p) ((p)->next)
#define prev(p) ((p)->prev)

static Point*           firstpoint=NULL;
static Point*           lastpoint=NULL;
static Point*            moving=NULL;
static int                  showingpolygon=1;
static int                  showingpoints=1;
static real                 xmin = 0, xmax = 1, ymin = 0, ymax = 1;
static real                 aspect = 1, tol = 0.1;
```

Defines:
   findpoint, never used.
   firstpoint, used in chunk 47.
   lastpoint, used in chunk 47.
   moving, used in chunk 47.
   new, used in chunks 37b and 47.
   next, used in chunks 36b, 37b, and 47.
   prev, used in chunk 47.
   real, used in chunks 18, 20–24, 33–36, 38a, 41, 42, 44, and 47.
   showingpoints, used in chunk 47.
   showingpolygon, used in chunk 47.
   TOL, used in chunk 47.
   X, used in chunk 47.
   Y, used in chunk 47.
Uses addpoint 47, delpoint 47, delpoints 47, do_addpoint 47, do_delpoint 47,
   do_endmove 47, do_movepoint 47, do_polygon 47, do_quit 47, do_redraw 47,
   do_startmove 47, endmove 47, movepoint 47, redraw 47, showchange 47, showpoint 47,
   showpoints 47, showpolygon 47, showside 47, and startmove 47.

47   ⟨*ple functions* 47⟩≡
```
     int main(int argc, char* argv[])
     {
     gpopen("polygonal line editor", 512 * aspect, 512);
     gpwindow(xmin,xmax, ymin,ymax);

     gpmark(0,"B"); /* filled box mark */
```

```
gpregister("kp",do_polygon,0);
gpregister("kq",do_quit,0);
gpregister("kr",do_redraw,0);
gpregister("k\f",do_redraw,0);
gpregister("b1+",do_addpoint,0);
gpregister("kd",do_delpoint,0);
gpregister("b3+",do_startmove,0);
gpregister("b3-",do_endmove,0);
gpregister("m3+",do_movepoint,0);

gpmainloop();
gpclose(0);
}

void redraw(int clear)
{
 if (clear)
   gpclear(0);
 if (showingpolygon)
   showpolygon();
 showpoints();
 gpflush();
}

void delpoints(void)
{
 firstpoint=lastpoint=NULL;       /* lazy! */
}

void addpoint(real x, real y)
{
 Point* p=new(Point);
 X(p)=x;
 Y(p)=y;
 next(p)=NULL;
 if (showingpoints) showpoint(p);
 if (firstpoint==NULL) {
  prev(p)=NULL;
  firstpoint=p;
 } else {
  prev(p)=lastpoint;    next(lastpoint)=p;
  if (showingpolygon) showside(lastpoint,p);
 }
 lastpoint=p;
}
```

```
void delpoint(real x, real y)
{
 Point* p=findpoint(x,y);
 if (p!=NULL) {
  if (prev(p)==NULL) firstpoint=next(p); else next(prev(p))=next(p);
  if (next(p)==NULL) lastpoint=prev(p);  else prev(next(p))=prev(p);
  redraw(1);
 }
}

void startmove(real x, real y)
{
 moving=findpoint(x,y);
 if (moving!=NULL) {
  x=X(moving); y=Y(moving);
  gpcolor(0);    gpplot(x,y); gpcolor(1);
  gpmark(0,"b"); gpplot(x,y);
 }
}

void movepoint(real x, real y)
{
 if (moving!=NULL) {
  showchange(moving,0);
  X(moving)=x; Y(moving)=y;
  showchange(moving,1);
 }
 else startmove(x,y);
}

void endmove(real x, real y)
{
 if (moving!=NULL) {
  gpmark(0,"B");
  redraw(0);
  moving=NULL;
 }
}

Point* findpoint(real x, real y)
{
 Point* p=firstpoint;
 for (p=firstpoint; p!=NULL; p=next(p)) {
  if ((fabs(X(p)-x)+fabs(Y(p)-y))<TOL) break;
 }
```

```
 return p;
}

void showpoints(void)
{
 Point* p;
 for (p=firstpoint; p!=NULL; p=next(p))
  showpoint(p);
 gpflush();
}

void showpolygon(void)
{
 Point* p;
 for (p=firstpoint; p!=NULL; p=next(p))
  showside(p,next(p));
 gpflush();
}

void showpoint(Point* p)
{
 gpplot(X(p),Y(p));
}

void showside(Point* p, Point *q)
{
 if (p!=NULL && q!=NULL) gpline(X(p),Y(p),X(q),Y(q));
}

void showchange(Point* p, int c)
{
 gpcolor(c);
 showpoint(p);
 if (showingpolygon) {
  showside(prev(p),p);
  showside(p,next(p));
 }
 gpflush();
}

int do_clear(char* e, real x, real y, void* p)
{
 delpoints();
 redraw(1);
 return 0;
}
```

```
int do_polygon(char* e, real x, real y, void* p)
{
 showingpolygon=!showingpolygon;
 redraw(1);
 return 0;
}

int do_quit(char* e, real x, real y, void* p)
{
 return 1;
}

int do_redraw(char* e, real x, real y, void* p)
{
 redraw(1);
 return 0;
}

int do_addpoint(char* e, real x, real y, void* p)
{
 addpoint(x,y);
 gpflush();
 return 0;
}

int do_startmove(char* e, real x, real y, void* p)
{
 startmove(x,y);
 gpflush();
 return 0;
}

int do_endmove(char* e, real x, real y, void* p)
{
 endmove(x,y);
 gpflush();
 return 0;
}

int do_delpoint(char* e, real x, real y, void* p)
{
 delpoint(x,y);
 gpflush();
 return 0;
}
```

```
int do_movepoint(char* e, real x, real y, void* p)
{
 movepoint(x,y);
 gpflush();
 return 0;
}
```

Defines:
   addpoint, used in chunk 46.
   delpoint, used in chunk 46.
   delpoints, used in chunk 46.
   do_addpoint, used in chunk 46.
   do_clear, never used.
   do_delpoint, used in chunk 46.
   do_endmove, used in chunk 46.
   do_movepoint, used in chunk 46.
   do_polygon, used in chunk 46.
   do_quit, used in chunk 46.
   do_redraw, used in chunk 46.
   do_startmove, used in chunk 46.
   endmove, used in chunk 46.
   findpoint, never used.
   main, used in chunks 313, 317, and 318c.
   movepoint, used in chunk 46.
   redraw, used in chunks 41c and 46.
   showchange, used in chunk 46.
   showpoint, used in chunk 46.
   showpoints, used in chunk 46.
   showpolygon, used in chunk 46.
   showside, used in chunk 46.
   startmove, used in chunk 46.
Uses firstpoint 46, lastpoint 46, moving 46, new 37a 46, next 37a 46, prev 46, real 46 46,
   showingpoints 46, showingpolygon 46, TOL 46, X 46, and Y 46.

3.7   Review

In this chapter we presented an architecture for interface design that has four layers, as show in Figure 3.5. The first layer is the graphics interactive program; the second layer is the interface toolkit, implemented by the tk package and the mvcb library. The third layer is the graphical input and output, implemented by the gp package. The fourth layer is the window system, which is platform-dependent, for example, X11 in the Linux platform, Vista in the Microsoft Windows platform, and Aqua/Cocoa for the MacOS X platform.

3.8   Comments and References

In this chapter we presented the implementation of a library for interface design in computer graphics. Some of the popular toolkit libraries are QT, GTK, FLTK, and GLUI.

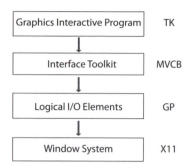

Figure 3.5. Implementation layers.

3.8.1 Summary

The external API of the MVCB library is composed of the following routines:

```
int     mvopen  (int n);
void    mvclose (void);
void    mvwindow(int n, real xmin, real xmax, real ymin, real ymax);
void    mvviewport(int n, real xmin, real xmax, real ymin, real ymax);
int     mvact   (int n);
void    mvclear (int c);
void    mvframe (void);
void    mvmake  (int nx, int ny);
void    mvdiv   (int nx, int ny, real xmin, real xmax, real ymin, real ymax);

char*        mvevent   (int wait, real* x, real* y, int* view);

void               mvmainloop(void);
MvCallback* mvregister(int v, char* s, MvCallback* f, void* d);
```

Exercises

1.   Incorporate map and unmap operations in the TK library.

2.   Extend the TK library to include a slider widget.

3.   Extend the TK library to include a choice widget.

4.   Extend the TK library to include a text widget.

4 | Geometry

In this chapter we study the geometry for computer graphics. Our objective is to develop computational tools that make possible the solution of several graphics problems.

4.1 Geometry for Computer Graphics

The first question we should ask is, What will be the most appropriate geometry for computing graphics? To answer this question, we have to take into account the types of problems to be resolved, as well as computational aspects.

4.1.1 Uses and Functionality

Geometry appears in different ways in the various computer graphics processes.

In modeling, geometry is used for representing the form of modeled objects; in operations with models; and in the calculation of most of their properties. The natural space for modeling 3D objects is the $\mathbb{R}^3$.

In viewing, geometry is used in the description of the virtual camera; in the simulation of illumination; and for the generation of images. These problems involve geometric optics, projections, and transformations between coordinate systems. In this way, the viewing process includes the space of the 3D scene, as well as the 2D space of the image.

We still have animation, which involves transformations of several scene parameters over time.

4.1.2 Computational Aspects

In terms of computation, we have different applications for the geometric elements and the geometric operations. Geometric elements should have a simple and natural description, partly because it is important to be able to easily construct more complex elements from basic ones. Geometric operations should constitute an unified schema for the manipulation of geometric elements. It is important that these operations have an efficient implementation. Ideally, we would like the primitive geometric elements, and their basic operations, to be implemented as extensions of the data types and operators of the adopted programming language.

4.1.3 Summary of the Adopted Solution

Considering the applications mentioned above, we can give two appropriate formulations for computer graphics: the Euclidean and projective geometries.

Euclidean geometry is the natural option for describing ambient space, be it 3D or 2D. However, in Euclidean geometry, transformations do not have a unified representation; besides, it is difficult to work with the projection concept in this geometry.

Projective geometry solves these limitations of Euclidean geometry. Euclidean space is contained in projective space; therefore, its natural structure can be used. Projective transformations make it possible to have a unified representation of every Euclidean transformations and still include the projections.

In this book we will adopt both Euclidean and projective geometries to solve graphics problems. We will explore compatibility between those two geometries to use the most appropriate formulation to each problem. More specifically, the geometric elements will be represented in Euclidean space. Basic operations and transformations with these elements will be, respectively, Euclidean and projective ones. To make such a schema possible, whenever necessary we will convert between Euclidean and projective representations.

4.2 Euclidean Space

We now examine the properties of Euclidean space, including its elements and basic operations.

4.2.1 Definitions

The Euclidean space $\mathbb{R}^n$ is a vector space of dimension n, with an inner product and an intrinsic coordinate system. These properties allow linear algebra tools to work with Euclidean space.

Here, we are mainly interested in the $\mathbb{R}^2$ and the $\mathbb{R}^3$, the Euclidean spaces of dimension 2 and 3, respectively.

4.2.2 Elements and Operations

The basic element of Euclidean space $\mathbb{R}^3$ is a vector $v = (x, y, z)$, represented by its coordinates in relation to the canonical basis.

We then define the type `Vector3` and the constructor `v3_make`:

56 ⟨*vector3* 56⟩≡
```
typedef struct Vector3 {
  Real x,y,z;
} Vector3;
```

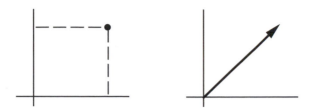

Figure 4.1. Absolute and relative interpretations of a vector.

Defines:
Vector3, used in chunks 57–59, 64, and 71–73.

57a   ⟨*v3 constructor* 57a⟩≡
```
Vector3 v3_make(Real x, Real y, Real z)
{
  Vector3 v;
  v.x = x; v.y = y; v.z = z;
  return v;
}
```
Defines:
v3_make, used in chunks 64b and 71.
Uses Vector3 56.

The origin of Euclidean space is the null vector $(0, 0, 0)$.

57b   ⟨*origin* 57b⟩≡
```
Vector3    v3_zero   = { 0.0, 0.0, 0.0 };
```
Defines:
v3_zero, never used.
Uses Vector3 56.

Notice, in Euclidean space, a vector represents a point in relation to the origin. To represent a vector relative to an arbitrary point, we perform a change of coordinate systems (see Figure 4.1).

The basic operations in $\mathbb{R}^3$ are the vector operations of addition between vectors and multiplication of a vector by a scalar:

57c   ⟨*v3 add* 57c⟩≡
```
Vector3 v3_add(Vector3 a, Vector3 b)
{
  a.x += b.x; a.y += b.y; a.z += b.z;
  return a;
}
```
Defines:
v3_add, used in chunk 72c.
Uses Vector3 56.

58a ⟨*v3 scale* 58a⟩≡
```
Vector3 v3_scale(Real t, Vector3 v)
{
  v.x *= t; v.y *= t; v.z *= t;
  return v;
}
```
Defines:
  v3_scale, used in chunks 59a and 72c.
Uses Vector3 56.

Notice that with these two basic operations, we can define other operations, such as subtraction between vectors.

```
#define v3_sub(a,b) v3_add(a, v3_scale(-1.0, v))
```

4.2.3 Metric Properties

The inner product defines a metric in $\mathbb{R}^3$ that allows to calculate several important properties. The inner product operation between two vectors is implemented by the routine v3_dot.

58b ⟨*v3 dot* 58b⟩≡
```
Real v3_dot(Vector3 u, Vector3 v)
{
  return (u.x * v.x + u.y * v.y + u.z * v.z);
}
```
Defines:
  v3_dot, used in chunk 58c.
Uses Vector3 56.

Starting from the inner product, we can calculate the length (or norm) of a vector, as well as the distance between two points.

58c ⟨*v3 norm alt* 58c⟩≡
```
Real v3_norm(Vector3 v)
{
  return sqrt(v3_dot(v, v));
}
```
Defines:
  v3_norm, used in chunk 59a.
Uses v3_dot 58b and Vector3 56.

```
#define v3_dist(a, b) v3_norm(v3_sub(a, b))
```

The cosine of the angle between two vectors is given by the quotient between the inner product and the product between the norms of the vectors.

```
double v3_angle(Vector3 u, Vector3 v)
{
  if (REL_EQ(0.0, v3_norm(u) * v3_norm(v)))
    error("(v3_angle) null vector");
  else
    return acos(v3_dot(u, v)/(v3_norm(u) * v3_norm(v)));
}
```

It follows that two vectors are orthogonal when the inner product between them is equal to zero; consequently, they form an angle of 90 degrees between themselves.

A non-null vector, divided by its norm, has unit length. Normalized vectors are useful for representing directions in space.

59a   ⟨*v3 unit* 59a⟩≡

```
   Vector3 v3_unit(Vector3 u)
   {
     Real  length = v3_norm(u);
     if(fabs(length) < EPS)
       error("(g3_unit) zero norm\n");
     else
       return v3_scale(1.0/length, u);
   }
```

Defines:
  v3_unit, never used.
Uses v3_norm 58c, v3_scale 58a, and Vector3 56.

4.2.4   Coordinates and Bases

Euclidean space has a natural coordinate system, given by the canonical basis $\{e_1, e_2, e_3\}$.

59b   ⟨*canonical basis* 59b⟩≡

```
   Vector3   v3_e1   = { 1.0, 0.0, 0.0 };
   Vector3   v3_e2   = { 0.0, 1.0, 0.0 };
   Vector3   v3_e3   = { 0.0, 0.0, 1.0 };
```

Defines:
  v3_e1, never used.
  v3_e2, never used.
  v3_e3, never used.
Uses Vector3 56.

Other coordinate systems in $\mathbb{R}^3$ can be constructed by taking bases formed by three linearly independent vectors. *Orthonormal bases*, formed by unit vectors orthogonal among themselves, are particularly important.

The cross product is a very useful operation, particularly for the construction of bases in $\mathbb{R}^3$.

59c   ⟨*v3 cross* 59c⟩≡

```
   Vector3 v3_cross(Vector3 u, Vector3 v)
```

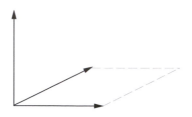

Figure 4.2. Cross product.

```
  {
    Vector3 uxv;
    uxv.x =    u.y * v.z - v.y * u.z;
    uxv.y =  - u.x * v.z + v.x * u.z;
    uxv.z =    u.x * v.y - u.y * v.x;
    return uxv;
  }
```
Defines:
  v3_cross, never used.
Uses **Vector3** 56.

This operation produces a vector normal to the plane defined by two vectors whose magnitude is given by the area of the parallelogram formed by these vectors (see Figure 4.2).

4.3   Transformations in Euclidean Space

We will now investigate several classes of transformations in Euclidean space.

4.3.1   Linear Transformations

A linear transformation in $\mathbb{R}^3$ is an operator $T : \mathbb{R}^3 \to \mathbb{R}^3$ with the following properties:

$$T(u + v) = T(u) + T(v),$$
$$T(\lambda v) = \lambda T(v),$$

where $u, v \in \mathbb{R}^3$ and $\lambda \in \mathbb{R}$.

This class of transformations has several desirable properties: they preserve linear structures, mapping subspaces into subspaces. Some important examples of linear transformations are scaling, rotation, reflection, and shear.

A relevant aspect, from the computational point of view, is that we can represent a linear transformation in $\mathbb{R}^3$ by a matrix M, 3×3. This means we can use matrices to implement transformations. To apply a linear transformation to a vector is equivalent to multiplying the associated matrix by this vector.

4.3.2 Isometries

Another important class of transformations is *isometries*. They have the property of preserving the metric; in other words, $||Tv|| = ||v||$.

Isometries in Euclidean space are rotations, reflections, and translations. Notice that, except for translations, isometries are a particular case of linear transformations. Unfortunately, representation by matrices does not include translations.

4.3.3 Affine Transformations

We saw above that both linear transformations and isometries are useful for computer graphics. This fact lead us to look for a broader class, the *affine transformations*, which includes both linear transformations and translations in space. Affine transformations also preserve ratios and proportions.

An affine transformation has the form $A(x) = M(x) + v$, where M is a matrix and v a vector. Notice that, given that A is not linear (unless $v = 0$), we cannot represent A by a matrix.

We reached the conclusion that affine transformations have the desired properties for geometric modeling operations in computer graphics. This class of transformations incorporates natural geometry concepts from the physical world, such as congruency and similarity.

It does have some disadvantages. Affine transformations do not admit an unified representation by matrices. A second disadvantage is that affine transformations do not allow us to implement certain fundamental viewing operations. It is enough simply to notice that the photograph of a 3D scene does not preserve parallel straight lines (see Figure 4.3). Therefore, this operation cannot be realized by affine transformations, which keep invariant relations of parallelism.

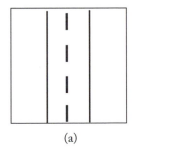 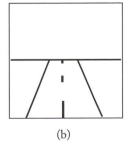

(a) (b)

Figure 4.3. Highway seem from (a) above and (b) ahead.

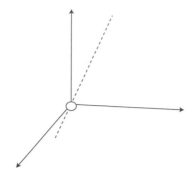

Figure 4.4. Projective space of dimension 2.

4.4 Projective Space

We want to work in Euclidean space and we want to use affine transformations. Further-more, we would like to have an unified representation for these operations, and we also need to incorporate viewing transformations to them. We can reach these two objectives with projective geometry.

4.4.1 Projective Space Model

The real projective space of dimension n, $\mathbb{RP}^n$, is the set of every straight line in $\mathbb{R}^{n+1}$ passing through the origin and excluding it. A projective point $p \in \mathbb{RP}^n$ is an equivalence class $p = (\lambda x_1, \lambda x_2, \ldots, \lambda x_{n+1})$, with $\lambda \neq 0$. In other words, $p = (x_1, x_2, \ldots, x_{n+1}) \equiv \lambda p$.

Notice we can associate the projective space of dimension n with Euclidean space of dimension $n + 1$. More specifically, $\mathbb{RP}^n := \mathbb{R}^{n+1} - \{(0, 0, \ldots, 0)\}$. In Figure 4.4, we show a schema of the $\mathbb{RP}^2$, the projective space of dimension 2, indicating a projective point (the dashed straight line) and omitting the origin.

The projective space $\mathbb{RP}^n$ can be decomposed in two sets: the affine space $\pi \equiv \mathbb{R}^n$ plunged within $\mathbb{RP}^n$, which is the set of projective points with $x_{n+1} = 1$, and the set of projective points having $x_{n+1} = 0$.

Notice that, from the equivalence relation, we can associate n-tuples in the plunged affine subspace (points in $\mathbb{R}^n$) to the projective points (straight line in $\mathbb{R}^{n+1}$) for which $x_{n+1} \neq 0$. This way, we have a natural partition

$$\mathbb{RP}^n = \{(x_1, \ldots, x_n, x_{n+1}), x_{n+1} \neq 0\} \cup \{(x_1, \ldots, x_n, 0)\}.$$

4.4.2 Normalized and Homogeneous Coordinates

Decomposition of the projective space allows us to identify the specific set of an element $p = \lambda p = (\lambda x_1, \lambda x_2, \lambda x_{n+1})$ of $\mathbb{RP}^n$, based on the value of its coordinate x_{n+1}. We then have:

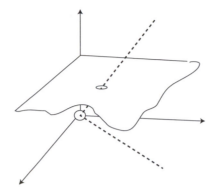

Figure 4.5. Decomposition of the projective plane.

□ Affine points: $p \in \pi$, in the form $p_a = (x_1, \ldots, x_n, 1)$ with $x_{n+1} \neq 0$, and $\lambda = \frac{1}{x_{n+1}}$.

□ Ideal points: $p \notin \pi$, in the form $p_i = (x_1, \ldots, x_n, 0)$ with $x_{n+1} = 0$, and $\lambda = 1$.

Figure 4.5 shows the decomposition of the projective space of dimension 2, $\mathbb{RP}^2$, in the plunged affine plane ($z = 1$) and the ideal plane ($z = 0$).

We can exploit the above decomposition in order to work with normalized coordinates. In fact, we can take a Euclidean point as being a projective point with $x_{n+1} = 1$. Despite that, in the general case, we have to work with the homogeneous coordinates calls, in the form $p = (x_1, \ldots, x_n, x_{n+})$, without making any distinction between affine and ideal points.

4.4.3 Homogeneous Representation

A point in projective space $\mathbb{RP}^3$ will be represented in homogeneous coordinates by the data structure **Vector4**, for which we have the constructor v4_make.

63a ⟨*vector4* 63a⟩≡
```
typedef struct Vector4 {
    double x,y,z,w;
} Vector4;
```
Defines:
   Vector4, used in chunks 63, 64, 66, and 71.

63b ⟨*v4 constructor* 63b⟩≡
```
Vector4 v4_make(Real x, Real y, Real z, Real w)
{
    Vector4 v;
    v.x = x; v.y = y; v.z = z; v.w = w;
    return v;
```

```
    }
```
Defines:
    v4_make, used in chunks 64a, 66b, and 71b.
Uses **Vector4** 63a.

We also define routines for the conversion between affine and projective points, making normalization necessary. Notice it is not possible to convert an ideal point into an affine one.

64a   ⟨*v4v3 conv* 64a⟩≡
```
    Vector4 v4_v3conv(Vector3 v)
    {
        return v4_make(v.x, v.y, v.z, 1.0);
    }
```
Defines:
    v4_v3conv, used in chunk 71a.
Uses **v4_make** 63b, **Vector3** 56, and **Vector4** 63a.

64b   ⟨*v3v4 conv* 64b⟩≡
```
    Vector3 v3_v4conv(Vector4 v)
    {
        if (REL_EQ(v.w, 0.)) v.w = 1;
        return v3_make(v.x/v.w, v.y/v.w, v.z/v.w);
    }
```
Defines:
    v3_v4conv, never used.
Uses **v3_make** 57a, **Vector3** 56, and **Vector4** 63a.

4.5   Projective Transformations in $\mathbb{RP}^3$

A projective transformation T in $\mathbb{RP}^3$ is a linear operator in $\mathbb{R}^4$

$$T : \mathbb{R}^4 \to \mathbb{R}^4.$$

In this way, T is given by a matrix M, 4×4. The projective transformation can be calculated as $T(p) = Mp$.

Notice that $T(p) = \lambda T(p)$, for $\lambda \neq 0$. This is a fundamental difference between projective and Euclidean transformations. For a better understanding of a projective transformation, we will analyze the anatomy of the associated matrix. We can identify four different blocks:

$$M = \left(\begin{array}{cc} A & T \\ P & S \end{array} \right);$$

☐ A: linear block (3×3),

☐ T: translation block (3×1),

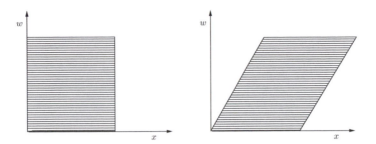

Figure 4.6. Translation in projective space.

☐ P: perspective block (1×3),

☐ S: scaling block (1×1).

Blocks A and T correspond to affine transformations in $\mathbb{R}^3$, thus leaving the plunged Euclidean space, π, invariant. Block P maps affine points into ideal ones and, consequently, does not leave π invariant. Block S is redundant, because if $s \neq 0$, then we can always assume that $s = 1$, once $T(p) \equiv \lambda T(p)$.

Finally, we have reached our objectives with projective transformations. In fact, we have incorporated translations, $T(p) = (x + cw, y + fw, z + gw, w)$, now starting to have a matrix representation. Note that translation works as a shear perpendicular to the direction w (see Figure 4.6).

Besides, projective transformations allow us to implement the perspective projection for viewing: $T(p) = (x, y, z, gx + hy + iz)$. Note that this transformation turns affine points into ideal points and vice versa. As a result, an ideal point $p \notin \pi$, is mapped into an affine point $p' \in \pi$, also called the *vanishing point*. Parallel straight lines, after the transformation, intersect one another at p' (see Figure 4.7).

We will represent projective transformations by 4×4 matrices. For this, we define the type `Matrix4`.

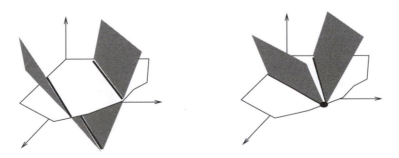

Figure 4.7. Perspective transformation.

66a   ⟨*matrix4* 66a⟩≡
```
typedef struct Matrix4 {
  Vector4 r1, r2, r3, r4;
} Matrix4;
```
Defines:
  Matrix4, used in chunks 66, 67, and 69–72.
Uses Vector4 63a.

The application of a projective transformation to a vector v is done by multiplying the associated matrix M by v. This calculation consists of taking the inner product between v and each line of M. The auxiliary routine v4_dot was created for this end.

66b   ⟨*v4m4 mult* 66b⟩≡
```
Vector4 v4_m4mult(Vector4 w, Matrix4 m)
{
  return v4_make(v4_dot(w, m.r1)
               , v4_dot(w, m.r2)
               , v4_dot(w, m.r3)
               , v4_dot(w, m.r4));
}
```
Defines:
  v4_m4mult, never used.
Uses Matrix4 66a, v4_dot 66c, v4_make 63b, and Vector4 63a.

66c   ⟨*v4 dot* 66c⟩≡
```
Real v4_dot(u,v)
     Vector4 u, v;
{
  return (u.x * v.x + u.y * v.y + u.z * v.z + u.w * v.w);
}
```
Defines:
  v4_dot, used in chunks 66b, 69, and 71.
Uses Vector4 63a.

We will now see the implementation of the basic transformations. The first transformation is the identity, m4_ident:

66d   ⟨*m4 ident* 66d⟩≡
```
Matrix4 m4_ident()
{
  Matrix4 m = {{1.0, 0.0, 0.0, 0.0},
               {0.0, 1.0, 0.0, 0.0},
               {0.0, 0.0, 1.0, 0.0},
               {0.0, 0.0, 0.0, 1.0}};
  return m;
}
```
Defines:
  m4_ident, used in chunk 67.
Uses Matrix4 66a.

The translation transformation is given by

$$M_t = \begin{pmatrix} 1 & 0 & 0 & t_x \\ 0 & 1 & 0 & t_y \\ 0 & 0 & 1 & t_z \\ 0 & 0 & 0 & 1 \end{pmatrix}$$

and is implemented by the routine m4_translate:

67a   ⟨*m4 translate* 67a⟩≡

```
Matrix4 m4_translate(Real tx, Real ty, Real tz)
{
  Matrix4 m = m4_ident();
  m.r1.w = tx;
  m.r2.w = ty;
  m.r3.w = tz;
  return  m;
}
```

Defines:
  m4_translate, never used.
Uses m4_ident 66d and Matrix4 66a.

The scaling transformation along the principal directions

$$M_s = \begin{pmatrix} s_x & 0 & 0 & 0 \\ 0 & s_y & 0 & 0 \\ 0 & 0 & s_z & 0 \\ 0 & 0 & 0 & 1 \end{pmatrix}$$

is implemented by the routine m4_scale:

67b   ⟨*m4 scale* 67b⟩≡

```
Matrix4 m4_scale(Real sx, Real sy, Real sz)
{
  Matrix4 m = m4_ident();
  m.r1.x= sx;
  m.r2.y= sy;
  m.r3.z= sz;
  return(m);
}
```

Defines:
  m4_scale, never used.
Uses m4_ident 66d and Matrix4 66a.

The routine m4_rotate implements rotations in $\mathbb{R}^3$ by Euler angles, along the main axes:

67c   ⟨*m4 rotate* 67c⟩≡

```
Matrix4 m4_rotate(char axis, Real angle)
```

```
{
  Matrix4 m = m4_ident();
  Real cost = (Real) cos(angle);
  Real sint = (Real) sin(angle);
  switch (axis) {
  case 'x' :
    m.r2.y=  cost; m.r2.z= -sint;
    m.r3.y=  sint; m.r3.z=  cost;
    break;
  case 'y' :
    m.r1.x=  cost; m.r1.z=  sint;
    m.r3.x= -sint; m.r3.z=  cost;
    break;
  case 'z' :
    m.r1.x=  cost; m.r1.y= -sint;
    m.r2.x=  sint; m.r2.y=  cost;
    break;
  default :
    error("(m4_rotate) invalid axis\n");
  }
  return  m;
}
```

Defines:
 m4_rotate, never used.
Uses m4_ident 66d and Matrix4 66a.

So far, we have seen the basic transformations in Euclidean space. We could also implement other useful transformations, such as reflections and shear. Besides the Euclidean transformations, the perspective transformation, given by the matrix below, will be necessary in the viewing processes (we will return to this subject in Chapter 11):

$$
M_p = \begin{pmatrix} 1 & 0 & 0 & 0 \\ 0 & 1 & 0 & 0 \\ 0 & 0 & 1 & 0 \\ m & n & p & 1 \end{pmatrix}.
$$

4.5.1 Composition of Transformations

A natural isomorphism exists between the algebra of matrices and the algebra of projective transformations. In this way, the composition of transformations is equivalent to the concatenation of matrices:

$$
\begin{aligned}
p' &= T_n(\cdots T_2(T_1(p))), \\
p' &= M_n \ldots M_2 M_1 p, \\
p' &= M p.
\end{aligned}
$$

In fact, we can use a single matrix to represent the transformation resulting from an arbitrary sequence of transformations. This is the great advantage of the unified representation by matrices.

Notice that the concatenation of matrices is a noncommutative operation. This reflects the fact that the result of a sequence of transformations depends on the order in which the individual transformations are applied:

$$M_1 M_2 \cdots M_n \neq M_n \cdots M_2 M_1.$$

The inverse of a sequence of transformations is given by the concatenation of the inverse of the matrices concatenated in the inverse order:

$$(M_1 M_2 \cdots M_n)^{-1} = M_n^{-1} \cdots M_2^{-1} M_1^{-1}.$$

The routine m4_m4prod implements the matrix product, which is the basic operation for the composition of transformations.

69     $\langle$ *m4m4 prod* 69$\rangle\equiv$

```
Matrix4 m4_m4prod(Matrix4 a, Matrix4 b)
{
  Matrix4 m, c = m4_transpose(b);

  m.r1.x = v4_dot(a.r1, c.r1);
  m.r1.y = v4_dot(a.r1, c.r2);
  m.r1.z = v4_dot(a.r1, c.r3);
  m.r1.w = v4_dot(a.r1, c.r4);

  m.r2.x = v4_dot(a.r2, c.r1);
  m.r2.y = v4_dot(a.r2, c.r2);
  m.r2.z = v4_dot(a.r2, c.r3);
  m.r2.w = v4_dot(a.r2, c.r4);

  m.r3.x = v4_dot(a.r3, c.r1);
  m.r3.y = v4_dot(a.r3, c.r2);
  m.r3.z = v4_dot(a.r3, c.r3);
  m.r3.w = v4_dot(a.r3, c.r4);

  m.r4.x = v4_dot(a.r4, c.r1);
  m.r4.y = v4_dot(a.r4, c.r2);
  m.r4.z = v4_dot(a.r4, c.r3);
  m.r4.w = v4_dot(a.r4, c.r4);
  return m;
}
```

Defines:
  m4_m4prod, never used.
Uses Matrix4 66a and v4_dot 66c.

For better clarity and simplicity, the routine `m4_m4prod` uses the transpose of one of the input matrices. Notice this is not the most efficient way to implement the product between matrices.

The routine `m4_transpose` implements the calculation of the transpose of a matrix, which is a useful operation for general calculations with matrices.

70   ⟨*m4 transpose* 70⟩≡

```
Matrix4 m4_transpose(Matrix4 m)
{
  Matrix4 mt;
  mt.r1.x= m.r1.x;
  mt.r1.y= m.r2.x;
  mt.r1.z= m.r3.x;
  mt.r1.w= m.r4.x;

  mt.r2.x= m.r1.y;
  mt.r2.y= m.r2.y;
  mt.r2.z= m.r3.y;
  mt.r2.w= m.r4.y;

  mt.r3.x= m.r1.z;
  mt.r3.y= m.r2.z;
  mt.r3.z= m.r3.z;
  mt.r3.w= m.r4.z;

  mt.r4.x= m.r1.w;
  mt.r4.y= m.r2.w;
  mt.r4.z= m.r3.w;
  mt.r4.w= m.r4.w;
  return mt ;
}
```

Uses `Matrix4` 66a.

4.6   Transformations of Geometric Objects

In this section we will discuss how to apply a transformation to the several elements used in the representation of graphics objects.

4.6.1   Revision on Transformations

The basic element to be transformed is a vector $p = (x, y, z) \in \pi \equiv \mathbb{R}^3$, belonging to the plunged affine space $\pi \in \mathbb{RP}^3$. Therefore, we will use the normalized representation $p = (x, y, z, 1)$.

To apply a transformation given by the projective matrix M to a homogeneous vector p, we perform the operation $p' = Mp$. Notice that after the transformation, if we want to maintain the normalized representation of the vectors, we have to perform the so-called homogeneous division of the coordinates by the component w. This operation indeed corresponds to a projection of the homogeneous vector in the plunged affine space:

$$p' = \frac{1}{w'}(x', y', z', w'),$$
$$p'' = (x'', y'', z'', 1).$$

4.6.2 Transforming Points and Directions

The routine v4_m4mult multiplies a homogeneous vector by a projective matrix. This routine should be used for generic projective transformations.

The routine v3_m4mult multiplies a Euclidean vector by a projective matrix. This routine can be used for the case of affine transformations.

71a   ⟨v3m4 mult 71a⟩≡
```
    Vector3 v3_m4mult(Vector3 v, Matrix4 m)
    {
        Vector4 w = v4_v3conv(v);
        return v3_make(v4_dot(w, m.r1), v4_dot(w, m.r2), v4_dot(w, m.r3));
    }
```
Defines:
   v3_m4mult, used in chunk 72b.
Uses Matrix4 66a, v3_make 57a, v4_dot 66c, v4_v3conv 64a, Vector3 56, and Vector4 63a.

The routine v3_m3mult multiplies a vector by the linear block of the projective matrix. This routine is useful to transform directional vectors not affected by translations.

71b   ⟨v3m3 mult 71b⟩≡
```
    Vector3 v3_m3mult(Vector3 v, Matrix4 m)
    {
        Vector4 w = v4_make(v.x, v.y, v.z, 0.0);
        return v3_make(v4_dot(w, m.r1), v4_dot(w, m.r2), v4_dot(w, m.r3));
    }
```
Defines:
   v3_m3mult, used in chunk 72b.
Uses Matrix4 66a, v3_make 57a, v4_dot 66c, v4_make 63b, Vector3 56, and Vector4 63a.

4.6.3 Transforming Rays

Many viewing operations involve the simulation of optic processes. The elementary geometric object in these simulations is the *ray*, r, defined by its origin o and direction d (see Figure 4.8).

Figure 4.8. Vector representing a ray.

We created the type Ray and the constructor `ray_make`.

```
typedef struct Ray {
  Vector3 o, d;
} Ray;
```

72a ⟨*ray constructor* 72a⟩≡

```
Ray ray_make(Vector3 o, Vector3 d)
{
  Ray r;
  r.o = o; r.d = d;
  return r;
}
```

Defines:
  ray_make, never used.
Uses Ray and Vector3 56.

To basic operations with a ray r are: to apply an affine transformation r and calculate a point along the ray corresponding to the parameter t, such that $p_t = o + td$.

72b ⟨*ray transform* 72b⟩≡

```
Ray ray_transform(Ray r, Matrix4 m)
{
  r.o = v3_m4mult(r.o, m);
  r.d = v3_m3mult(r.d, m);
  return r;
}
```

Defines:
  ray_transform, never used.
Uses Matrix4 66a, Ray, v3_m3mult 71b, and v3_m4mult 71a.

72c ⟨*ray point* 72c⟩≡

```
Vector3 ray_point(Ray r, Real t)
{
  return v3_add(r.o, v3_scale(t, r.d));
}
```

Defines:
  ray_point, never used.
Uses Ray, v3_add 57c, v3_scale 58a, and Vector3 56.

In several viewing problems, it will also be necessary to calculate the intersection between a ray and a surface. To this end, we will use the data structure Inode, containing the necessary information, such as the parameter t, corresponding to the intersection point; the vector n, normal to the surface at this point; etc. This structure can be used as an element of a linked list containing all the intersections along a ray.

72d ⟨*inode* 72d⟩≡

```
typedef struct Inode {
  struct Inode    *next;
```

```
      double          t;
      Vector3         n;
      int             enter;
      struct Material *m;
    } Inode;
```
Defines:
  Inode, used in chunk 73.
Uses Vector3 56.

We defined the constructor `inode_alloc`, as well as the destructor `inode_free`, since this type of information is quite volatile.

73a ⟨*inode constructor* 73a⟩≡
```
    Inode *inode_alloc(Real t, Vector3 n, int enter)
    {
      Inode *i = NEWSTRUCT(Inode);
      i->t = t;
      i->n = n;
      i->enter = enter;
      i->next = (Inode *)0;
      return i;
    }
```
Defines:
  inode_alloc, never used.
Uses Inode 72d and Vector3 56.

73b ⟨*inode destructor* 73b⟩≡
```
    void inode_free(Inode *l)
    {
      Inode *i;
      while (l) {
        i = l; l = l->next; free(i);
      }
    }
```
Defines:
  inode_free, never used.
Uses Inode 72d.

4.6.4   Transformation on the Tangent Plane

Transformation on the tangent plane to a surface at a point has different characteristics from transformations over points and vectors.

We can represent a plane n, by a row vector $n = (a, b, c, d)$, corresponding to the coefficients of the implicit equation of the plane. Therefore, every point $p \in n$, satisfies the equation

$$\{p = (x, y, z, 1) \quad | \quad ax + by + cz + d = 0\},$$

which can be formulated in a concise way using the inner product, $\langle n, p \rangle = 0$.

If we apply a transformation given by the matrix M to the plane n, the condition of a point p belonging to n corresponds, after the transformation by M, $(nM^{-1})(Mp) = 0$; that is, the transformed point Mp is on the transformed plane nM^{-1}.

In this case we see that, to transform tangent planes using as a column vector, we should use the transpose of the inverse matrix:

$$n' = (M^{-1})^T n.$$

Notice that for orthogonal matrices, $(M^{-1})^T = M$. This is the only case in which we can transform tangent planes as vectors.

4.6.5   Dual Interpretation of Transformations

Transformations can be understood either as a transformation of vectors or as a change between coordinate systems.

The first interpretation consists of considering a transformation as a mapping between points in a same- coordinate system. In this way, point p is mapped in $T(p)$. This interpretation helps us understand the parametric description of graphics objects, where the geometry is specified by a function $p = g(u, v)$ defining the points of the object. To transform parametric objects, we directly apply the transformation matrix to these points, i.e., $p' = T(g(u, v))$ (see Figure 4.9).

The second interpretation consists of considering a transformation as a change of coordinate system. In this way, a vector v, in the canonical basis $\{e_1, e_2, e_3\}$, is mapped in the vector corresponding to the transformed basis $v' = xT(e_1) + yT(e_2) + zT(e_3)$. This interpretation helps us understand the implicit description of graphics objects, where the geometry is specified by a function $h(v) = 0$ of the environment space, $v \in \mathbb{R}^3$. To transform implicit objects, we apply the inverse of the transformation to the points of the transformed space, and these will be evaluated in the original environment space, i.e., $h(T^{-1}(v)) = 0$ (see Figure 4.10).

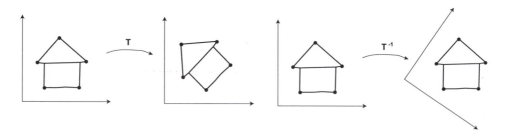

Figure 4.9.   Direct transformation: mapping points.

Figure 4.10. Inverse transformation: change of coordinate systems.

4.7 Comments and References

In this chapter we presented the implementation of a library for basic geometric operations in computer graphics.

One of the first references about viewing transformations is the article "The Geometry Engine" by Jim Clark, founder of Silicon Graphics [Clark 82]. In this work he describes a graphics processor implementing geometric transformations.

4.7.1 Summary

The external API of the GEOM library is composed of the following routines:

```
Vector3 v3_make(Real x, Real y, Real z);
Vector3 v3_scale(Real t, Vector3 v);
Vector3 v3_add(Vector3 a, Vector3 b);
Vector3 v3_sub(Vector3 a, Vector3 b);
Vector3 v3_cross(Vector3 u, Vector3 v);
Vector3 v3_unit(Vector3 u);
Real v3_dot(Vector3 u, Vector3 v);
Real v3_norm(Vector3 v);

Vector4 v4_make(Real x, Real y, Real z, Real w);
Vector3 v3_v4conv(Vector4 w);
Vector4 v4_v3conv(Vector3 v);

Vector3 v3_m4mult(Vector3 v, Matrix4 m);
Vector3 v3_m3mult(Vector3 v, Matrix4 m);
Vector4 v4_m4mult(Vector4 w, Matrix4 m);

Matrix4 m4_ident();
Matrix4 m4_translate(Real tx, Real ty, Real tz);
Matrix4 m4_scale(Real sx, Real sy, Real sz);
Matrix4 m4_rotate(char axis, Real angle);
Matrix4 m4_transpose(Matrix4 m);
Matrix4 m4_m4prod(Matrix4 a, Matrix4 b);

Ray ray_make(Vector3 o, Vector3 d);
Ray ray_transform(Ray r, Matrix4 m);
Vector3 ray_point(Ray r, Real t);

Inode *inode_alloc(Real t, Vector3 n, int enter);
void inode_free(Inode *l);
```

4.7.2 Programming Layer

The GEOM library implements the basic geometric operations for 3D computer graphics. The data structures `Vector3` and `Matrix4` are essential and constitute the data types most used in graphics programs. The geometric transformations are implemented directly in hardware on the graphics boards (in particular, on the boards supporting the OpenGl and DirectX standards).

Exercises

1. Using the GEOM library, implement the program vexpr to calculate vector expressions. The operands are 3D vector in the format x y, z. The set of operators should include, at least, vector addition, multiplication of a vector by a scalar, inner product, cross product, and equality test between vectors.

   The program should read one of the operands from stdin and the others from the command line. The operations should be specified by name and passed as parameters in the command line (e.g., add, mult). The result should be sent to stdout. For example,

   ```
   echo 1 3 0.4 | vexpr add 2 1 0.1
   3 4 0.5
   ```

2. Using the GP and GEOM libraries, implement an interactive program to transform and plot polygonal lines. The following transformations should be implemented: translation, rotation, and scaling.

3. Extend the GEOM library to include the functions below:

   (a) Linear interpolation between two vectors.

   (b) Normal projection of a vector u on a vector v.

   (c) Tangential projection of a vector u on a vector v.

   (d) Add the components of a vector.

   (e) Calculate the perpendicular unit vector to a given vector.

   (f) Calculate the normal vector to a plane determined by three points.

   (g) Calculate the matrix of an orthogonal transformation mapping a given unit vector u into a given unit vector v.

   (h) Place the elements of a 4×4 matrix in the Matrix4 data structure (using the C language).

   (i) Calculate the rotation matrix along an arbitrary axis.

   (j) Calculate the inverse of a 4×4 matrix.

5 | Color

Color is one of the most important elements in computer graphics. It is the basic stimulus used by our visual system for perceiving the physical world. Consequently, color information is the main attribute of an image. Besides, the simulation of illumination involves calculations with color. In this chapter, we will study color and its applications in computer graphics.

5.1 Color Foundations

We will use the paradigm of the four universes to study color in computer graphics. In this way, starting from color in the physical world, we will define mathematical models of color, establish a representation for color, and give structures for its implementation in the computer.

Color is the sensation provoked by an electromagnetic radiation through the human visual system. Therefore, color is a psychophysics phenomenon. This fact has great relevance, leading us to consider both perceptual and physical aspects in the study of the color.

5.1.1 Color Wavelength Model

From a physical point of view, color is produced by an electromagnetic radiation whose wavelength λ is in the visible band of the spectrum, from 400 to 800 nanometers approximately (see Figures 5.1 and 5.2).

Figure 5.1. Colors in the visible spectrum. (See Plate I.)

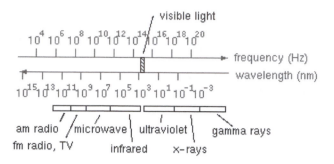

Figure 5.2. Bands of the electromagnetic spectrum.

The perception of color is established by the combination of electromagnetic radiation in several wavelengths received by the visual system. This way, a color is characterized by its *spectral distribution function*, which associates an energy value to each wavelength λ (see Figure 5.3).

The characterization of color by its spectral distribution leads us to conclude that a function is the appropriate mathematical model to describe color. More specifically, a given color is an element of the space of spectral distributions $D = \{f : [\lambda_0, \lambda_1] \in \mathbb{R}^+ \to \mathbb{R}^+\}$, where $[\lambda_0, \lambda_1]$ is the interval defining the visible band of the spectrum. Notice the space of spectral distributions is a function space and therefore has infinite dimension.

5.1.2 Physical Color Systems

In the physical world, color is processed by physical color systems. These systems are divided into color-receiving and color-emitting systems. Examples include a camera (a receiving system) and a monitor (an emitting system).

A *color-receiving system* consists of a set of sensors, $\{s_i\}$, $i = 1, \ldots, n$, that performs sampling in n degrees of the visible spectrum. The response of each sensor is given by $c_i = \int c(\lambda) s_i(\lambda) d\lambda$. In this way, a color-receiving system associates, to each spectral distribution, a vector of samples (i.e., $c(\lambda) = (c_1, \ldots c_n)$).

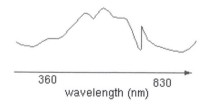

Figure 5.3. Spectral distribution function.

A *color-emitting system* consists of a set of emitters, $\{e_i\}$, $i = 1, \ldots, n$, producing electromagnetic energy with a certain spectral distribution, $e_i = d_i(\lambda)$. The color produced by the system is given by the linear combination of the distribution functions of each emitter (i.e., $c(\lambda) = \sum c_i d_i(\lambda)$).

Notice that physical color systems have finite dimension, and they indicate a natural way of discretizing the spectral model of color. The receiving systems perform sampling, and the emitter systems perform reconstruction. In this way, we transform a spectral distribution function into samples and vice versa. The spectral distribution functions associated with receivers and emitters are called *primary colors* of the system. The vector of samples $(c_1, \ldots c_n)$ provide the color representation in this system.

5.1.3 Psychophysics Study of Color

We have seen that physical color systems require into a discretization of the continuous model of spectral distribution. We therefore have a space of finite dimension associated with the entire physical color system.

To understand the perceptual aspects of color, we should study the human visual system. The human eye can be considered a physical color-receiving system. It has three types of sensors responding to low (red), medium (green), and high (blue) wavelength bands. Color experiments conducted with human observers show the color space of the visual system has an underlying linear structure. This verification is expressed by *Grassman's law*, based on empirical results in which color matches obey the rules of linearity and additivity [Malacara-Hernandez 02]. It was discovered by Hermann Günther Grassmann (1809–1877), a German polymath.

An immediate consequence of a perceptual approach to color is that we can use a vector space of dimension 3 as a mathematical model of the visual system. More specifically, we take the Euclidean space $\mathbb{R}^3$, where the vectors of the basis $\{e_1, e_2, e_3\}$ are associated with the primary colors of the system.

Analogously, we define color spaces for other physical color systems. This task has been accomplished by the CIE (Commission Internationale d'Eclairage), which defined several standard color systems. Among them, we have the CIE-RGB and CIE-XYZ systems.

These facts lead us to conclude we can use the tools of the Euclidean geometry to work with color spaces. We represent a color by a 3D vector whose coordinates correspond to the components of the primary colors of the system. We will mainly use the RGB system, based on the primary colors red, green, and blue.

79 ⟨*color* 79⟩≡

```
typedef Vector3 Color;

#define RED(c) (c.x)
#define GRN(c) (c.y)
#define BLU(c) (c.z)
```

Defines:
  BLU, used in chunks 83b and 88a.
  Color, used in chunks 83b and 86–88.

GRN, used in chunks 83b and 88a.
RED, used in chunks 83b and 88a.

We define a color constructor, c_make, the operations color addition, c_add, color multiplication by scalar, c_scale, and color product, c_mult. These operations have a physical interpretation: sum corresponds to merging colors; scaling corresponds to increasing the color luminance; and the product between two color vectors is equivalent to filtering.

On the other hand, except for the product of colors, these operations are natural to a vector space.

```
#define c_make(r,g,b) v3_make(r,g,b)
#define c_add(a, b)    v3_add(a,b)
#define c_scale(a, b)  v3_scale(a, b)
#define c_mult(a, b)   v3_mult(a, b)
```

The product between two colors is given by

80a   ⟨*v3 mult* 80a⟩≡
```
Vector3 v3_mult(Vector3 a, Vector3 b)
{
  Vector3 c;
  c.x = a.x * b.x;   c.y = a.y * b.y;   c.z = a.z * b.z;
  return c;
}
```
Defines:
  v3_mult, never used.

5.1.4   Computing with Color

The routines defined in the previous subsection implement the basic operations with color.

In addition to these basic operations, we will use the operation of matrix multiplication by a vector v3_m4mult to accomplish basis changes. This type of transformation corresponds to the conversion between physical systems of different colors whose color space is linear, of dimension 3.

80b   ⟨*col convert* 80b⟩≡
```
Vector3 col_convert(Vector3 c, Matrix m)
{
  return v3_m4mult(c, m);
}
```
Defines:
  col_convert, never used.

Notice that to calculate the matrix m_{AB} that performs the conversion between two physical systems A and B, we have to use the spectral distribution functions associated with the primary colors of the two systems.

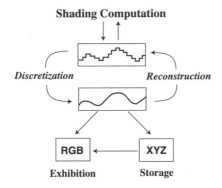

Figure 5.4. Computing with color.

In computer graphics, most color problems can be solved by working directly with trichromatic color spaces. However, certain problems demand more complicated calculations, which can involve nonlinear transformations or even the reconstruction of the spectral distribution function with subsequent resampling.

The first case includes the conversion between color spaces with different dimensions or nonlinear structures. The second case happens in the simulation of wavelength-dependent illumination phenomena. Figure 5.4 illustrates the various computational processes with color.

5.2 Device Color Systems

In a physical color system, the color representation coordinates are generally positive and limited. This is because both sensors and emitters have a physical limitation in terms of the amount of electromagnetic energy with which they can operate. Thus, it is convenient to associate a color solid to the physical system of a device. This solid defines the set of valid colors for the device.

5.2.1 Process of Color Formation

Another important aspect of physical color systems is the process of color formation they use. This process of color formation is related to the way the spectral distribution functions of the primary colors are combined. This process can be additive or subtractive. In the additive process, the combination is performed by overlapping (sum) the spectral distributions. In the subtractive process, the combination is performed from the white color by filtering (multiplication) the spectral distributions.

An example of additive system is the mRGB system of monitors and video projectors. The mRGB system uses s mixing of the primary colors red, blue, and green. Normalizing

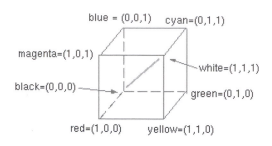

Figure 5.5. RGB color solid. (See Plate II.)   **Figure 5.6.** CMYK color cube.

the color coordinates within the interval $[0, 1]$ turns the mRGB color solid in the unit cube (see Figure 5.5). The origin corresponds to black because it is an additive system.

```
#define C_WHITE c_make(1,1,1)
#define C_BLACK c_make(0,0,0)
```

An example of a system in which the process of color formation is subtractive can be seen in the CMY system of color printers and of the photography process. In the CMY system, cyan, magenta and yellow ink filter white. The color solid of the CMY system is also a unit cube. In this system, the origin corresponds to white.

5.2.2   RGB–CMY Conversion

The conversion between the RGB and CMY systems is quite simple, and it consists of a basis change. A scaling by   1 in each one of the principal directions performs the change between the additive and subtractive process. The origin of the system is mapped by a translation along the diagonal of the cube $(1, 1, 1)$ (see Figure 5.6).

The matrix `rgb_cmy_m` implements this transformation.

82a   ⟨*rgb cmy matrix* 82a⟩≡
```
Matrix4 rgb_cmy_m = {{-1.0,   0.0,   0.0, 1.0},
                     { 0.0,  -1.0,   0.0, 1.0},
                     { 0.0,   0.0,  -1.0, 1.0},
                     { 0.0,   0.0,   0.0, 0.0}
};
```
Defines:
  rgb_cmy_m, used in chunks 82b and 83a.

The conversion is performed by the routines `rgb_to_cmy` and `cmy_to_rgb`, which use the same matrix.

82b   ⟨*rgb to cmy* 82b⟩≡
```
Vector3 rgb_to_cmy(Vector3 c)
{
```

```
      return v3_m4mult(c, rgb_cmy_m);
   }
```
Defines:
 rgb_to_cmy, never used.
Uses rgb_cmy_m 82a.

83a   ⟨*cmy to rgb* 83a⟩≡

```
   Vector3 cmy_to_rgb(Vector3 c)
   {
      return v3_m4mult(c, rgb_cmy_m);
   }
```
Defines:
 cmy_to_rgb, never used.
Uses rgb_cmy_m 82a.

5.3   Color Specification Systems

Color specification systems are intended to allow the intuitive identification of different colors. Exploring perceptual characteristics is key to achieving this goal. The question in place is, What are the significant parameters for color identification by a human being? By first answering this question, we can then define proper color spaces for color specification.

5.3.1   Luminance: Chrominance Decomposition

Intuitively, we know that a certain color can be more or less luminous. This fact corresponds to the variation on the amount of energy associated with a spectral distribution. Given a spectral distribution function $c(\lambda)$ and a real number $t > 0$, the product $c' = tc(\lambda)$ corresponds to another spectral distribution having non-null energy only for the wavelengths λ in which $c(\lambda)$ is also non-null. If $t > 1$, c' then has larger energy; otherwise, if $0 < t < 1$, c' has smaller energy. From a perceptual point of view, the scaling of function $c(\lambda)$ alters a psychophysical measurement denominated *luminance*, or brightness of the color.

The luminance of a color is given by the operator $L(c) = \sum l_i c_i$, where l_i depends on the primaries of the color system. In the mRGB system of the monitor, $l_r = 0.299$, $l_g = 0.587$, and $l_b = 0.114$.

83b   ⟨*rgb to y* 83b⟩≡

```
   Real c_rgb_to_y(Color c)
   {
      return 0.299 * RED(c) + 0.587 * GRN(c) + 0.114 * BLU(c);
   }
```
Defines:
 c_rgb_to_y, never used.
Uses BLU 79, Color 79, GRN 79, and RED 79.

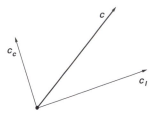

Figure 5.7. Decomposition of a color vector c in its components of luminance c_l and chrominance c_c.

We can divide color information into two components: *luminance* and *chrominance*. The former, as we saw above, is related to the brightness of the color, while the latter to the chroma, that is, the color independent of intensity variation.

In a color space of dimension 3, a color $c \in \mathbb{R}^3$ is represented by its coordinates $c = (c_1, c_2, c_3)$. As we saw above, for $t > 0$, the vector $tc = (tc_1, tc_2, tc_3)$ represents the same chroma information with variable brightness. We can then conclude that the chroma space is a projective chroma.

To simplify the chroma representation, we would like to determine a subset of $\mathbb{R}^3$ in which each point corresponds to a distinct chroma information. An appropriate choice is the plane given by the equation $c_1 + c_2 + c_3 = 1$, in which every color, produced by a combination of the primary colors of the space, has a representative. This plane is called the *Maxwell plane*.

The coordinates of the radial projection of a color on the Maxwell plane are called *chromaticity coordinates*. Calculation of these coordinates is immediate. Given that two colors with same chrome and different brightness have only one representative c' on the Maxwell plane, their coordinates satisfy $c'_1 + c'_2 + c'_3 = 1$. In this way, we can find t for an arbitrary color, such that $tc = c'$. Therefore,

$$t(c_1 + c_2 + c_3) = c'_1 + c'_2 + c'_3 = 1,$$

and so,

$$t = \frac{1}{c_1 + c_2 + c_3},$$

and

$$c'_i = \frac{c_i}{c_1 + c_2 + c_3}.$$

The decomposition of a color into its luminance and chrominance components has great importance from a perceptual point of view. This means we can represent a color vector c as the sum of two vectors $c = c_l + c_c$, where c_l describes the luminance of the color and c_c describes the chroma information (see Figure 5.7). This decomposition will be explored in the next subsection to elaborate a space for color specification.

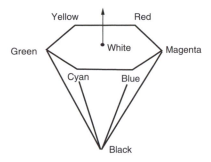

Figure 5.8. HSV color solid.

5.3.2 HSV Systems for Color Selection

The luminance/chrominance decomposition allows the introduction of intuitive coordinates for color selection. The process consists of first choosing the color chrominance and then determining the color luminance.

Chrominance is chosen through a point in a representative chroma space of the system. As the chroma set is 2D, we can establish a system of polar coordinates on the plane. In this system, the origin corresponds to white. As we distance ourselves from the origin, we have more saturated, or pure, colors. Radially about the origin we have the various color shades.

The HSV system (*hue*, or shade; *saturation*; and *value*, related to luminance) is based on these intuitive parameters, from a perceptual point of view. The HSV space can be naturally associated with a straight pyramid of hexagonal basis with a vertex at the origin. In this color solid, the value varies between 0 and 1, from the apex to the basis of the pyramid. On the planes orthogonal to the pyramid axis, we describe shade and saturation using polar coordinates (see Figure 5.8).

RGB-HSV conversion. To perform the conversion between the RGB and HSV systems, we have to map between the color solids of the two systems. This task is simplified by the existence of a natural correspondence between the vertices of the RGB cube and the HSV pyramid.

We define the coordinate value v and a color $c = (r, g, b)$ as $v(c) = \max(r, g, b)$. In this way, for each value v, we have a cube C_v parallel to the unit RGB cube (see Figure 5.9). The apex of the inverted pyramid corresponds to black $(0, 0, 0)$, and the center of its basis corresponds to white $(1, 1, 1)$. We therefore obtain a correspondence between the axis of the HSV pyramid and the diagonal of the RGB cube.

By making the orthogonal projection of a cube C_v on a plane π_v perpendicular to the diagonal and passing through the point (v, v, v), we obtain a hexagon in which each vertex corresponds to either one of the primary RGB colors or to the complementary CMY colors. That is, the remaining vertices of the RGB cube are mapped into the vertices of the hexagonal basis of the HSV pyramid (see Figure 5.10).

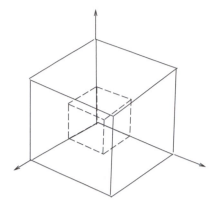
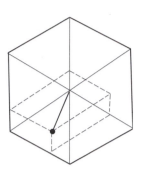

Figure 5.9. Cube parallel to unit RGB cube.   **Figure 5.10.** Hexagon.

The routine `rgb_to_hsv` converts between the systems RGB and HSV. The calculation of the color value trivially proceeds from the definition $v = \max(r, g, b)$.

The saturation calculation consists of determining the fraction between the orthogonal projection c_c of the vector $c = (r, g, b)$ on the plane π_v, and the boundary. It is easy to see that, by normalizing $s \in [0, 1]$,

$$s = \frac{v - \min(r, g, b)}{v}.$$

The hue calculation consists of determining the angle between the projected vector c and the vector R. Notice that, depending on which is the smallest component of c, its projection c_c will be located in a pair of triangular sectors of the hexagon. More precisely, let $x = \min(r, g, b)$: if $x = r$ then $c_c \in \{(R, Y, W) \cup (Y, G, W)\}$, if $x = g$ then $c_c \in \{(R, M, W) \cup (M, B, W)\}$, and if $x = b$ then $c_c \in \{(G, C, W) \cup (C, B, W)\}$. In these sectors, the relative coordinate to one of the CMY vertices is given by

$$h = \frac{a - b}{v - x},$$

where a and b are, respectively, the corresponding components to the initial and final vertices of the pair of sectors.

86   ⟨*rgb to hsv* 86⟩≡

```
Color rgb_to_hsv(Real r, Real g, Real b)
{
  Real v, x, f;
  int i;

  x = MIN(r, MIN(g, b));
  v = MAX(r, MAX(g, b));
```

```
    if (v == x)
       return v3_make(UNDEFINED, 0, v);
    f = (r == x) ? g - b : ((g == x) ? b - r : r - g);
    i = (r == x) ? 3 : ((g == x) ? 5 : 1);
    return c_make(i - f /(v - x), (v - x)/v, v);


}
```

Defines:
  rgb_to_hsv, never used.
Uses c_make and Color 79.

The routine hsv_to_rgb converts from HSV to RGB.

87   ⟨hsv to rgb 87⟩≡
```
    Color hsv_to_rgb(Real h, Real s, Real v)
    {
      Real m, n, f;
      int i;

      if(h == UNDEFINED)
         return c_make(v, v, v);
      i = floor(h);
      f = h - i;
      if(EVEN(i))
         f = 1 - f;
      m = v * (1 - s);
      n = v * (1 - s * f);
      switch (i) {
      case 6:
      case 0: return c_make(v, n, m);
      case 1: return c_make(n, v, m);
      case 2: return c_make(m, v, n);
      case 3: return c_make(m, n, v);
      case 4: return c_make(n, m, v);
      case 5: return c_make(v, m, n);
      }
    }
```

Defines:
  hsv_to_rgb, never used.
Uses c_make and Color 79.

5.4   Discretizing the Color Solid

Color in graphics devices is represented by integer numbers. This means that, in practice, graphics devices work with a discretized color space. In general, color information in the devices is given by a vector whose components are integer numbers with a precision of n bits.

Notice that the color space discretization described above corresponds to a uniform partition of the color solid of the device. In the next chapter we will discuss the problem of color discretization in the context of digital images and will explore methods to create nonuniform partitions of the color solid.

Some graphics devices use a single integer number of m bits to represent the color information. In this case, it is necessary to have a method to wrap and unwrap the color components in this representation. We therefore define routines to calculate the integer color value starting from the RGB coordinates and vice versa.

88a   ⟨*rgb to index* 88a⟩≡

```
int rgb_to_index(Color c, int nr, int ng, int nb)
{
  unsigned int r = CLAMP(RED(c), 0, 255);
  unsigned int g = CLAMP(GRN(c), 0, 255);
  unsigned int b = CLAMP(BLU(c), 0, 255);

  r = (r >> (8 - nr)) & MASK_BITS(nr);
  g = (g >> (8 - ng)) & MASK_BITS(ng);
  b = (b >> (8 - nb)) & MASK_BITS(nb);

  return ((r << (ng + nb))| (g << nb)| b);

}
```

Defines:
  rgb_to_index, never used.
Uses BLU 79, Color 79, GRN 79, MASK_BITS 88b, and RED 79.

88b   ⟨*index to rgb* 88b⟩≡

```
Color index_to_rgb(int k, int nr, int ng, int nb)
{
  unsigned int r, g, b;
  r = ((k >> (ng + nb)) & MASK_BITS(nr)) << (8 - nr);
  g = ((k >> (nb)) & MASK_BITS(ng)) << (8 - ng);
  b = ((k) & MASK_BITS(nb)) << (8 - nb);

  return c_make(r, g, b);
}

#define MASK_BITS(n) ((01 << (n))-1)
```

Defines:
  index_to_rgb, never used.
  MASK_BITS, used in chunk 88a.
Uses c_make and Color 79.

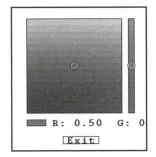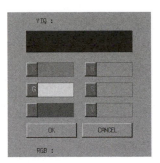

Figure 5.11. Color selection and conversion. (See Plate III.)

5.5   Comments and References

In this chapter we studied the representation of color and the implementation of a library to manipulate it. Figure 5.11 shows two examples of interfaces for color selection and conversion.

Color is one of the most important attributes present in many graphics objects. In a graphics system, the library routines are used for conversion between different color representations and also for the color specification by the user.

The original article describing the HSV system is authored by Alvy Ray Smith [Smith 81]. A more recent article by the same author is "HWB: A More Intuitive Hue-Based Color Model" [Smith and Lyons 96].

5.5.1   Links

There are two important international organizations for color standardization: CIE and ICC. More information on them can be found in:

  □ CIE. Commission Internationale d'Eclairage (International Commission on Illumination). http://www.hike.te.chiba-u.ac.jp/ikeda/CIE/home.html

  □ ICC. The International Color Consortium. http://www.color.org/

  Charles Poyton's webpage has interesting material on color: *Charles A. Poynton's Colour FAQ*, http://www.inforamp.net/~poynton/notes/colour_and_gamma/ColorFAQ.html

5.5.2   Review

The API of the color library consists of the following routines:

```
Vector3 rgb_to_cmy(Vector3 c);
Vector3 cmy_to_rgb(Vector3 c);
Vector3 rgb_to_yiq(Vector3 c);
```

```
Vector3 yiq_to_rgb(Vector3 c);

Vector3 rgb_to_hsv(Real r, Real g, Real b)
Vector3 hsv_to_rgb(Real h, Real s, Real v)
```

Exercises

1. Write a program to construct a color table with 256 colors. The program should implement at least two discretization methods for the RGB color solid.

2. Using the GP library, write a program to display the color tables produced in the previous exercise. Compare the two solutions.

3. Design and implement a widget for color selection.

4. Write a function that, given an arbitrary RGB color and a color map, finds the color in the map best representing it.

5. Write a program to convert colors between the RGB and HSV systems.

6 Digital Image

Images, as the end result of the viewing process, have fundamental importance in computer graphics. They are an indispensable part of interactive systems and therefore also play a role in the modeling process. In this chapter we will study the digital image, its representation, and operations with images.

6.1 Foundations

To develop a conceptualization for the study of images, we will once again use the paradigm of the four universes. We analyze the characteristics of images in the physical universe; define a mathematical model for images; establish a representation schema for images; and develop a data format for coding images (see Figure 6.1).

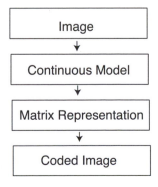

Figure 6.1. Abstract levels for images.

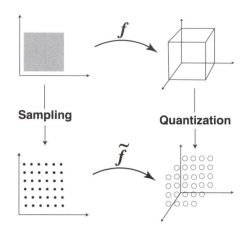

Figure 6.2. Discretization of images.

6.1.1 Continuous and Discrete Models of Images

An image consists of a 2D support where for each point we associate color information. In this way, we can use as a mathematical model of image the function $f : U \subset \mathbb{R}^2 \to C$. The set U is the *image support* and the set of values of f is called the *image gamut*. In this model the domain of the image function is usually a rectangle $U = [a, b] \times [c, d]$, and the counterdomain is a trichromatic space $C = \mathbb{R}^3$, as for example, the RGB space.

To represent an image on the computer, we have to discretize both the domain and the counterdomain of the image function. *Sampling* is discretization of the geometric support; *quantization* is discretization of the color space, or the process of reducing the color gamut (see Figure 6.2).

6.1.2 Image Quantization

Quantization is the transformation $q : \mathbb{R}^n \to M_k$, where $M_k = \{c_1, c_2, \ldots c_k\}$ is a finite subset of $\mathbb{R}^n$. The set M_k is called a *color map* of the quantization (or *code book*) transformation. When $k = 2^l$, we say that q is a quantization of l bits. Given the discrete representation of images, it is common to have a quantization among finite color subsets of the type $q : R_j \to M_k$. If $j = 2^n$ and $k = 2^m$, we have a quantization from n to m bits.

Consider a quantization transformation $q : \mathbb{R}^n \to M_k$. The elements c_i of M_k are called *quantization levels*. At each quantization level, $c_i \in M_k$ corresponds to one subset of colors $C_i \subset \mathbb{R}^n$, which are the colors mapped to the color c_i by the transformation q; that is,

$$C_i = q^{-1}(c_i) = \{c \in C \; ; q(c) = c_i\}.$$

The family of sets C_i constitutes a partition of the color space. Each of the sets C_i of this partition is called a *quantization cell*. Notice that the quantization function q assumes a constant equal to c_i in each cell C_i.

Note that the quantization function q is entirely determined by the quantization cells C_i and by the quantization levels c_i. By using geometric arguments we can obtain c_i starting from C_i and vice versa. In this way, some quantization methods perform calculations first at the c_i level and later at the cells C_i, while others use the opposite strategy.

If q is given by the quantization cells C_i, the levels c_i correspond to the centroid of the cells. If q is given by the quantization levels of c_i, the geometry of the cells C_i corresponds to the Voronoi diagram associated with the levels c_i; in other words, each cell C_i is formed by the set of points in the color space closer to the level c_i than to any of the other levels.

6.1.3 Matrix Representation

Sampling of the image support is usually based on a uniform grid $F_\Delta = \{(u_i, v_j) \in \mathbb{R}^2\}$, where $u_i = a + i\Delta u$ and $v_j = c + j\Delta v$ with $\Delta u = (b - a)/m$, $\Delta v = (d - c)/n$, and $i = 0, \ldots m$, $j = 0, \ldots n$. The points (u_i, v_j) are called sample points.

We can represent a discrete image by a 2D matrix. In the matrix representation, we associate to the image function $f(u, v)$ a matrix $A_{m \times n} = \{a_{ij}\}$, where $i = 1, m$ and $j = 1, n$.

The elements $a_{ij} = f(u_i, v_j)$ of the discrete image are called *pixels* (from "picture elements"). In a monochrome image, $a_{i,j} = x$ is a scalar, while in a trichromatic image, $a_{i,j} = (r, g, b)$ is a vector. What is more, $a_{i,j} = k$ can be an index of the corresponding color $c_k = (r, g, b)$ in a color map.

The *spatial resolution* of an image is given by the number of samples, or by the number m of lines and n of columns of the matrix A. The *color resolution* of an image is given by the number of color levels, or by the number of bits of a_{ij}.

6.2 Format of the Image Representation

Starting from the above conceptualization, we establish a format for image representation.

6.2.1 Data Structure

We adopt matrix representation as the image format. To implement this format, we need two types of information:

□ **Header.** Specifies representation data, such as spatial resolution and quantization type.

□ **Pixel matrix.** The elements of the image matrix. The pixel is an RGB color vector.

We define the data structure `Image`, composed of a header with spatial and color resolution, and a pointer to the pixel matrix.

94a   ⟨*image structure* 94a⟩≡

```
typedef struct Image {
  int w, h;
  unsigned int maxval;
  Bcolor *c;
} Image;
```

Defines:
   Image, used in chunks 94–97.
Uses Bcolor 94b.

The elements of an image are defined by integer numbers of 8 bits, unsigned. The pixel is a 3D vector `Bcolor`, where each component is a `Byte`.

94b   ⟨*image elements* 94b⟩≡

```
typedef unsigned char Byte;

typedef struct Bcolor {
  Byte z, y, x;
} Bcolor;
```

Defines:
   Bcolor, used in chunk 94.
   Byte, never used.

We also define the interval of valid values for a `Byte` by the macros `PIX_MIN` and `PIX_MAX`.

94c   ⟨*pixel values* 94c⟩≡

```
#define PIX_MIN 0
#define PIX_MAX 255
```

Defines:
   PIX_MAX, used in chunk 95c.
   PIX_MIN, used in chunk 95c.

The routine `img_init` is the constructor for the structure `Image`. Its parameters are the spatial resolution and the image type.

94d   ⟨*img init* 94d⟩≡

```
Image *img_init(int type, int w, int h)
{
  Image *i = NEWSTRUCT(Image);

  i->w = w; i->h = h;
  i->maxval = 255;
  i->c = NEWTARRAY(w*h, Bcolor);
  img_clear(i, C_BLACK);
  return i;
}
```

Defines:
  img_init, used in chunk 97.
Uses Bcolor 94b, Image 94a, and img_clear.

The routine img_free is the destructor for the structure Image.

95a   ⟨*img free* 95a⟩≡
```
void img_free(Image *i)
{
   efree(i->c); efree(i);
}
```
Defines:
  img_free, never used.
Uses Image 94a.

6.2.2   Access to the Image Matrix

We chose to store the image elements in a contiguous memory area. In this way, addressing the (u, v) elements of the image matrix is done by the macros PIXRED, PIXGRN, and PIXBLU.

95b   ⟨*image array access* 95b⟩≡
```
#define PIXRED(I,U,V) I->c[U + (((I->h - 1) - (V)) * I->w)].x
#define PIXGRN(I,U,V) I->c[U + (((I->h - 1) - (V)) * I->w)].y
#define PIXBLU(I,U,V) I->c[U + (((I->h - 1) - (V)) * I->w)].z
```
Defines:
  PIXBLU, used in chunks 95c and 96a.
  PIXGRN, used in chunks 95c and 96a.
  PIXRED, used in chunks 95c and 96a.

The routines img_putc and img_getc enable access to the image matrix by color.

95c   ⟨*img putc* 95c⟩≡
```
void img_putc(Image *i, int u, int v, Color c)
{
   if (u >= 0 && u < i->w && v >= 0 && v < i->h) {
     PIXRED(i,u,v) = CLAMP(RED(c), PIX_MIN, PIX_MAX);
     PIXGRN(i,u,v) = CLAMP(GRN(c), PIX_MIN, PIX_MAX);
     PIXBLU(i,u,v) = CLAMP(BLU(c), PIX_MIN, PIX_MAX);
   }
}
```
Defines:
  img_putc, used in chunk 97.
Uses Image 94a, PIX_MAX 94c, PIX_MIN 94c, PIXBLU 95b, PIXGRN 95b, and PIXRED 95b.

96a   ⟨*img getc* 96a⟩≡
```
Color img_getc(Image *i, int u, int v)
{
  if (u >= 0 && u < i->w && v >= 0 && v < i->h)
    return c_make(PIXRED(i,u,v),PIXGRN(i,u,v),PIXBLU(i,u,v));
  else
    return C_BLACK;
}
```
Defines:
  img_getc, used in chunk 96b.
Uses Image 94a, PIXBLU 95b, PIXGRN 95b, and PIXRED 95b.

6.3   Image Coding

We chose *PPM* format (portable pixel map) for external image representation. This format is supported by most Unix systems and in Windows by several commercial and public domain programs.

6.3.1   PPM Format

PPM format is quite simple, supporting the type of images we used in the matrix representation defined in this chapter. A PPM file, which by convention has the extension ".ppm," consists of a header and the pixel matrix. The header includes the usual information about the matrix representation, such as spatial resolution. The first 2 bytes of the file correspond to the integer PPM_MAGIC, which allows us to identify whether a file is in PPM format.

```
#define PPM_MAGIC       P6
```

6.3.2   Direct Coding

As we saw above, a PPM file consists of a header and a pixel matrix. The direct coding of an image matrix is given by the list of the matrix elements sorted by lines. The routines to read and write PPM images use the open source library *libnetpbm* (http://netpbm.sourceforge.net).

The routine img_write writes a PPM file with the image data.

96b   ⟨*img write* 96b⟩≡
```
void img_write(Image *i, char *fname, int cflag)
{
  FILE *fp;
  int row, col;
  pixval maxval;
  pixel **pixels;

  fp = (strcmp("stdout", fname) == 0)? stdout : fopen(fname, "wb");
```

```
      pixels = ppm_allocarray(i->w, i->h);
      for ( row = 0; row < i->h; ++row ) {
        for ( col = 0; col < i->w; ++col ) {
          Color c = img_getc(i, col, i->h - row - 1);
          pixel p = pixels[row][col];
          (pixels[row][col]).r  = RED(c);
          (pixels[row][col]).g  = GRN(c);
          (pixels[row][col]).b  = BLU(c);
        }
      }
      ppm_writeppm(fp, pixels, i->w, i->h, i->maxval, TRUE);
      pnm_freearray(pixels, i->h);
      if  (strcmp("stdout", fname) != 0)
        fclose(fp);
    }
```
Defines:
   img_write, never used.
Uses Image 94a and img_getc 96a.

The routine `img_read` reads a PPM file to the Image structure.

97   ⟨img read 97⟩≡
```
    Image *img_read(char *fname)
    {
      FILE *fp, *fp2;
      int row, col, cols, rows;
      pixval maxval;
      pixel **pixels;
      Image *i;

      fp =  (strcmp("stdin", fname) == 0)? stdin : fopen(fname, "rb");
      pixels = ppm_readppm(fp, &cols, &rows, &maxval);
      i = img_init(0, cols, rows);
      i->maxval = maxval;
      for ( row = 0; row < rows; ++row ) {
        for ( col = 0; col < cols; ++col ) {
          pixel const p = pixels[row][col];
          img_putc(i, col, rows-row-1, c_make(PPM_GETR(p), PPM_GETG(p),
                  PPM_GETB(p)));
        }
      }
      pnm_freearray(pixels, rows);
      fclose(fp);
      return i;
    }
```
Defines:
   img_read, never used.
Uses Image 94a, img_init 94d, and img_putc 95c.

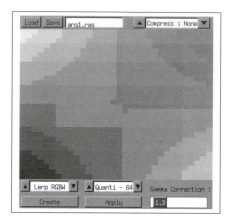

Figure 6.3. Program for visualizing images. (See Plate IV.)

6.4   Comments and References

In this chapter we discussed representation of images and presented a library for the manipulation of images. Figure 6.3 shows an example of a program for visualizing images. Two references on image processing for computer graphics are [Gomes and Velho 95, Gomes and Velho 97].

6.4.1   Revision

The API of the images library consists of the following routines:

```
Image *img_init(int type, int w, int h);
void  img_clear(Image *i, Color c);
Image *img_read(char *fname);
void  img_write(Image *i, char *fname, int cflag);

void  img_putc(Image *i, int u, int v, Color c);
Color img_getc(Image *i, int u, int v);

void img_free(Image *i);
```

6.4.2   Image Format

The most important image formats are

   □ TIFF,

   □ GIF,

□ JPEG,

□ PhotoCD.

Some public domain packets for images are

□ Utah Raster Toolkit,

□ PBM,

□ LibTIFF,

□ IRIS Tools.

The most popular public domain programs for viewing images are GIMP, ImageMagic, and XV.

Exercises

1. Write a program to generate images with the following patterns:

   (a) squared,

   (b) ramps of grey tones,

   (c) interpolation of four colors at the corners of the image,

   (d) white noise.

2.

   (a) Use a public domain program (GIMP, for instance) to visualize the images of the previous exercise.

   (b) Write a program to visualize images using the GP library.

   (c) Compare the results of (a) and (b) and discuss the limitations of your program.

3. Write a program to perform gamma correction on an image. Using your program, try to empirically determine the gamma factor of your monitor.

4. Write a dithering program. Using the gray tone patterns created in Exercise 6.1, test the program with quantization for 6, 4, 2, and 1 bits.

5. Write a quantization program. Using the patterns created in Exercise 6.1, test the program with quantization for 6, 4, 2, and 1 bits.

6. Write a program to compress images using the RLE method. Test the program with the images generated in Exercise 6.1. Verify the compression factors for each image and explain the results.

7.   Write a program to combine the methods of color quantization and dithering.

8.   Write a program to convert a colored image into an a gray tone image.

7 Description of 3D Scenes

Along with digital images, 3D scenes are one of the fundamental elements of computer graphics. The viewing process, which ends with the production of a digital image, starts from the description of a 3D scene. The modeling process creates the representation of a scene starting from the user's guidelines. In this chapter, we study the representation of, and computational methods to create, 3D scenes.

7.1 3D Scenes

A 3D scene describes a virtual world in computer graphics applications. The main purpose of this representation is to capture the aspects relevant for both modeling and visualization of the objects in the virtual world.

The scene description establishes the interface between the processes of modeling and visualization (see Figure 7.1). Besides, this representation is used for both the storage and transmission of the scene, for instance in a CAD system or in a distributed virtual reality system.

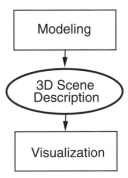

Figure 7.1. Interface between modeling and visualization.

7.1.1   Elements of a 3D Scene

Description of a 3D scene consists of the specification of its elements and how they are structured, including configuration information. The components of a 3D scene are the *objects* inhabiting the virtual world. These objects can be organized into three categories:

- □ **Object models.** Describes the geometry and visual properties.

- □ **Light sources.** Describes the illumination.

- □ **Virtual camera.** Describes the observer.

The *structure* of the objects in a 3D scene corresponds to groups of objects with relations, such as geometric links, among themselves. These groups can be structured in a hierarchical way. The *configuration* of a 3D scene is determined by several other parameters specifying the way in which the description can be manipulated (e.g., the name of the scene, data on the image of the scene, etc.).

Note that description of a 3D scene involves several types of information, as well as many diverse parameters. This diversity is one of the fundamental characteristics that should be taken into account in the representation of a 3D scene.

7.1.2   Representation of 3D Scenes

Just as we defined a format for digital images (see Chapter 6), we could do the same for 3D scenes. But defining this would not be adequate: 3D scenes contain many types of information, which may or may not be present in a certain scene. Consequently, setting a fixed data format would be very complex and, therefore, inefficient.

Another proposal that certainly would provide total flexibility, would be to adopt a procedural representation, based in a generic programming language, such as C or Lisp. This solution is also unsatisfactory since it would require the use of constructions lacking a semantic contextualization of 3D scenes.

The ideal alternative for representing 3D scenes lies between these two extremes and offers the best compromise between specificity and generality allowing a representation that is flexible and simultaneously has great expression power. It consists of adopting a *scene description language*.

7.1.3   Scene Description Language

A language for describing 3D scenes should meet the following requirements:

- □ Intuitive notation,

- □ Uniform syntax,

- □ Extensible semantics,

- □ Simple implementation.

Besides, this language should incorporate concepts from existing area standards; of particular importance are Open Inventor SDL (scene description language) and VRML (Virtual Reality Modeling Language). Based on these two standards, we will develop a 3D scene description language that meets the requirements listed above. This language allows us to describe the elements of a scene through simple and effective constructions. We will give a concrete example to clarify this statement:

Example 7.1. Simple 3D Scene

```
scene {
   camera = view { from = {0, 0, -2.5}, fov = 90},
   light = ambi_light { intensity = 0.2 },
   light = dist_light { direction = {0, 1, -1} },
   object = group{
            material = plastic { kd = 0.8, ks = 0.0 },
            transform = { translate {v = {0, .0, 0}}},
            children = {
               primobj{ shape = sphere{radius = .1 }},
               primobj{ shape = cylinder { center = {2, 2, 2}}}}}},
}
```
                                                                                   □

This example describes a 3D scene composed of a virtual camera, two light sources, and a group with two primitive objects. Notice this information is encoded in a clear and precise way, still presenting a regular structure.

In the following sections, we will study the computational concepts related to programming languages. From these concepts, we will specify the implementation of the 3D scene description language and demonstrate its use.

7.2 Language Concepts

A language is a systematic schema for describing information. The *syntax* of the language determines its formal structure and the *semantics* of the language is related to its content. An expression consists of a set of symbols structured according to the syntactic rules, whose content is defined by the semantic definition. In a programming language, the content is a computational process.

7.2.1 Expression Languages

Several types of programming languages exist. We will concentrate on the *expression languages*. An expression language is based on two fundamental abstractions: *operators* and *operands*.

In this type of language, a program is formed by a sequential set of expressions. The syntax consists of the rules to build expressions and the semantics of the evaluation of those expressions. Notice that, as evaluation implies a computational process, the content effectively takes place through the execution of that process.

Expression languages are intimately related to functional computing. In fact, we can associate operators with functions and operands with parameters. In an expression language, every expression has a *value*. Expressions can be either *primitive* or *composed*. A primitive expression has its value defined directly (in other words, a given constant for a basic type of the language). A composed expression has its value defined by the result of the recursive evaluation of the set (that is, the application of the function and its parameters).

We use the *substitution model* to implement the *evaluation of an expression*. The basic procedure has the following structure:

> if simple expression
>
>> returns value
>
> if composed expression
>
>> finds values of the operands
>> returns the value of the applied operator to the operands

7.2.2   Syntax and Semantics in Expressions

In a expression language, the goal of the syntactic rules is to identify operators and operands to form expressions. Notice we can have different syntaxes for the same semantic content. For example, consider the binary expressions made up of an operator and two operands. We therefore have three possibilities for structuring binary expressions, determined by the position of the operator relative to the operands. They correspond to the prefix, postfix, and infix operators.

Example 7.2. Sum Operation

- □ **Prefix notation.** $(+\quad a\quad b)$
- □ **Postfix notation.** $(a\quad b\quad +)$
- □ **Infix notation.** $(a\quad +\quad b)$

□

The syntactic analysis should produce a representation of expressions independent of the notation used. This representation is given by a *expression tree*. The internal nodes of the tree contain operators, while the leaves of the tree contain basic types. The hierarchical structure is formed by the clustering of subexpressions. We will give an example.

Example 7.3. The tree of the expression

$$((a + b) * (c - (d + e)))$$

is shown in Figure 7.2. This expression uses the infix notation. Notice that the same tree would be used to represent that expression given in a postfix or prefix notation.   □

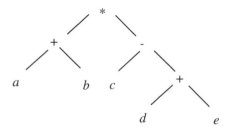

Figure 7.2. Expression tree.

Expressions identified by the syntactic analyzer are sent to the expression evaluator implementing the substitution model presented in Section 7.2.1. In this way, the execution consists of sequentially evaluating the expression trees forming the program. The pseudocode below shows the structure of an interpreter for expression languages:

While (more expressions)

    Read expression

    Evaluate expression

7.2.3　Compilation and Interpretation of Programs

A program is normally encoded through alphanumeric characters composing the text, or *source code*, of the program. This text should be analyzed so higher-level language structures can be extracted from it. Those structures should be then processed, therefore executing the meaning of the program.

The source code analysis phase is called *compilation*. In this phase, an analysis of the lexical and syntactic structures takes place. The processing phase is called *execution*. In this phase, computing by the attribution of semantic content to the computational structures takes place.

In certain computational systems, the analysis and execution phases are accomplished by a single program called *interpreter*. A compiler (or interpreter) is composed of the following modules implementing the various phases of analysis and execution of the program code:

□ Lexical analyzer (or scanner);

□ Syntactic analyzer (or parser);

□ Expression evaluator (or evaluator).

Beyond these three modules, we also have modules for managing symbols (symbol manager) and for error handling (error handler).

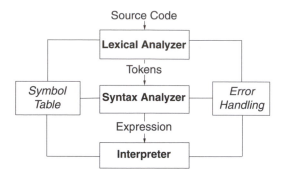

Figure 7.3. Anatomy of an interpreter.

In the lexical analysis, sequences of characters are grouped to form the basic language types: numbers, names, etc. The syntactic analyzer has as input the source code and as output the identifiers (or tokens) of the basic types. Names are stored in a table by the symbol manager. In expression languages, the syntax determines the way the composed expressions are constructed, starting from the basic types. The syntactic analyzer has identifiers as input and expression trees as output.

As we said in the previous section, the semantics is given by the language operators. The expression evaluator runs the program, applying operators to its operands. Figure 7.3 shows the anatomy of a program interpreter, its modules and the interrelations among them.

7.2.4   Tools for Developing Languages

The development environment of UNIX programs has several tools to facilitate implementation of languages. These tools were improved by Open Software Foundation and are part of the GNU programming packet. The tools below are programs to generate programs implementing the modules of an interpreter (or compiler). These modules are specified by the lexical, syntactic, and semantic rules of the designed language.

- □ **lex.** Scanner generator (lexical analysis)

- □ **yacc.** Parser generator (syntactic analysis)

- □ **CPP / M4.** Macro translator (preprocessing)

7.3   An Extension Language

Instead of directly implementing a 3D scene description language, we are going to develop a "metalanguage" that will allow incremental and flexible specification of our language.

We will use a type of metalanguage called *extension language*, which has closed and uniform syntax and open and minimum semantics. The advantages of this schema is that the extension language incorporates the entire computational environment necessary for syntactic analysis; at the same time it also allows for specification of the application semantics, such as the description of scenes.

The extension language provides the computational support for "sublanguages" (or *embedded languages*). These sublanguages extend the semantics of the language kernel through primitives provided by the application, as well as functions defined by the user.

In this section, we will develop all of the modules comprising the interpreter of our extension language.

7.3.1 Syntactic Analyzer

We will use UNIX tools to develop the extension language. In particular, we will use the yacc program to generate the syntactic analyzer. The yacc has as input a specification of the syntactic rules for the construction of the expression trees of the language. The expression tree is constituted by *terminal symbols* and *nonterminal symbols*.

Terminal symbols (or tokens) are basic language types corresponding to the tree leaves. Our language has the following basic types: numbers, strings, names, and classes. Strings are character strings between quotation marks, and classes are identifiers for operators.

107a ⟨*tokens* 107a⟩≡
```
%token <dval> NUMBER
%token <sval> STRING NAME
%token <fval> CLASS
```

Nonterminal symbols (or types) are syntactic structures of the language, also called "productions," corresponding to the internal tree nodes. Our language has the following productions: value, pv, pvlist, expression, and input.

107b ⟨*types* 107b⟩≡
```
%type <nval> node input
%type <pval> pvlist pv
%type <vval> val
```

The structure below represents a node of the expression tree, being either internal or external. For this reason, the data structure consists of the union of all of the basic and derived types.

107c ⟨*parser data structure* 107c⟩≡
```
%union {
    char    ival;
    double  dval;
    char    *sval;
    Pval    *pval;
    Val     vval;
    Node    *nval;
```

```
    Val    (*fval)();
  }
```
Uses **Node** 115b, **Pval** 113b, and **Val** 114a.

We specify the grammar of our language by the syntactic rules below:

108   ⟨*grammar rules* 108⟩≡
```
    %%
    input:    /* empty */          { $$ = root = NULL;}
            | input node    ';'    { $$ = root = $2;}
            | input error   ';'    { yyerrok; $$ = root = NULL;}
            ;
    node:     CLASS '{' pvlist '}'  { $$ = t_node($1, $3); }
            | '{' pvlist '}'        { $$ = t_node(t_pvl, $2); }
            ;
    pvlist:   /* empty */          { $$ = (Pval *)0;}
            | pvlist ','           { $$ = $1;}
            | pvlist pv            { $$ = pv_append($1, $2);}
            ;
    pv:       NAME '=' val         { $$ = pv_make($1, $3);}
            | val                  { $$ = pv_make(NULL, $1);}
            ;
    val:      NUMBER               { $$ = pv_value(V_NUM, $1, NULL, NULL);}
            | '-' NUMBER           { $$ = pv_value(V_NUM, - $2, NULL, NULL);}
            | STRING               { $$ = pv_value(V_STR, 0., $1, NULL);}
            | node                 { $$ = pv_value(V_NOD, 0., NULL, $1);}
            ;
    %%
```
Uses **pv_append** 115a, **pv_make** 114b, **pv_value** 114c, **Pval** 113b, **root**, **t_node** 115c,
   t_pvl 117a, **V_NOD** 113c, **V_NUM** 113c, and **V_STR** 113c.

Those rules define an extremely simple and powerful grammar. It allows constructions
of the type:

```
class { name = value, name = value }
```

This construction is quite appropriate for describing n-ary expressions. The operator
is of the type `class`. The operands are pairs `name` and `value`, which allows us to name
them.

As `value` can also be an expression, we can group subexpressions to form expressions.
Furthermore, we can omit both `class` and `name` from the basic construction, resulting
in the variants `{ name = value, name = value }`, `class { value, value }`, and
`{ value, value }`. Note that, as `value` can be a number, this last construction can
represent n-dimensional vectors.

An important observation concerns the error management problem. In the first syntactic rule, we have a production of the form `input error;`. This means that, when a

syntax error is detected, the partial data will be discarded and the routine `yyerror` will be called. This routine simply informs us that an error happened at a line of the input file.

109a   ⟨*yyerror* 109a⟩≡
```
int yyerror()
{
  extern int lineno;
  fprintf(stderr, "lang: syntax error in , near line %d\n",lineno);
}
```
Defines:
  `yyerror`, never used.
Uses `lineno` 109c.

7.3.2 Lexical Analyzer

The lexical analyzer is responsible for processing the source code, grouping the input characters to form symbols (or tokens).

We could use the program **lex** to generate the lexical analyzer. However, we prefer to implement it directly to have more control over the processing.

The program is relatively simple and works as a finite state machine. Based on the current character, the algorithm determines whether it continues in the current state, or changes the state. Each state corresponds to a type of symbol. The states are indicated by the names of the macros in the `yylex` routine.

109b   ⟨*yylex* 109b⟩≡
```
yylex()
{
  Symbol *s;

  SCAN_WHITE_SPACE
  SCAN_NUMBER
  SCAN_STRING
  SCAN_NAME_CLASS
  SCAN_MARK
}
```
Uses `SCAN_MARK` 111b, `SCAN_NAME_CLASS` 111a, `SCAN_NUMBER` 110b, `SCAN_STRING` 110c, `SCAN_WHITE_SPACE` 110a, `Symbol` 112b, and `yylex`.

The information internal to the lexical analyzer is stored in the variable `fin`, which is a pointer to the input file and in `lineno` and `c`, which indicate, respectively, the current line and character of the source code. These variables are accessible to other routines of the lexical analyzer.

109c   ⟨*internal state* 109c⟩≡
```
static FILE *fin = stdin;
static int c;
int lineno = 0;
```

Defines:
  c, used in chunks 110, 111, and 117a.
  fin, used in chunks 110–12.
  lineno, used in chunks 109a and 111b.

The macro SCAN_WHITE_SPACE has the purpose of detecting the "white spaces" of the code, which are separators formed by whites and tabulations. It also detects the condition EOF, indicating the end of the file.

110a   ⟨*scan white space* 110a⟩≡

```
#define SCAN_WHITE_SPACE
  while ((c = getc(fin)) == ' '|| c == '\t')
    ;
  if (c == EOF) return 0;
```

Defines:
  SCAN_WHITE_SPACE, used in chunk 109b.
Uses c 109c and fin 109c.

The macro SCAN_NUMBER constructs numbers formed by a sequence of floating point numerical digits.

110b   ⟨*scan number* 110b⟩≡

```
#define SCAN_NUMBER
  if (c == '.'|| isdigit(c)) { double d;
    ungetc(c, fin);
    fscanf(fin, "%lf", &d);
    yylval.dval = d;
    return NUMBER;
  }
```

Defines:
  SCAN_NUMBER, used in chunk 109b.
Uses c 109c and fin 109c.

The macro SCAN_STRING assembles character strings delimited by quotation marks.

110c   ⟨*scan string* 110c⟩≡

```
#define SCAN_STRING
  if (c == '"') { char sbuf[320], *p;
    for (p = sbuf; (c = getc(fin)) != '"'; *p++ = c) {
      if (c == '\\')
        c = ((c = getc(fin)) == '\n')? ' ' : c;
      if (c == '\n'|| c == EOF) {
        fprintf(stderr,"missing quote, sbuf\n"); break;
      }
      if (p >= sbuf + sizeof(sbuf) - 1) {
        fprintf(stderr,"sbuffer overflow\n"); break;
      }
    }
    *p = '\0';
    yylval.sval = malloc(strlen(sbuf) + 1);
```

```
      strcpy(yylval.sval, sbuf);
      return STRING;
    }
```

Defines:
  SCAN_STRING, used in chunk 109b.
Uses c 109c and fin 109c.

The macro SCAN_NAME_CLASS identifies a name with the aid of the symbol manager, which we will describe further on.

111a   ⟨*scan name class* 111a⟩≡

```
    #define SCAN_NAME_CLASS
      if (isalpha(c)) { char sbuf[1024], *p = sbuf; int t;
        do {
          if (p >= sbuf + sizeof(sbuf) - 1) {
            *p = '\0';
            fprintf(stderr,"name too long %s (%x:%x)\n", sbuf, p, sbuf);
          }
          *p++ = c;
        } while ((c = getc(fin)) != EOF && (isalnum(c)|| c == '_' ));
        ungetc(c, fin);
        *p = '\0';
        if ((s = sym_lookup(sbuf)) == (Symbol *)0)
          s = sym_install(sbuf, NAME, NULL);
        if (s->token == CLASS)
          yylval.fval = s->func;
        else
          yylval.sval = s->name;
        return s->token;
      }
```

Defines:
  SCAN_NAME_CLASS, used in chunk 109b.
Uses c 109c, fin 109c, sym_install 112c, sym_lookup 113a, and Symbol 112b.

The macro SCAN_MARK detects alphanumeric and special characters, such as end of line (\n).

111b   ⟨*scan mark* 111b⟩≡

```
    #define SCAN_MARK
      switch (c) {
      case '\\': if ((c = getc(fin)) != '\n')
                   return c;
                 else
                   return yylex();
      case '\n': lineno++; return yylex();
      default:   return c;
      }
    }
```

Defines:
SCAN_MARK, used in chunk 109b.
Uses c 109c, fin 109c, lineno 109c, and yylex.

The routine yyfile is used to specify the input file of the lexical analyzer.

112a ⟨*yyfile* 112a⟩≡
```
void yyfile(FILE *fd)
{
    fin = fd;
}
```
Defines:
yyfile, never used.
Uses fin 109c.

7.3.3   Symbol Manager

The symbol manager maintains the name table of the program. The data structure Symbol is used to represent the elements of the table. A symbol can be a name or the identifier of an operator. In this last case, the table contains a pointer to the function implementing the operator.

112b ⟨*symbol table* 112b⟩≡
```
typedef struct Symbol {
    char          *name;
    int           token;
    Val           (*func)();
    struct Symbol *next;
} Symbol;
```
Defines:
Symbol, used in chunks 109b and 111–13.
Uses Val 114a.

The symbol table is a single linked list stored in the internal variable symlist. The routine sym_install installs a symbol in the table.

112c ⟨*symbol install* 112c⟩≡
```
static Symbol *symlist = (Symbol *)0;

Symbol *sym_install(char *s, int t, Val (*func)())
{
    Symbol *sp = (Symbol *) malloc(sizeof(Symbol));

    sp->name = malloc(strlen(s) + 1);
    strcpy(sp->name, s);
    sp->token = t;
    sp->func = func;
    sp->next = symlist;
    return symlist = sp;
```

```
  }
```
Defines:
  sym_install, used in chunks 111a and 118c.
  symlist, used in chunk 113a.
Uses Symbol 112b and Val 114a.

The routine sym_lookup verifies if a name corresponds to an existing symbol in the table. If the symbol exists, then it returns its pointer; otherwise it returns a null pointer.

113a   ⟨*symbol lookup* 113a⟩≡

```
  Symbol *sym_lookup(char *s)
  {
    Symbol *sp;
    for (sp = symlist; sp != (Symbol *)0; sp = sp->next) {
      if (strcmp(sp->name, s) == 0)
        return sp;
    }
    return (Symbol *)0;
  }
```
Defines:
  sym_lookup, used in chunks 111a and 118c.
Uses Symbol 112b and symlist 112c.

7.3.4   Parameters and Values

The operands of a language expression are given by a list of parameters. A parameter consists of the pair name and value. The structure Pval is used to represent this pair. Notice it is the element of a single linked list.

113b   ⟨*parameter value structure* 113b⟩≡

```
    typedef struct Pval {
      struct Pval   *next;
      char          *name;
      struct Val     val;
    } Pval;
```
Defines:
  Pval, used in chunks 107c, 108, and 114–18.
Uses Val 114a.

The values correspond to the various basic and derived types of the language. As we previously saw, they are numbers, strings, expressions, and lists of parameters. We also define the type V_PRV used by the sublanguage.

113c   ⟨*value types* 113c⟩≡

```
    #define V_NUM    1
    #define V_STR    2
    #define V_NOD    3
    #define V_PVL    4
    #define V_PRV    5
```

Defines:
  V_NOD, used in chunks 108, 114c, and 116.
  V_NUM, used in chunks 108, 114c, and 117–19.
  V_PRV, never used.
  V_PVL, used in chunks 117a and 118a.
  V_STR, used in chunks 108 and 114c.

The structure **Val** represents a value. It is the union of the above types.

114a ⟨*value structure* 114a⟩≡
```
typedef struct Val {
  int type;
  union { double  d;
          char    *s;
          Node    *n;
          void    *v;
  } u;
} Val;
```
Defines:
  Val, used in chunks 107c and 112–19.
Uses **Node** 115b.

The routine **pv_make** constructs a parameter given by name and value.

114b ⟨*pv make* 114b⟩≡
```
Pval *pv_make(char *name, Val v)
{
  Pval *pv = (Pval *)malloc(sizeof(Pval));
  pv->name = name;
  pv->val = v;
  pv->next = (Pval *)0;
  return pv;
}
```
Defines:
  pv_make, used in chunks 108 and 116b.
Uses **Pval** 113b and **Val** 114a.

The routine **pv_value** returns a value of a certain type.

114c ⟨*pv value* 114c⟩≡
```
Val pv_value(int type, double num, char *str, Node *nl)
{
  Val v;
  switch (v.type = type) {
  case V_STR: v.u.s = str; break;
  case V_NUM: v.u.d = num; break;
  case V_NOD: v.u.n = nl; break;
  }
  return v;
}
```

Defines:
    pv_value, used in chunks 108 and 119.
Uses **Node** 115b, **V_NOD** 113c, **V_NUM** 113c, **V_STR** 113c, and **Val** 114a.

The routine **pv_append** appends a parameter at the end of a list of parameters. It is used for the construction of the operands list of an expression.

115a   ⟨*pv append* 115a⟩≡

```
Pval *pv_append(Pval *pvlist, Pval *pv)
{
  Pval *p = pvlist;
  if (p == NULL)
    return pv;
  while (p->next != NULL)
    p = p->next;
  p->next = pv;
  return pvlist;
}
```

Defines:
    pv_append, used in chunks 108 and 116b.
Uses **Pval** 113b.

7.3.5   Nodes and Expressions

An expression corresponds to a tree where the internal nodes are operators of the language. The structure **Node** represents a tree node and consists of (1) a pointer to the function implementing the operator and (2) a list of parameters defining its operands.

115b   ⟨*node structure* 115b⟩≡

```
typedef struct Node {
  struct Val   (*func)();
  struct Pval  *plist;
} Node;
```

Defines:
    Node, used in chunks 107c, 114–16, and 119d.
Uses **Pval** 113b and **Val** 114a.

The routine **t_node** constructs a node of the expression tree.

115c   ⟨*node construtor* 115c⟩≡

```
Node *t_node(Val (*fun)(), Pval *p)
{
  Node *n = (Node *) emalloc(sizeof(Node));
  n->func = fun;
  n->plist = p;
  return n;
}
```

Defines:
    t_node, used in chunk 108.
Uses **Node** 115b, **Pval** 113b, and **Val** 114a.

To evaluate an expression, we should apply the substitution model. This process essentially consists of traversing the expression tree in depth. To make the language yet more versatile, we implement the expression evaluation by traversing the tree in width and depth. In this way, we visit each tree node, and we execute the function implementing the operator twice. The first corresponds to preprocessing (action T_PREP), and the second corresponds to the execution itself (action T_EXEC).

```
#define T_PREP    0
#define T_EXEC    1
```

What is more, we implement two types of expression evaluation: destructive and non-destructive. The routine t_eval performs the destructive expression evaluation. It replaces subexpressions by their value in the recursive evaluation process.

116a   ⟨eval 116a⟩≡
```
Val t_eval(Node *n)
{
  Pval *p;

  (*n->func)(T_PREP, n->plist);
  for (p = n->plist; p != NULL; p = p->next)
    if (p->val.type == V_NOD)
      p->val = t_eval(p->val.u.n);
  return (*n->func)(T_EXEC, n->plist);
}
```
Defines:
  t_eval, used in chunk 119b.
Uses Node 115b, Pval 113b, T_EXEC, T_PREP, V_NOD 113c, and Val 114a.

The routine t_nd_eval makes the nondestructive evaluation of expressions. It preserves the trees of subexpressions, creating lists separate from operands already appraised that are last for the operators.

116b   ⟨non destructive eval 116b⟩≡
```
Val t_nd_eval(Node *n)
{
  Pval *p, *qlist = NULL;

  (*n->func)(T_PREP, n->plist);
  for (p = n->plist; p != NULL; p = p->next)
    qlist = pv_append(qlist, pv_make(p->name,
                (p->val.type == V_NOD)? t_nd_eval(p->val.u.n) : p->val));
  return (*n->func)(T_EXEC, qlist);
}
```
Defines:
  t_nd_eval, used in chunk 119c.
Uses Node 115b, pv_append 115a, pv_make 114b, Pval 113b, T_EXEC, T_PREP, V_NOD 113c,
  and Val 114a.

The routine t_pvl is the function implementing the operator "list," which corresponds to the syntactic construction { pv, pv, . . . }. Notice this is the only semantics effectively implemented in the kernel of the extension language.

117a   ⟨pvl 117a⟩≡

```
Val t_pvl(int c, Pval *pvl)
{
  Val v;
  v.type = V_PVL;   v.u.v = pvl;
  return v;
}
```

Defines:
  t_pvl, used in chunk 108.
Uses c 109c, Pval 113b, V_PVL 113c, and Val 114a.

7.3.6   Auxiliary Functions

We define several auxiliary routines to work with parameter lists. The routine pvl_to_array converts a list of numerical values to an array.

117b   ⟨pvl to array 117b⟩≡

```
void pvl_to_array(Pval *pvl, double *a, int n)
{
  int k = 0;
  Pval *p = pvl;

  while (p != NULL && k < n) {
    a[k++] = (p->val.type == V_NUM) ? p->val.u.d : 0;
    p = p->next;
  }
}
```

Defines:
  pvl_to_array, used in chunk 117c.
Uses Pval 113b and V_NUM 113c.

The routine pvl_to_v3 converts a list with three numbers to a 3D vector.

117c   ⟨pvl to v3 117c⟩≡

```
Vector3 pvl_to_v3(Pval *pvl)
{
  double a[3] = {0, 0, 0};
  pvl_to_array(pvl, a, 3);
  return v3_make(a[0], a[1], a[2]);
}
```

Defines:
  pvl_to_v3, used in chunk 118a.
Uses Pval 113b and pvl_to_array 117b.

The routine `pvl_get_v3` extracts a parameter from the list indicated by `pname`, which has a vector as value. If this parameter does not exist, the routine returns the default value `defval`.

118a   ⟨*pvl get v3* 118a⟩≡
```
Vector3 pvl_get_v3(Pval *pvl, char *pname, Vector3 defval)
{
  Pval *p;
  for (p = pvl; p != (Pval *)0; p = p->next)
    if (strcmp(p->name, pname) == 0 && p->val.type == V_PVL)
      return pvl_to_v3(p->val.u.v);
  return defval;
}
```
Defines:
  `pvl_get_v3`, never used.
Uses **Pval** 113b, `pvl_to_v3` 117c, and **V_PVL** 113c.

The routine `pvl_get_num` extracts a parameter of scalar value from the list.

118b   ⟨*pvl get num* 118b⟩≡
```
Real pvl_get_num(Pval *pvl, char *pname, Real defval)
{
  Pval *p;
  for (p = pvl; p != (Pval *)0; p = p->next)
    if (strcmp(p->name, pname) == 0 && p->val.type == V_NUM)
      return p->val.u.d;
  return defval;
}
```
Defines:
  `pvl_get_num`, never used.
Uses **Pval** 113b and **V_NUM** 113c.

7.4   Sublanguages and Applications

In this section, we show how to use resources from the extension language to define application-oriented sublanguages.

7.4.1   Interface with the Extension Language

To specify a sublanguage, we define the operators implementing the desired semantics. The routine `lang_defun` is used to define a new operator. It installs, in the symbol table, the name of the operator and the function implementing it.

118c   ⟨*lang defun* 118c⟩≡
```
void lang_defun(char *name, Val (*func)())
{
  if (sym_lookup(name))
```

```
        fprintf(stderr,"lang: symbol %s already defined\n", name);
      else
        sym_install(name, CLASS, func);
    }
```
Defines:
  lang_defun, never used.
Uses sym_install 112c, sym_lookup 113a, and Val 114a.

We call the lexical and syntactic analyzers to perform an analysis of the source code and to produce an expression tree.

The routine lang_parse executes the syntactic analyzer generated by yacc, which in turn calls the lexical analyzer.

119a   ⟨*lang parse* 119a⟩≡
```
    int lang_parse()
    {
      return yyparse();
    }
```
Defines:
  lang_parse, never used.

To run the program we evaluate the expression tree, whose root is stored in the internal variable root. The routine lang_eval runs the program evaluating its tree in a destructive way.

119b   ⟨*lang eval* 119b⟩≡
```
    Val lang_eval()
    {
      return (root != NULL)? t_eval(root) : pv_value(V_NUM, 0, NULL, NULL);
    }
```
Defines:
  lang_eval, never used.
Uses pv_value 114c, root, t_eval 116a, V_NUM 113c, and Val 114a.

The routine lang_nd_eval runs the program evaluating its tree in a nondestructive way.

119c   ⟨*lang nd eval* 119c⟩≡
```
    Val lang_nd_eval(void)
    {
      return (root != NULL)? t_nd_eval(root) : pv_value(V_NUM, 0, NULL, NULL);
    }
```
Defines:
  lang_nd_eval, never used.
Uses pv_value 114c, root, t_nd_eval 116b, V_NUM 113c, and Val 114a.

The routine lang_ptree returns the expression tree.

119d   ⟨*lang parse tree* 119d⟩≡
```
    Node *lang_ptree(void)
    {
```

```
  return root;
 }
```
Defines:
   lang_ptree, never used.
Uses **Node** 115b and **root**.

7.4.2   Implementing the Semantics

To implement the language semantics, we define operators through functions executing
the actions T_PREP and T_EXEC.

   These functions follow the structure below:

```
Val f(int call, Pval *pl)
{
  Val v;

  if (call == T_EXEC) {
    /* execute and return value */
  } else if (call == T_PREP) {
    /* preprocess and return null */
  }
  return v;
}
```

7.4.3   Generating the Interpreter

We create a main program to generate the language interpreter, which includes the kernel
of the extension language and the sublanguage.

   That program can be divided into three parts:

   1. definition of the operators of the sublanguage,

   2. compilation of the source code,

   3. execution of the program.

   The program below shows an example of the structure of the interpreter:

```
main(int argc, char **argv)
{
  lang_define("f", f);
  ...

  if (lang_parse() == 0)
    lang_eval();

  exit(0);
}
```

7.5 Comments and References

In this chapter we discussed concepts related to languages and procedural descriptions. We presented an extension language to specify the data of a 3D scene. Finally, we developed a library with the computational support for implementing this language.

The concepts discussed in this chapter can be seen in more detail in the excellent book by Aho and Ullman [Aho and Ullman 79].

7.5.1 Revision

The API of the language library consists of the following routines:

```
Pval *pv_make(char *name, Val v);
Pval *pv_append(Pval *pvlist, Pval *pv);
Val  pv_value(int type, double num, char *str, Node *nl);

Node *t_node(Val (*fun)(), Pval *p);
Val  t_eval(Node *n);
Val  t_pvl(int c, Pval *pl);

Node *yyptree();

void lang_define(char *name, Val (*func)());
int  lang_parse();
Val  lang_eval();

void pvl_to_array(Pval *pvl, double *a, int n);
Vector3 pvl_to_v3(Pval *pvl);
Real pvl_get_num(Pval *pvl, char *pname, Real defval);
Vector3 pvl_get_v3(Pval *pvl, char *pname, Vector3 defval);
```

7.5.2 Extensions

The expression language we developed in this chapter is quite powerful and contains practically all the ingredients of a programming language. The only important resource of a programming language that is not present in our language is the possibility of creating new functions using the language itself. The functions of the language are defined in C as primitive operators. This engine allows efficient implementation.

However, the extension language could be enhanced with constructions for defining macros and functions. The former would allow the definition of *macros*. In this case we could use the preprocessor CPP of the C language. In this way, we would have the command `defines` in the language. CPP allows the definition of macros with the following form:

```
#define M(P1, P2, PN) macro code
```

The preprocessor identifies all the occurrences of the defined macros and performs the *macro expansion*, replacing the macro call by its text with the corresponding parameters. For instance, the macro call M (the, b, c) is replaced by the macro code, with a, b, c in the place of P1, P2, P3.

Another advantage of using CPP is that it allows the inclusion of multiple files through the command include.

The construction for defining functions demands a significant change in the language. It could be done with the construction defun, which associates an expression to the name of a function (operator) of the language.

7.5.3   Related Information

Examples of important extension languages include Lisp, TCL, and Moon. Other scene description languages (besides VRML and OpenInventor) in which the syntax of our language is based, are Geomview (formats OOGL, OFF), Renderman, PovRay, and Radiance.

Exercises

1.   Use the LANG library to create a language for a calculator. The following operations must be implemented: sum, subtraction, multiplication, and division.

2.   Extend the calculator of the previous exercise to allow variables with values to be passed in the command line. Use the format arg { var = num } , where var is the variable name and num is the *default* value that will be used in case the variable does not appear in the command line.

8   3D Geometric Models

A 3D scene is formed by set of 3D objects. From this point of view, the form of the objects is one of the most important aspects in computer graphics processes and applications. In this chapter, we will study models and representations of 3D objects.

8.1   Foundations of Modeling

Once again we will use the paradigm of the four universes. In the physical universe we have 3D objects whose form we want to characterize. In the mathematical universe we define models for the geometry of those objects. In the representation universe we create the schema and parameters associated with those geometric models. In the implementation universe we establish data structures and procedures to support those representations in the computer (see Figure 8.1).

8.1.1   Models and Geometric Descriptions

The geometric support of an object consists of a set of points in the ambient space, $S = \{p \subset \mathbb{R}^3 : p \in O\}$. Certain constraints are necessary to best characterize the geometry of this set of points.

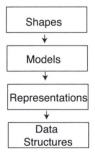

Figure 8.1. Four abstraction levels in geometric modeling.

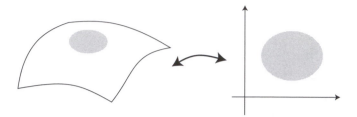

Figure 8.2. Mappings preserving the topological properties of a given space.

Manifolds. We will assume the form of the objects we will work with consists of a *homogeneous* set of points that can be modeled as *manifolds* of dimension 1 (curves), 2 (surfaces), and 3 (solids), embedded in the 3D Euclidean space. This means that, locally, our set of n-dimensional points is homeomorphic to an open ball in $\mathbb{R}^n$. In Figure 8.2, we illustrate this concept for a surface.

Parametric and implicit descriptions. Once we have chosen the mathematical model for the object geometry, we need to specify it concretely. In other words, we need mathematical tools to describe n-dimensional manifolds. The functional description fits our purposes. We will use functions to specify the set of points of the objects. There are two types of geometric functional description: parametric and implicit.

In the parametric description, the set of points $p \in S$, is defined directly by a function $p = f(u)$ defined in a parametric space with dimension m of the object, i.e., $u \in U \subset \mathbb{R}^m$. Figure 8.3 illustrates this concept for the case of a parametric curve.

In the implicit description, the geometry is indirectly defined as the set of points $p \in \mathbb{R}^3$ satisfying the equation $g(p) = c$. In this way, we say that $S = g^{-1}(c)$ is the inverse image of g. Figure 8.4 illustrates these concepts for the case of an implicit curve.

Notice that the parametric and implicit descriptions are complementary. The parametric description allows the *enumeration* of points in S, while the implicit description makes it possible to perform the *classification* of points in the ambient space in relation to S.

Another important observation is that, besides primitive functions (parametric and implicit), we can make our modeling system more powerful by also including operations with those functions in a way to generate composition of functions.

Figure 8.3. Parametric curve.   Figure 8.4. Implicit curve.

8.1.2 Representation Schema

Based on the functional geometry model presented in the previous subsection, we can develop a schema to represent the form of the objects. The most common representation schema are the following:

☐ primitive families,

☐ constructive schema,

☐ decomposition schema.

Representation by primitives. In the representation schema by primitives, we define a family of functions to describe a class of objects. In addition, we can include geometric transformations (see Chapter 4). The implementation of a modeling system by primitives means we are using the definition of a library for shapes, support functions, and transformations.

Example 8.1 (Family of Spheres). A primitive-based system of this type could be used in modeling marbles. Let us see how such a system is framed in the paradigm of the four universes:

☐ **Object.** spherical shapes.

☐ **Model.** functional description.

  – parametric form: $(x, y, z) = r(\cos u \cos v, \sin u \cos v, \sin v)$
  – implicit form: $x^2 + y^2 + z^2 = r^2$

☐ **Representation.** parameters of the description: name and radius, (id, r).

☐ **Data structure.** associative list: $id_k \mapsto r_k$, for $k = 1, \ldots M$.   ☐

Constructive representation. In the constructive representation schema, we use geometric primitive and operations of point set combination. In this way we can construct more complex composed objects from simpler primitive objects. The combination operators define an algebra.

To implement a constructive modeling system, we have to define the primitives as well as the combination operators. The representation of an object in the system is given by an algebraic expression.

Example 8.2 (CSG System–Constructive Solid Geometry). The CSG system is based on boolean operations of union, intersection and difference between sets of points. A CSG system based on spheres, according to the paradigm of the four universes, would have:

- □ **Object.** Combination of spherical shapes.

- □ **Model.** Primitive: spheres; operators: $\cup, \cap, /$.

- □ **Representation.** CSG boolean expression.

- □ **Data structure.** Binary tree of the expression. □

Representation by decomposition. In the representation schema by decomposition, we adopt a strategy opposite to that of the constructive schema. Instead of using simple shapes to construct more complex ones, we decompose complex shapes into simpler parts that can be described using either the parametric or implicit forms. Therefore, in this schema, we need to define operations for assembling the pieces. In general, we have a stratification of the topological elements of the model (vertices, edges, faces, shells). Assembly is given by a graph describing the incidence relations between those elements (see Figure 8.5).

The implementation of a modeling system by decomposition means we have defined a class of patches to be used, as well as the type of assembling between them.

Example 8.3 (Polyhedra). Faceted objects can be decomposed into polygonal patches. The representation is a mesh of polygons. Let us see how such a system is framed in the paradigm of the four universes:

- □ **Objects.** Faceted shapes.

- □ **Model.** Linear piecewise decomposition of the geometry.

- □ **Representation.** Surface given as a polygonal mesh.

- □ **Data structure.** List of vertices and faces. □

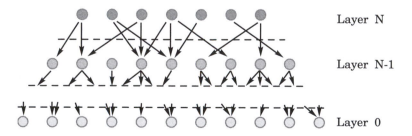

Figure 8.5. Graph with incidence relations for assembling topological elements of a model.

8.2   Geometric Primitives

For one of the bases of our geometric modeling system, we will use families of primitives. We will make only two demands in relation to the classes of valid objects. They should have a dual functional description: parametric and implicit. And they should support a pre-established set of functions. In this way, to include a new family of primitives in the system, it is necessary to implement such functionality.

The basic primitives include: sphere, cone, cylinder, quadrics and superquadrics, torus, box, and height surface.

Representation of those objects consists of the set of parameters specific to each family of models. For instance, center and radius for the sphere. The operations with those objects consist of geometric transformations, such as rigid motions in space.

We will also associate to each primitive object a bounding box, aligned with the main directions. This information is given by the structure Box3d, indicating the inferior-left and superior-right vertices of the box.

127a   ⟨*box3d struct* 127a⟩≡

```
typedef struct Box3d {
  Vector3 ll, ur;
} Box3d;
```

Defines:
   Box3d, used in chunks 127–29 and 135a.

8.2.1   Definition of Primitive Objects

The implementation of primitive models will follow the *object-oriented* approach. In this way, the representation of a primitive in the system uses the data structure Prim made up of support functions; bounding box; direct and inverse transformation matrices; and parameters of the object.

127b   ⟨*prim struct* 127b⟩≡

```
typedef struct Prim {
  struct PrimFuncs *f;
  Box3d   b;
  Matrix4 td, ti;
  void   *d;
} Prim;
```

Defines:
   Prim, used in chunks 128–40.
Uses Box3d 127a and PrimFuncs 128a.

Support functions of the primitive implement the interface between the object and the modeling system. These functions correspond to the set of operations that can be accomplished with primitive models. In this way, object orientation makes the specific implementation of each primitive family independent from the rest of the modeling system.

The structure `PrimFuncs` contains pointers to each of the functions of the primitive family.

128a   ⟨*prim funcs* 128a⟩≡

```
typedef struct PrimFuncs {
    Prim    *(*instance)();
    void    (*destroy)();
    Box3d   (*bbox)();
    int     (*classify)();
    Vector3 (*point)();
    Vector3 (*normal)();
    Vector3 (*gradient)();
    Inode   *(*intersect)();
    Prim    *(*transform)();
    Poly    *(*uv_decomp)();
    Vector3 (*texc)();
    Vector3 (*du)();
    Vector3 (*dv)();
    Matrix4 (*local)();
    int     (*id)();
    void    (*write)();
    void    (*draw)();
} PrimFuncs;
```

Defines:
    `PrimFuncs`, used in chunks 127b, 128b, and 133.
Uses `Box3d` 127a, `Poly` 142a, and `Prim` 127b.

8.2.2 Generic Interface

Object-oriented programming requires a generic interface for all members of a class. This interface consists of generic functions for encapsulating the specific support functions to each primitive family. The implementation of these functions is trivial: they simply call the function corresponding to the primitive passed as parameter.

Next, we give a description of each of these generic functions, specifying the operation each one accomplishes. The routines `prim_instance` and `prim_destroy` are, respectively, the constructor and destructor of primitive objects. Notice the constructor creates an instance of the primitive, with default parameters, starting from the support functions of the family.

128b   ⟨*prim instance* 128b⟩≡

```
Prim *prim_instance(PrimFuncs *f)
{
    return f->instance(f);
}
```

Defines:
    `prim_instance`, never used.
Uses `Prim` 127b and `PrimFuncs` 128a.

129a   ⟨*prim destroy* 129a⟩≡
```
void prim_destroy(Prim *p)
{
    (*p->f->destroy)(p);
}
```
Defines:
  prim_destroy, never used.
Uses Prim 127b.

The routine `prim_bbox` returns the bounding box of the primitive.

129b   ⟨*prim bbox* 129b⟩≡
```
Box3d prim_bbox(Prim *p)
{
    return (*p->f->bbox)(p);
}
```
Defines:
  prim_bbox, never used.
Uses Box3d 127a and Prim 127b.

The routine `prim_classify` classifies the point q in relation to the primitive. It uses the implicit description to determine whether the point is in the interior, exterior, or on the boundary of the object.

129c   ⟨*prim classify* 129c⟩≡
```
int prim_classify(Prim *p, Vector3 q)
{
    return (*p->f->classify)(p, q);
}
```
Defines:
  prim_classify, never used.
Uses Prim 127b.

The routine returns the classification according to the codes below:

```
#define PRIM_IN   1
#define PRIM_OUT -1
#define PRIM_ON   0
```

The routine `prim_point` uses the parametric description to perform an enumeration of the points of the primitive.

129d   ⟨*prim point* 129d⟩≡
```
Vector3 prim_point(Prim *p, Real u, Real v)
{
    return (*p->f->point)(p, u, v);
}
```
Defines:
  prim_point, never used.
Uses Prim 127b.

The routine `prim_normal` calculates the normal vector to the surface of the primitive corresponding to the parameter (u, v).

130a   ⟨*prim normal* 130a⟩≡

```
Vector3 prim_normal(Prim *p, Real u, Real v)
{
  return (*p->f->normal)(p, u, v);
}
```

Defines:
  prim_normal, never used.
Uses Prim 127b.

The routine `prim_gradient` returns the gradient of the implicit function of the primitive at point q.

130b   ⟨*prim gradient* 130b⟩≡

```
Vector3 prim_gradient(Prim *p, Vector3 q)
{
  return (*p->f->gradient)(p, q);
}
```

Defines:
  prim_gradient, never used.
Uses Prim 127b.

The routine `prim_intersect` calculates the intersection between a ray and the primitive by using its implicit description.

130c   ⟨*prim intersect* 130c⟩≡

```
Inode *prim_intersect(Prim *p, Ray r)
{
  return (*p->f->intersect)(p, r);
}
```

Defines:
  prim_intersect, never used.
Uses Prim 127b.

The routine `prim_transform` applies a geometric transformation to the primitive. Notice that matrix md specifies the direct transformation and matrix mi specifies the inverse one.

130d   ⟨*prim transform* 130d⟩≡

```
Prim *prim_transform(Prim *p, Matrix4 md, Matrix4 mi)
{
  return (*p->f->transform)(p, md, mi);
}
```

Defines:
  prim_transform, never used.
Uses Prim 127b.

The routine `prim_uv_decomp` produces a polygonal approximation of the primitive, starting from the uniform decomposition of its parametric domain. It returns a list of polygons (see Section 8.3 for more details).

131a   ⟨*prim uvdecomp* 131a⟩≡
```
Poly    *prim_uv_decomp(Prim *p, Real level)
{
  return (*p->f->uv_decomp)(p,level);
}
```
Defines:
  prim_uv_decomp, never used.
Uses Poly 142a and Prim 127b.

The routine `prim_texc` calculates the texture coordinates of the primitive, normalized in the interval $[0, 1]$, corresponding to the parametric coordinates given by (u, v).

131b   ⟨*prim texc* 131b⟩≡
```
Vector3 prim_texc(Prim *p, Real u, Real v)
{
  return (*p->f->texc)(p, u, v);
}
```
Defines:
  prim_texc, never used.
Uses Prim 127b.

The routines `prim_du` and `prim_dv` calculate the partial derivatives of the parameterization function in relation to u and v, respectively.

131c   ⟨*prim du* 131c⟩≡
```
Vector3 prim_du(Prim *p, Real u, Real v)
{
  return (*p->f->du)(p, u, v);
}
```
Defines:
  prim_du, never used.
Uses Prim 127b.

131d   ⟨*prim dv* 131d⟩≡
```
Vector3 prim_dv(Prim *p, Real u, Real v)
{
  return (*p->f->dv)(p, u, v);
}
```
Defines:
  prim_dv, never used.
Uses Prim 127b.

The routine `prim_local` returns the transformation matrix performing the change of coordinates from the global to the local system of the primitive.

132a   ⟨*prim local* 132a⟩≡
```
Matrix4 prim_local(Prim *p)
{
    return (*p->f->local)(p);
}
```
Defines:
  prim_local, never used.
Uses Prim 127b.

The routine `prim_id` returns the identifier of the family the primitive belongs to.

132b   ⟨*prim id* 132b⟩≡
```
int prim_id(Prim *p)
{
    return p->type;
}
```
Defines:
  prim_id, never used.
Uses Prim 127b.

The routine `prim_write` writes the representation of the primitive to the file given by `fp` using the 3D scene language description.

132c   ⟨*prim write* 132c⟩≡
```
void prim_write(Prim *p, FILE *fp)
{
    (*p->f->write)(p, fp);
}
```
Defines:
  prim_write, never used.
Uses Prim 127b.

Beyond these functions, each family of primitives has a function to create the primitive starting from its representation in the 3D scene language description.

8.2.3   Example of a Primitive

We will now show how to define a primitive object in the modeling system and give an example using a *sphere* primitive. We will take as basis the unit sphere S^2 centered at the origin. From this canonical model, we will use translation and scaling transformations to obtain instances of the sphere with both arbitrary center and radius. The advantage of this strategy is that the calculations can be performed in a simpler and more efficient way in the local coordinate system of the primitive.

The data structure `Sphere` encapsulates the center and radius parameters of the sphere primitive.

133a ⟨*sphere struct* 133a⟩≡
```
typedef struct Sphere {
  Vector3 c;
  double  r;
} Sphere;
```
Defines:
  Sphere, used in chunks 133c, 134b, and 140b.

The table `sphere_func` defines the functionality of the sphere primitive. Its elements are pointers to functions implementing each of the basic operations of the primitive. We will see those functions next.

133b ⟨*sphere funcs* 133b⟩≡
```
PrimFuncs sphere_funcs = {
    sphere_instance,
    sphere_destroy,
    sphere_bbox,
    sphere_classify,
    sphere_point,
    sphere_normal,
    sphere_gradient,
    sphere_intersect,
    sphere_transform,
    sphere_uv_decomp,
    sphere_texc,
    sphere_du,
    sphere_dv,
    sphere_local,
    sphere_id,
    sphere_write,
    sphere_draw,
};
```
Defines:
  sphere_funcs, used in chunk 140a.
Uses PrimFuncs 128a, sphere_bbox 135a, sphere_classify 135b, sphere_destroy 134a, sphere_draw, sphere_du 139b, sphere_dv 139c, sphere_gradient 136c, sphere_id 139e, sphere_instance 133c, sphere_intersect 137, sphere_local 139d, sphere_normal 136b, sphere_point 136a, sphere_texc 139a, sphere_transform 138a, sphere_uv_decomp 138b, and sphere_write 140b.

The routine `sphere_instance` is the constructor of the sphere primitive. It allocates the data structures and returns a canonical sphere with center $c = (0, 0, 0)$ and radius $r = 1$.

133c ⟨*sphere instance* 133c⟩≡
```
Prim *sphere_instance(PrimFuncs *f)
```

```
{
  Vector3 ll = {-1,-1,-1}, ur = {1,1,1};
  Prim *p = NEWSTRUCT(Prim);
  Sphere *s = NEWSTRUCT(Sphere);

  p->f = f;
  p->b.ll = ll; p->b.ur = ur;
  p->ti = p->td = m4_ident();
  s->c = v3_make(0,0,0); s->r = 1;
  p->d = s;
  return p;
}
```

Defines:
  sphere_instance, used in chunks 133b and 140a.
Uses Prim 127b, PrimFuncs 128a, and Sphere 133a.

The routine sphere_destroy is the destructor of instances of the sphere primitive. It frees the memory allocated by sphere_instance.

134a   ⟨sphere destroy 134a⟩≡
```
void sphere_destroy(Prim *p)
{
  free(p->d);
  free(p);
}
```

Defines:
  sphere_destroy, used in chunk 133b.
Uses Prim 127b.

The routine sphere_set modifies the parameters of an already existing sphere. Notice this routine uses translation and scaling transformations to calculate the change of coordinates to the local system of the primitive. The routine also updates the bounding box of the primitive.

134b   ⟨sphere set 134b⟩≡
```
Prim *sphere_set(Prim *p, Vector3 c, double  r)
{
  Sphere *s = p->d;
  s->c = c; s->r = r;
  p->td = m4_m4prod(m4_translate(c.x.y.z),m4_scale(r,r,r));
  p->ti = m4_m4prod(m4_scale(1/r,1/r,1/r), m4_translate(-c.x,-c.y,-c.z));
  p->b = sphere_bbox(p);
  return p;
}
```

Defines:
  sphere_set, used in chunk 140a.
Uses Prim 127b, Sphere 133a, and sphere_bbox 135a.

The routine `sphere_bbox` generates a bounding box for the sphere primitive. First, it changes the vertices of the cube containing the canonical sphere to the global coordinate system. A bounding box for that cube is then calculated. Observe that, in the case of arbitrary transformations, the box is not the smallest possible one.

135a ⟨*sphere bbox* 135a⟩≡

```
Box3d sphere_bbox(Prim *p)
{
  Box3d b;
  Vector3 v;
  double x, y, z;

  for (x = -1; x <= 1; x +=2) {
    for (y = -1; y <= 1; y +=2) {
      for (z = -1; z <= 1; z +=2) {
        v = v3_m4mult(v3_make(x, y, z), p->td);
        if (x == -1 && y == -1 && z == -1) {
          b.ll = b.ur = v;
        } else {
          if (v.x < b.ll.x) b.ll.x = v.x;
          if (v.y < b.ll.y) b.ll.y = v.y;
          if (v.z < b.ll.z) b.ll.z = v.z;
          if (v.x > b.ur.x) b.ur.x = v.x;
          if (v.y > b.ur.y) b.ur.y = v.y;
          if (v.z > b.ur.z) b.ur.z = v.z;
        }
      }
    }
  }
  return b;
}
```

Defines:
  `sphere_bbox`, used in chunks 133b and 134b.
Uses `Box3d` 127a and `Prim` 127b.

The routine `sphere_classify` performs the point-set classification. First, it transforms the point q to the local coordinate system of the sphere. It then uses the implicit equation $x^2 + y^2 + z^2 - 1 = 0$ to determine whether the point $q = (x, y, z)$ is in the interior, exterior, or on the surface of the sphere.

135b ⟨*sphere classify* 135b⟩≡

```
int sphere_classify(Prim *p, Vector3 q)
{
  Vector3 w = v3_m4mult(q, p->ti);
  Real d = v3_sqrnorm(w);
  return (d < 1)? PRIM_IN : ((d > 1)? PRIM_OUT : PRIM_ON);
}
```

Defines:
 sphere_classify, used in chunk 133b.
Uses Prim 127b, PRIM_IN, PRIM_ON, and PRIM_OUT.

The routine `sphere_point` returns the point at the sphere corresponding to the parametric coordinates (u, v). The chosen parameterization uses spherical coordinates with $u \in [0, 2\pi]$ and $v \in [-\pi/2, \pi/2]$. Notice this parameterization is singular at the poles of the sphere, i.e., $v = \pm\pi/2$. Also, note that the calculation is performed in the local coordinate system and the result is subsequently transformed to the global coordinate system.

136a   ⟨*sphere point* 136a⟩≡
```
Vector3 sphere_point(Prim *p, Real u, Real v)
{
  Vector3 w;
  w.x = cos(u)*cos(v);
  w.y = sin(u)*cos(v);
  w.z = sin(v);
  return v3_m4mult(w, p->td);
}
```
Defines:
 sphere_point, used in chunk 133b.
Uses Prim 127b.

The routine `sphere_normal` calculates the vector normal to the sphere at the point $w = f(u, v)$. This vector is in the local system and must be transformed to the global system (see Chapter 4).

136b   ⟨*sphere normal* 136b⟩≡
```
Vector3 sphere_normal(Prim *p, Real u, Real v)
{
  Vector3 w;
  w.x = cos(u)*cos(v);
  w.y = sin(u)*cos(v);
  w.z = sin(v);
  return v3_m4mult(w, m4_transpose(p->ti));
}
```
Defines:
 sphere_normal, used in chunk 133b.
Uses Prim 127b.

The routine `sphere_gradient` returns the gradient at the point q of the implicit function $f(x, , z) = x^2 + y^2 + z^2 - 1$ associated with the sphere $\nabla f = (\frac{f}{x}, \frac{f}{y}, \frac{f}{z}) = (2x, 2y, 2z)$. Before the calculation, the point $q = (x, y, z)$ is transformed to the local coordinate system of the sphere.

136c   ⟨*sphere gradient* 136c⟩≡
```
Vector3 sphere_gradient(Prim *p, Vector3 q)
{
```

```
    Vector3 w = v3_scale(2.0, v3_m3mult(q, p->ti));
    return v3_m3mult(w, m4_transpose(p->ti));
  }
```

Defines:
  sphere_gradient, used in chunks 133b and 137.
Uses Prim 127b.

The routine sphere_intersect calculates the intersection between a ray s and a sphere. First, the ray is transformed to the local coordinate system. The intersection is then calculated by replacing the parametric equation of the ray $r(t) = o + td$ in the implicit equation of the sphere $x^2 + y^2 + z^2 - 1 = 0$, thus obtaining the quadratic equation in t,

$$at^2 + 2bt + c - 1 = 0, \tag{8.1}$$

where $a = d_x^2 + d_y^2 + d_z^2$, $b = o_x d_x + o_y d_y + o_z d_z$, and $c = o_x^2 + o_y^2 + o_z^2$.

The intersection points between the ray and sphere are obtained by finding the roots of the equation, i.e., the parameters t_0 and t_1 of $r(t)$ satisfying (8.1).

137   ⟨sphere intersect 137⟩≡

```
    Inode *sphere_intersect(Prim *p, Ray rs)
    {
      double a, b, c, disc, t0, t1;
      Inode *in, *out;
      Ray r = ray_transform(rs, p->ti);

      a = SQR(r.d.x) + SQR(r.d.y) + SQR(r.d.z);
      b = 2.0 * (r.d.x * r.o.x + r.d.y * r.o.y + r.d.z * r.o.z);
      c = SQR(r.o.x) + SQR(r.o.y) + SQR(r.o.z) - 1;
      if ((disc = SQR(b) - 4 * a * c) <= 0)
        return (Inode *)0;
      t0 = (-b + sqrt(disc)) / (2 * a);
      t1 = (-b - sqrt(disc)) / (2 * a);
      if (t1 < RAY_EPS)
        return (Inode *)0;
      if (t0 < RAY_EPS) {
        Vector3 n1 = v3_unit(sphere_gradient(p, ray_point(rs, t1)));
        return inode_alloc(t1, n1, FALSE);
      } else {
        Vector3 n0 = v3_unit(sphere_gradient(p, ray_point(rs, t0)));
        Vector3 n1 = v3_unit(sphere_gradient(p, ray_point(rs, t1)));
        i0 = inode_alloc(t0, n0, TRUE);
        i1 = inode_alloc(t1, n1, FALSE);
        i0->next = i1;
        return i0;
      }
    }
```

Defines:
  sphere_intersect, used in chunk 133b.
Uses Prim 127b and sphere_gradient 136c.

The routine `sphere_transform` applies a geometric transformation to the sphere. Notice that both direct and inverse transformation matrices should be provided.

138a ⟨*sphere transform* 138a⟩≡

```
Prim *sphere_transform(Prim *p, Matrix4 md, Matrix4 mi)
{
  p->td = m4_m4prod(md, p->td);
  p->ti = m4_m4prod(p->ti, mi);
  return p;
}
```

Defines:
  `sphere_transform`, used in chunk 133b.
Uses `Prim` 127b.

The routine `sphere_uv_decomp` generates a polygonal approximation of the sphere by making a regular decomposition of its parametric domain.

138b ⟨*sphere uv decomp* 138b⟩≡

```
Poly *sphere_uv_decomp(Prim *p)
{
  Real u, v, nu = 20, nv = 10;
  Real iu = ULEN/nu, iv = VLEN/nv;
  Poly *l = NULL;

  for (u = UMIN; u < UMAX; u += iu) {
    for (v = VMIN; v < VMAX; v += iv) {
      l = poly_insert(l,
          poly3_make(v3_make(u,v,1),v3_make(u,v+iv,1),v3_make(u+iu,v,1)));
      l = poly_insert(l,
          poly3_make(v3_make(u+iu,v+iv,1),v3_make(u+iu,v,1),
                     v3_make(u,v+iv,1)));
    }
  }
  return l;
}
```

Defines:
  `sphere_uv_decomp`, used in chunk 133b.
Uses `Poly` 142a, `poly3_make` 144b, `poly_insert` 143d, `Prim` 127b, `ULEN`, `UMAX`, `UMIN`, `VLEN`, `VMAX`, and `VMIN`.

```
#define UMIN (0)
#define UMAX (PITIMES2)
#define ULEN (UMAX - UMIN)
#define VEPS (0.01)
#define VMIN ((-PI/2.0) + VEPS )
#define VMAX ((PI/2.0) - VEPS)
#define VLEN (VMAX - VMIN)
```

The routine `sphere_texc` returns the texture coordinates of the sphere, normalized in the interval $[0, 1]$.

139a ⟨*sphere texc* 139a⟩≡
```
Vector3 sphere_texc(Prim *p, Real u, Real v)
{
  return v3_make((u - UMIN)/ULEN, (v - VMIN)/VLEN, 0);
}
```
Defines:
  sphere_texc, used in chunk 133b.
Uses Prim 127b, ULEN, UMIN, VLEN, and VMIN.

The routines `sphere_du` and `sphere_dv` return the partial derivatives of the parameterization function of the sphere.

139b ⟨*sphere du* 139b⟩≡
```
Vector3 sphere_du(Prim *p, Real u, Real v)
{
  return v3_make(- sin(u) * cos(v), cos(u) * cos(v), 0);
}
```
Defines:
  sphere_du, used in chunk 133b.
Uses Prim 127b.

139c ⟨*sphere dv* 139c⟩≡
```
Vector3 sphere_dv(Prim *p, Real u, Real v)
{
  return v3_make(- cos(u) * sin(v), - sin(u) * sin(v), cos(v));
}
```
Defines:
  sphere_dv, used in chunk 133b.
Uses Prim 127b.

The routine `sphere_local` returns the transformation matrix to the local coordinate system of the sphere.

139d ⟨*sphere local* 139d⟩≡
```
Matrix4 sphere_local(Prim *p)
{
  return p->ti;
}
```
Defines:
  sphere_local, used in chunk 133b.
Uses Prim 127b.

The routine `sphere_id` returns the class identifier of the sphere primitive.

139e ⟨*sphere id* 139e⟩≡
```
int sphere_id(Prim *p)
{
  return SPHERE;
```

```
  }
```

Defines:
  sphere_id, used in chunk 133b.
Uses Prim 127b and SPHERE.

The representation of a sphere in the 3D scene description language language has the following syntax:

```
primobj = sphere { center = {1,2,3}, radius = 4}
```

The routine sphere_parse performs interpretation of the sphere primitive.

140a   ⟨*sphere parse* 140a⟩≡
```
Val sphere_parse(int pass, Pval *pl)
{
  Val v;

  if (pass == T_POST) {
    Vector3 c = pvl_get_v3(pl, "center", v3_make(0,0,0));
    double r = pvl_get_num(pl, "radius", 1);
    v.type = PRIM;
    sphere_set(v.u.v = sphere_instance(&sphere_funcs), c, r);
  }
  return v;
}
```

Defines:
  sphere_parse, never used.
Uses sphere_funcs 133b, sphere_instance 133c, and sphere_set 134b.

The routine sphere_write writes the representation of the sphere to a file.

140b   ⟨*sphere write* 140b⟩≡
```
void sphere_write(Prim *p, FILE *fp)
{
  Sphere *s = p->d;
  fprintf(fp, "sphere { \n");
  fprintf(fp, "\t\t center = {%g, %g, %g},\n",s->c.x,s->c.y,s->c.z);
  fprintf(fp, "\t\t radius = %g \n}\n",s->r);
}
```

Defines:
  sphere_write, used in chunk 133b.
Uses Prim 127b and Sphere 133a.

8.3   Approximation of Surfaces and Polygonal Meshes

In this section we will discuss the problem of approximating surfaces. This problem has a strong relation with the representation schema by decomposition presented in Section 8.1.2. Although decomposition schema are also used to represent surfaces in an exact way, usually the approximation of surfaces is based on decomposition. Several methods for approximating surfaces exist. Most use polynomial patches of degree n. An important case are representations based on *splines*.

8.3.1 Approximation Methods

Surface approximation methods start from an initial description, which can be given in parametric or implicit form, or even by a dense point-sampling obtained by sensors or simulation.

Starting from the initial description, the approximation methods calculate a decomposition of the surface in which each patch approximates a piece of the surface.

Approximation methods apply two basic operations: sampling and structuring. *Sampling* consists of obtaining points on the surface to produce the patches. *Structuring* involves the stitching of patches to form a mesh. Depending on the sampling pattern, we have two methods: *uniform* and *adaptive*. Depending on the structuring, we have the following types of meshes: *generic*, *rectangular*, and *simplicial*.

8.3.2 Piecewise Linear Approximation

Piecewise linear approximation is the most common schema for approximating surface representations. The fact that approximation is piecewise makes this method produce a model by decomposition. This method has the following advantages: simplicity of algorithms and representations, computational support of software and hardware, and compatibility among systems.

The representation used for piecewise linear approximation of surfaces is a polygon mesh. Polygonal meshes represent topology by the incidence relations among the various topological elements of the mesh, including vertices, edges, faces, and shells. The geometry is given by the position of the vertices. The surface as a whole is reconstructed by linear interpolation of the vertices through the topological structures.

The data structures for meshes can be classified according to the types of topological relations explicitly represented. The structures most commonly used are direct list of polygons, vertex and face lists, and edge-based graphs.

8.4 Polygonal Surfaces

In our modeling system we will adopt polygonal meshes as a decomposition scheme. This representation allows an exact description of polyhedra and an approximate description of generic surfaces. The data structure chosen is the simplest possible: the mesh is given by a list of polygons, where each polygon consists of an array with the coordinates of its vertices. Besides position, other useful information associated with the vertices (not represented in this structure) include: normal vector to the surface, texture coordinates, color, and material. In the next chapters, we will provide a different solution to represent this information.

8.4.1   Polygons of *n* Sides

The basic data structure of a polygonal mesh represents a polygon of n sides and, at the same time, is the element of single linked list constituting the mesh.

142a   ⟨*poly struct* 142a⟩≡

```
typedef struct Poly {
  struct Poly *next;
  int          n;
  Vector3     *v;
} Poly;
```

Defines:
  Poly, used in chunks 128a, 131a, 138b, and 142–49.

The routine `poly_alloc` is the constructor of polygons.

142b   ⟨*poly alloc* 142b⟩≡

```
Poly *poly_alloc(int n)
{
  Poly *p = NEWSTRUCT(Poly);
  p->n = n;
  p->v = NEWARRAY(n, Vector3);
  p->next = NULL;
  return p;
}
```

Defines:
  poly_alloc, used in chunks 144b, 145b, and 149b.
Uses Poly 142a.

The routines `poly_transform` and `poly_homoxform` apply affine and projective transformations, respectively, to the vertices of a polygon.

142c   ⟨*poly transform* 142c⟩≡

```
Poly *poly_transform(Poly *p, Matrix4 m)
{
  int i;
  for (i = 0; i < p->n; i++)
    p->v[i] = v3_m4mult(p->v[i], m);
  return p;
}
```

Defines:
  poly_transform, never used.
Uses Poly 142a.

143a   ⟨*poly homoxform* 143a⟩≡
```
Poly *poly_homoxform(Poly *p, Matrix4 m)
{
  int i;
  for (i = 0; i < p->n; i++)
    p->v[i] = v3_v4conv(v4_m4mult(v4_v3conv(p->v[i]), m));
  return p;
}
```
Defines:
  poly_homoxform, never used.
Uses Poly 142a.

The routine `poly_normal` calculates the normal vector to a polygon.

143b   ⟨*poly normal* 143b⟩≡
```
Vector3 poly_normal(Poly *p)
{
  return v3_unit(v3_cross(v3_sub(p->v[1], p->v[0]), v3_sub(p->v[2], p->v[0])));
}
```
Defines:
  poly_normal, used in chunk 146b.
Uses Poly 142a.

The routine `poly_centr` calculates the centroid of a polygon.

143c   ⟨*poly centr* 143c⟩≡
```
Vector3 poly_centr(Poly *p)
{
  int i;  Vector3 c = v3_make(0,0,0);
  for (i = 0; i < p->n; i++)
    c = v3_add(c, p->v[i]);
  return v3_scale((Real)(p->n), c);
}
```
Defines:
  poly_centr, never used.
Uses Poly 142a.

The routine `poly_insert` adds a polygon to a list of polygons.

143d   ⟨*poly insert* 143d⟩≡
```
Poly *poly_insert(Poly *pl, Poly *p)
{
  p->next = pl;
  return p;
}
```
Defines:
  poly_insert, used in chunks 138b, 148b, and 149b.
Uses Poly 142a.

The routine `poly_copy` copies the content of the vertices of a polygon to another polygon.

144a ⟨*poly copy* 144a⟩≡

```
int poly_copy(Poly *s, Poly *d)
{
  int i;
  for (i = 0; i < s->n; i++)
    d->v[i] = s->v[i];
  return (d->n = s->n);
}
```

Defines:
  poly_copy, never used.
Uses Poly 142a.

8.4.2   Triangles

Triangles are a particular case of n-sided polygons, where $n = 3$. We will use the structure Poly to represent triangles and dedicated routines to work with them.

The routine `poly3_make` is the constructor of triangles.

144b ⟨*poly3 make* 144b⟩≡

```
Poly *poly3_make(Vector3 v0, Vector3  v1, Vector3  v2)
{
  Poly *p = poly_alloc(3);
  p->v[0] = v0;  p->v[1] = v1;  p->v[2] = v2;
  return p;
}
```

Defines:
  poly3_make, used in chunk 138b.
Uses Poly 142a and poly_alloc 142b.

We will use a list of lists to represent a triangle in the 3D scene description language. In this way, a triangle is given by the list of their three vertices (given by the (x, y, z) coordinates). The description has the following format:

```
{ { NUM,   NUM,   NUM},   { NUM,   NUM,   NUM},   { NUM,   NUM,   NUM} }
```

The routine `poly3_read` reads a triangle from a file specified by `fp`.

144c ⟨*poly3 read* 144c⟩≡

```
int poly3_read(Poly *p, FILE* fp)
{
  char *fmt = "{%lf, %lf, %lf},";
  int i, n;

  fscanf(fp,"{");
  for (i = 0; i < 3; i++) {
```

```
    if ((n=fscanf(fp, fmt,&(p->v[i].x),&(p->v[i].y),&(p->v[i].z))) == EOF)
      return EOF;
    else if (n != 3)
      fprintf(stderr,"Error reading polyfile");
  fscanf(fp,"}\n");
  }
  return (p->n = 3);
}
```

Defines:
  poly3_read, never used.
Uses Poly 142a.

The routine poly3_write writes a triangle to a file.

145a ⟨*poly3 write* 145a⟩≡
```
void poly3_write(Poly *p, FILE* fp)
{
  if ( (v3_norm(v3_sub(p->v[0], p->v[1])) < EPS)
    ||(v3_norm(v3_sub(p->v[1], p->v[2])) < EPS)
    ||(v3_norm(v3_sub(p->v[2], p->v[0])) < EPS))
    fprintf(stderr, "(poly3_write) WARNING: degenerate polygon\n");
  fprintf(fp, "{{%g, %g, %g}, ",  p->v[0].x, p->v[0].y, p->v[0].z);
  fprintf(fp, " {%g, %g, %g}, ",  p->v[1].x, p->v[1].y, p->v[1].z);
  fprintf(fp, " {%g, %g, %g}}\n", p->v[2].x, p->v[2].y, p->v[2].z);
}
```

Defines:
  poly3_write, used in chunk 148a.
Uses Poly 142a.

The routine poly3_parse performs the parsing of a triangle from its expression in the scene description language.

145b ⟨*poly3 parse* 145b⟩≡
```
Poly *poly3_parse(Pval *plist)
{
  Pval *pl;
  int k;

  for (pl = plist, k = 0; pl !=NULL; pl = pl->next, k++)
    ;
  if (k != 3) {
    fprintf(stderr, "(poly3): wrong number of vertices %d\n", k);
    return NULL;
  } else {
    Poly *t = poly_alloc(3);
    for (pl = plist, k = 0; pl !=NULL; pl = pl->next, k++)
      if (pl->val.type == V_PVL)
        t->v[k] = pvl_to_v3(pl->val.u.v);
      else
```

```
                    fprintf(stderr, "(poly3): error in vertex\n");
                return t;
            }
        }
```

Defines:
  poly3_parse, used in chunk 148b.
Uses Poly 142a and poly_alloc 142b.

The routine `poly3_area` calculates the area of a triangle.

146a   ⟨*poly3 area* 146a⟩≡
```
        Real poly3_area(Poly *p)
        {
          return v3_norm(v3_cross(v3_sub(p->v[1],p->v[0]), v3_sub(p->v[2],p->v[0])))/2;
        }
```
Defines:
  poly3_area, never used.
Uses Poly 142a.

The routine `poly3_plane` calculates the equation of the support plane of a triangle.

146b   ⟨*poly3 plane* 146b⟩≡
```
        Vector4 poly3_plane(Poly *p)
        {
          Vector3 n = poly_normal(p);
          Real d = v3_dot(n, p->v[0]);
          return v4_make(n.x, n.y, n.z, d);
        }
```
Defines:
  poly3_plane, used in chunk 147a.
Uses Poly 142a and poly_normal 143b.

The routine `plane_ray_inter` computes the intersection point between a ray and a plane.

146c   ⟨*poly intersect* 146c⟩≡
```
        Real plane_ray_inter(Vector4 h, Ray r)
        {
          Vector3 n = {h.x, h.y, h.z};
          Real denom = v3_dot(n, r.d);
          if (REL_EQ(denom, 0))
            return MINUS_INFTY;
          else
            return (h.w + v3_dot(n, r.o)) / denom;
        }
```
Defines:
  plane_ray_inter, used in chunk 147a.

The routine `poly3_ray_inter` computes the intersection between a ray and a triangle. It uses the previous routines in the calculation.

147a   ⟨*poly3 ray inter* 147a⟩≡

```
Real poly3_ray_inter(Poly *p, Ray r)
{
  Vector4 h; Vector3 q0, q1, q2;
  Real t, d, a, b;

  t = plane_ray_inter((h = poly3_plane(p)), r);
  if (t < 0)
    return MINUS_INFTY;

  q0 = v3_sub(ray_point(r, t), p->v[0]);
  q1 = v3_sub(p->v[1], p->v[0]);
  q2 = v3_sub(p->v[2], p->v[0]);

  switch (max3_index(fabs(h.x), fabs(h.y), fabs(h.z))) {
  case 1:
    PROJ_BASE(a, b, q0.y, q0.z, q1.y, q1.z, q2.y, q2.z); break;
  case 2:
    PROJ_BASE(a, b, q0.x, q0.z, q1.x, q1.z, q2.x, q2.z); break;
  case 3:
    PROJ_BASE(a, b, q0.x, q0.y, q1.x, q1.y, q2.x, q2.y); break;
  }
  if ((a >= 0 && b >= 0 && (a+b) <= 1))
    return t;
  else
    return MINUS_INFTY;
}
```

Defines:
  `poly3_ray_inter`, never used.
Uses `plane_ray_inter` 146c, `Poly` 142a, `poly3_plane` 146b, and `PROJ_BASE` 147b.

The macro `PROJ_BASE` projects a vector on a plane formed by two vectors on this plane.

147b   ⟨*proj base* 147b⟩≡

```
#define PROJ_BASE(A, B, Q0_S, Q0_T, Q1_S, Q1_T, Q2_S, Q2_T) \
{ Real d = (Q1_S * Q2_T - Q2_S * Q1_T); \
  A = (Q0_S * Q2_T - Q2_S * Q0_T) / d;  \
  B = (Q1_S * Q0_T - Q0_S * Q1_T) / d;  \
}
```

Defines:
  `PROJ_BASE`, used in chunk 147a.

8.4.3   Lists of Triangles

The representation of a triangle mesh in the 3D scene description language follows the
format below:

```
polyprim = trilist {
        {{3,2,3}, {4,5,6}, {7,8,9}},
        {{5,2,3}, {4,9,6}, {7,2,9}}
        {{1,4,3}, {3,5,6}, {7,3,9}}
        {{7,2,3}, {4,2,6}, {1,8,9}}
        {{6,2,3}, {4,1,6}, {3,8,9}}
        {{8,2,3}, {4,2,6}, {3,8,9}}
        {{1,5,3}, {4,5,3}, {1,7,9}}
    }
```

The routine `trilist_write` writes a triangle mesh to a file.

148a
⟨*trilist write* 148a⟩≡

```
void trilist_write(Poly *tlist, FILE* fp)
{
  Poly *p = tlist;

  fprintf(fp, "trilist {\n");
  while (p != NULL) {
    poly3_write(p, fp);
    if ((p = p->next) != NULL)
      fprintf(fp, ",\n");
  }
  fprintf(fp, "}\n");
}
```

Defines:
  `trilist_write`, never used.
Uses `Poly` 142a and `poly3_write` 145a.

The routine `trilist_parse` interprets the expression corresponding to a triangle
mesh in the 3D scene description language.

148b
⟨*trilist parse* 148b⟩≡

```
Val trilist_parse(int pass, Pval *plist)
{
  Val v;

  if (pass == T_POST) {
    Pval *pl;
    Poly *tl = NULL;

    for (pl = plist; pl != NULL; pl = pl->next) {
      if (pl->val.type == V_PVL)
        tl = poly_insert(tl, poly3_parse(pl->val.u.v));
```

```
       else
          fprintf(stderr, "(trilist): syntax error\n");
     }
     v.type = POLYLIST;
     v.u.v = tl;
   }
   return v;
 }
```

Defines:
  trilist_parse, never used.
Uses Poly 142a, poly3_parse 145b, and poly_insert 143d.

Other auxiliary routines for triangle meshes include the routine `plist_lenght` that calculates the number of elements of a triangle list and the routine `plist_alloc` that allocates memory for a polygon list.

149a   ⟨plist lenght 149a⟩≡
```
   int plist_lenght(Poly *p)
   {
     int n = 0;
     while (p != NULL) {
       n++; p = p->next;
     }
     return n;
   }
```

Defines:
  plist_lenght, never used.
Uses Poly 142a.

149b   ⟨plist alloc 149b⟩≡
```
   Poly *plist_alloc(int n, int m)
   {
     Poly *l = NULL;
     while (n--)
       l = poly_insert(l, poly_alloc(m));
     return l;
   }
```

Defines:
  plist_alloc, never used.
Uses Poly 142a, poly_alloc 142b, and poly_insert 143d.

8.5 Comments and References

In this chapter, we discussed the representation of 3D geometric shapes and presented libraries for the construction of primitives and polygonal meshes. Figure 8.6 shows an

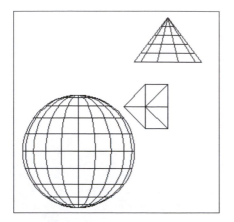

Figure 8.6. Orthogonal projection of geometric primitives.

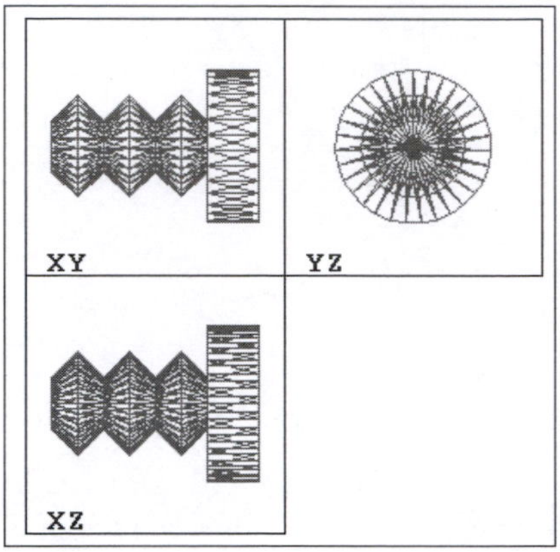

Figure 8.7. Orthogonal projection of polygonal meshes.

example of a program that draws the orthogonal projection of geometric primitives. Figure 8.7 shows an example of a program that draws the orthogonal projection of polygonal meshes.

8.5.1   Revision

The API of the library of primitive includes the following routines:

```
Prim *prim_instance(int class);
Box3d prim_bbox(Prim *p);
int prim_classify(Prim *p, Vector3 q);
Vector3 prim_gradient(Prim *p, Vector3 q);
Vector3 prim_point(Prim *p, Real u, Real v);
Vector3 prim_normal(Prim *p, Real u, Real v);
Inode *prim_intersect(Prim *p, Ray r);
Prim *prim_transform(Prim *p, Matrix4 md, Matrix4 mi);
Poly   *prim_uv_decomp(Prim *p, Real level);
Vector3 prim_texc(Prim *p, Real u, Real v);
Vector3 prim_du(Prim *p, Real u, Real v);
Vector3 prim_dv(Prim *p, Real u, Real v);
Matrix4 prim_local(Prim *p);
int prim_id(Prim *p);
void prim_write(Prim *p, FILE *fp);
```

The API of the library of polygonal meshes includes the following routines:

```
Poly *poly_alloc(int n);
Poly *poly_transform(Poly *p, Matrix4 m);
```

```
Vector3 poly_normal(Poly *p);
Poly *poly_insert(Poly *pl, Poly *p);
Inode *poly_intersect(Poly *p, Vector4 plane, Ray r);
void trilist_write(Poly *tlist, FILE* fp);
Val trilist_parse(int pass, Pval *plist);
```

Exercises

1. Write a program to scan and write the primitive SPHERE using the scene description language.

2. Implement a new geometric primitive. For instance, a cone.

3. Write a program to draw the orthogonal projection of a primitive.

4. Write a program to test if a point is contained in the interior of a solid primitive.

5. Write a program to calculate the approximate volume of a solid primitive. Hint: use ray tracing.

6. Write a program to scan and write a polygonal mesh.

7. Write a program to draw the orthogonal projection of a polygonal mesh.

8. Implement a description of polygonal meshes using a vertex and polygon list structure.

9. Write a program to create, edit, and transform geometric primitives.

10. Write a program to create, edit, and transform polygonal meshes.

9 | Modeling Techniques

In the previous chapter we presented mathematical models to describe the geometry of 3D objects, as well as representation schema to implement them on the computer. Another important problem in geometric modeling is how to specify the form of the objects once a representation schema is chosen. In this chapter we will study modeling techniques that aim to allow intuitive manipulation of a model's degrees of freedom.

9.1 Foundations of Modeling Systems

We will use the paradigm of the four universes to conceptualize modeling systems. In this sense, the modeling process begins in the physical universe through the user interface. The user's actions correspond to methods and geometric operations defined in the mathematical universe. Those operations are translated into procedures and modeling techniques in the representation universe. Finally, those techniques are mapped into modeling system architectures in the implementation universe (see Figure 9.1). We will now discuss each of those levels.

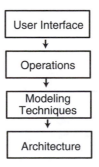

Figure 9.1. Abstraction levels of a modeling system.

9.1.1   User Interface

The user interface in a modeling system is related to the means made available by the system for specifying model parameters. Two basic interface modes exist: *textual* (noninteractive) and *graphic* (interactive).

In an noninteractive textual mode, the user specifies the model through commands to the system. This type of interface is, in general, based on a language that defines the format of the commands (syntax), as well as its functionality (semantic). An object is specified by an expression in that modeling language.

In an interactive graphics mode, the user specifies the model through a graphical interface, usually implemented in an interactive graphics workstation with a windowing system. The system makes available mechanisms for viewing and controlling the parameters of the model. An object is modeled by direct manipulation of such controls.

We can also have hybrid systems combining these two basic interface modes, such as interactive textual systems and graphics systems based on procedural representations.

9.1.2   Operations with Models

In a modeling system, geometric models are based on one of the representation schema presented in the previous chapter. There are representations by primitive families, constructive schema, and by decomposition schema.

A set of operations is associated with each of those representations, allowing us to generate the model; this set is also an integral part of the description of the model. Using these operations, we can build objects in the modeling system and modify the form of existing objects. Other operations are for analyzing object properties and creating simulations.

Modeling operations can be separated in two classes: geometric and combination operations. The geometric operations include the affine transformations and general deformations. The combination operations include operations with a set of points and also blending operations.

9.1.3   Modeling Techniques

We saw above that a geometric model can be realized as the result of a sequence of modeling operations. A modeling technique consists of representing, through a computational procedure, the necessary modeling operations to construct a certain type of geometry. The components of the model are the geometric elements and the operations with those elements. The modeling techniques define the composition rules used to apply operations to geometric elements. The result is a description of the object by a valid expression according to a representation schema.

Notice we can work with several models of the same object, providing either an exact or approximate representation of the object geometry.

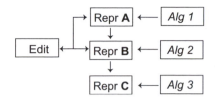

Figure 9.2. Modeling systems with multiple representations.

9.1.4   System Architecture

The architecture of a modeling system is largely determined by the choice of representation schema and the associated modeling techniques.

We have two architecture options for modeling systems: systems based on a single representation or systems based on multiple representations. In the second case, depending on the possibilities of conversion between representations, we can have a main representation and secondary representations (see Figure 9.2).

9.2   Constructive Models

In this section, we will present techniques for the creation of CSG (constructive solid geometry) models.

Constructive models are based on geometric primitives and on the operations with a set of points. To define those operations, we use logic operators and the point membership classification function, inside(C, p), which determines whether point $p \in \mathbb{R}^3$ is at the interior, exterior, or boundary of solid C.

- Union: $A \cup B = \text{inside}(A) \,||\, \text{inside}(B)$

- Intersection: $A \cap B = \text{inside}(A)\,\&\&\, \text{inside}(B)$

- Complement: $\overline{A} = \overline{\text{inside}(A)}$

- Difference: $A \backslash B = A \cap \overline{B} = \text{inside}(A)\,\&\&\, \overline{\text{inside}(B)}$

Notice we can use tables to implement the CSG operations. In fact, as the difference operation is given in terms of the intersection operation, we only have to define tables for the union and intersection operations (see Tables 9.1 and 9.2).

$\cup$	in	on	out
in	in	in	in
on	in	?	on
out	in	on	out

$\cap$	in	on	out
in	in	on	out
on	on	?	out
out	out	out	out

Table 9.1. Union operation.   **Table 9.2.** Intersection operation.

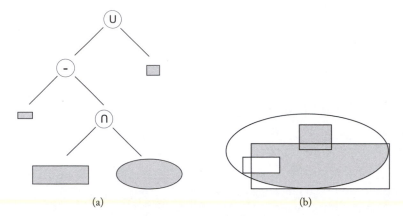

(a)   (b)

Figure 9.3. (a) CSG tree. (b) CSG object.

An important case is when point classification at the boundary of the solid is not well determined. To solve this problem, we would have to define regularized CSG operations [Requicha 80].

The model of a CSG object is a combination of geometric primitives using the Boolean point membership operations defined above. External representation of the object is given by a CSG expression, while internal representation of the object is given by the tree of the expression.

Notice we have defined only the semantics of the CSG operators. To implement this representation, we still have to define their syntax.

Example 9.1 (CSG Object). Expression of the CSG object using infix syntax:

$$(A \cup (B - (C \cap D))).$$

We show the CSG tree of the object in Figure 9.3(a) and the resulting geometry in Figure 9.3(b).   □

A final observation is that we can see CSG modeling as both a representation schema and a modeling technique. In other words, CSG modeling is at the same time a constructive representation and a language-based modeling technique.

We will now present the CSG representation and the CSG modeling techniques in our system.

9.2.1   CSG Structures

The internal representation of a CSG model is a binary tree where the leaves are primitive objects and the intermediate nodes are CSG operators. The structure `CsgNode` represents a node of the CSG tree.

157a   ⟨*csg node* 157a⟩≡
```
    typedef struct CsgNode {            /* CSG Tree Node */
      int     type;                     /* CSG_PRIM or CSG_COMP */
      union {
        struct CsgComp  c;              /* Composite */
        struct Prim     *p;             /* Primitive */
      } u;
    } CsgNode;
```
Defines:
  CsgNode, used in chunks 157–60.
Uses CSG_COMP, CSG_PRIM, and CsgComp 157b.

The nodes can be of the types primitive object (CSG_PRIM) or composition operation (CSG_COMP).

```
#define CSG_PRIM    0
#define CSG_COMP    1
```

Primitive objects are represented by the structure Prim, defined in Chapter 8. The CSG composition operations are represented by the structure CsgComp, which consists of the code of the operation and the operands given by CSG subtrees.

157b   ⟨*csg comp* 157b⟩≡
```
    typedef struct CsgComp{            /* CSG Composite */
      char            op;              /* Boolean Operation + - * */
      struct CsgNode *lft, *rgt;       /* Pointer to Children */
    } CsgComp;
```
Defines:
  CsgComp, used in chunk 157a.
Uses CsgNode 157a.

To produce CSG trees we will use routines for the construction of the two different types of tree node. The routine csg_prim encapsulates a primitive object as a leaf of the CSG tree.

157c   ⟨*csg prim* 157c⟩≡
```
    CsgNode *csg_prim(Prim *p)
    {
      CsgNode *n = (CsgNode *) NEWSTRUCT(CsgNode);
      n->type = CSG_PRIM;
      n->u.p = p;
      return n;
    }
```
Defines:
  csg_prim, used in chunks 159–61.
Uses CSG_PRIM and CsgNode 157a.

The routine `csg_link` constructs a composed CSG object formed by a CSG operator applied to two CSG subtrees.

158a   ⟨*csg link* 158a⟩≡
```
CsgNode *csg_link(int op, CsgNode *lft, CsgNode *rgt)
{
  CsgNode *n = NEWSTRUCT(CsgNode);
  n->type = CSG_COMP;
  n->u.c.op = op;
  n->u.c.lft = lft;
  n->u.c.rgt = rgt;
  return n;
}
```
Defines:
  `csg_link`, used in chunks 159c and 162.
Uses `CSG_COMP` and `CsgNode` 157a.

9.2.2   A Simple CSG Expression Language

We will adopt a simple syntax for the representation of CSG expressions. The elements of the language are primitive objects and CSG and grouping operators. The primitive objects have the following format: `c {p1 p2...}`, where `c` is a letter identifying the class of the primitive and `p2` are numeric values of the primitive parameters. The CSG operators are indicated by the characters | for union, & for intersection, and / for difference. Grouping of expressions is done with parentheses.

Example 9.2 (CSG Expression). The code below is the representation of a CSG expression corresponding to the intersection between a sphere of radius 2 and the union of two spheres, with radius 4 and center $(1,1,1)$ and with radius 3 and center $(2,2,2)$, respectively.

```
( s{0 0 0 2} & ( s{1 1 1 4}| s{2 2 2 3} ) )
```                                                                                    □

The interpreter of this simple CSG expression language will be implemented using the tools `lex` and `yacc`.

The lexical analyzer is generated by `lex`, starting from the specification below.

158b   ⟨*csg lex* 158b⟩≡
```
D    [0-9]
S    [-]
%%
[ \t\n]  ;
{S}?{D}*"."{D}+  |
{S}?{D}+"."{D}*  |
{S}?{D}+                    { yylval.dval = atof( yytext ); return NUM;}
                           { return yytext[0]; }
```

This description defines two categories of symbols: numeric digits (D) and negative signs (S). The patterns of the following symbols correspond, respectively, to white space, numbers, and individual characters.

The syntactic analyzer is generated by yacc, starting from the specification below. The terminal symbols of the grammar are numbers (NUM) and letters. The nonterminal symbols are the productions prim_obj, csg_obj, and bop.

159a   ⟨*csg union* 159a⟩≡

```
%union {
    char    cval;
    double  dval;
    CsgNode *nval;
}
```

Uses CsgNode 157a.

159b   ⟨*csg classes* 159b⟩≡

```
%token <dval> NUM
%type <cval> bop
%type <nval> prim_obj csg_obj
```

The grammar consists of the syntactic production rules of the language.

159c   ⟨*csg grammar* 159c⟩≡

```
csg_obj: '(' csg_obj bop csg_obj ')'  {$$ = root = csg_link($3, $2, $4);}
       | prim_obj
       ;
bop:        '|'                       {$$ = '+';}
       | '&'                          {$$ = '*';}
       | '\\'                         {$$ = '-';}
       ;
prim_obj: 's' '{' NUM NUM NUM NUM '}' {$$ = csg_prim(sphere_set(
                                         sphere_instance(&sphere_funcs),
                                         v3_make($3, $4, $5), $6));}
       ;
```

Uses csg_link 158a and csg_prim 157c.

Notice we defined a single primitive class: the sphere. Other primitives can be added to the production by prim_obj.

The routine csg_parse interprets an expression in this CSG language, calling the routine generated by yacc, yyparse.

159d   ⟨*csg parse* 159d⟩≡

```
CsgNode *csg_parse()
{
  if (yyparse() == 0)
    return root;
  else
    return NULL;
```

```
  }
```
Defines:
  csg_parse, never used.
Uses CsgNode 157a.

9.2.3   CSG Representation in the 3D Scene Description Language

The boolean expression language chosen for CSG objects is an appropriate representation for a modeling program. It is simple and yet captures the relevant aspects of this class of objects. However, this representation is not compatible with our 3D scene description language. For this reason, we have to develop an engine to translate the description of an object from one language to another. This translation will be done starting from the CSG expression tree.

Representation of a CSG object in the scene description language obeys the syntax of pre-fixed expressions and uses the following operators: csg_prim, csg_union, csg_inter, and csg_diff. For example:

```
csg_union { csg_prim{ sphere { center = {0, 0,  0}}},
            csg_prim{ sphere { center = {1, 1, -1}}}
          }
```

The routine csg_write writes a CSG object to a file given by its binary tree. It recursively visits the tree in depth. When it reaches a leaf of the tree, the routine writes its corresponding primitive using the routine prim_write, defined in Chapter 8. In each internal node of the tree, the routine writes the name of the corresponding CSG operator, using the routine csg_opname, and performs a recursion for each of the subtrees. Notice that this processing type, which traverses the CSG tree in depth, is the basis of most calculations with CSG objects.

160   ⟨csg write 160⟩≡
```
  void csg_write(CsgNode *t, FILE *fd)
  {
    switch(t->type) {
    case CSG_PRIM: {
      fprintf(fd, "csg_prim{ "); prim_write(t->u.p, fd); fprintf(fd, " }\n");
      break;}}
    case CSG_COMP:
      fprintf(fd, "%s {\n", csg_opname(t->u.c.op));
      csg_write(t->u.c.lft, fd); fprintf(fd, ",\n");
      csg_write(t->u.c.rgt, fd); fprintf(fd, "\n }");
      break;
    }
  }
```
Defines:
  csg_write, never used.
Uses CSG_COMP, csg_opname 161a, CSG_PRIM, csg_prim 157c, and CsgNode 157a.

Plate I. Colors in the visible spectrum. (See page 77.)　　**Plate II.** RGB color solid. (See page 82.)

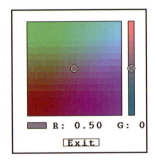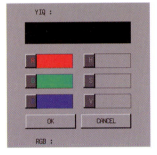

Plate III. Color selection and conversion. (See page 89.)

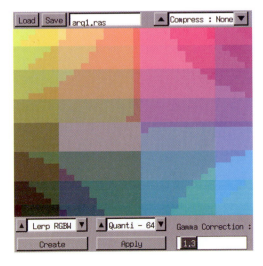

Plate IV. Program for visualizing images. (See page 98.)

Plate V. Ray tracing. (See page 287.)

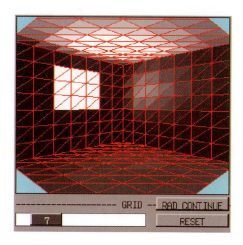

Plate VI. Radiosity. (See page 287.)

Plate VII. Test images "Mandrill" (left) and "Lenna" (right). (See page 325.)

The routine `csg_opname` returns a string with the name of the CSG operators in the 3D scene description language.

161a

⟨*csg opename* 161a⟩≡

```
char *csg_opname(char c)
{
  switch (c) {
  case '+': return "csg_union";
  case '*': return "csg_inter";
  case '-': return "csg_diff";
  default: return "";
  }
}
```

Defines:
  csg_opname, used in chunk 160.

9.2.4 Interpretation of CSG Objects in the 3D Scene Description Language

Besides writing CSG objects in the 3D scene description language, we also need to interpret CSG expressions in that language. For this, it is enough to implement the functions related to the CSG operators in the language; the rest will be done by the interpreter `lang_parse`.

The routine `csg_prim_parse` interprets a CSG primitive by encapsulating the object as a leaf in the CSG tree.

161b

⟨*csg prim parse* 161b⟩≡

```
Val csg_prim_parse(int pass, Pval *p)
{
  Val v;

  switch (pass) {
  case T_EXEC: {
    v.type = CSG_NODE;
    if (p != NULL && p->val.type == PRIM)
      v.u.v = csg_prim(p->val.u.v);
    else
      fprintf(stderr,"(csg_op): syntax error\n");
    break; }
  default:
  }
  return v;
}
```

Defines:
  csg_prim_parse, never used.
Uses csg_prim 157c.

The CSG operators in the 3D scene description language are interpreted by the routines `csg_union_parse`, `csg_inter_parse`, and `csg_diff_parse`. All of them have the same structure except for the code of the CSG operation. Therefore, we will show only the routine `csg_union_parse`.

162   ⟨*csg union parse* 162⟩≡

```
Val csg_union_parse(int pass, Pval *p)
{
  Val v;
  switch (pass) {
   case T_EXEC: {
     if ((p != NULL && p->val.type == CSG_NODE)
         && (p->next != NULL && p->next->val.type == CSG_NODE)) {
       v.type = CSG_NODE;
       v.u.v = csg_link('+', p->val.u.v, p->next->val.u.v);
     } else {
       fprintf(stderr,"(csg_op): syntax error\n");
     }
     break; }
   default:
   }
   return v;
}
```

Defines:
  csg_union_parse, never used.
Uses csg_link 158a.

Notice that all of the above routines use the constructor functions of the CSG structure defined in Section 9.2.

9.3   Generative Modeling

Generative modeling is a powerful technique for defining complex shapes using transformation groups and geometric elements.

A *generative model*, $\mathcal{G} = (\gamma, \delta)$, has a parametric functional description given by

$$S(u, v) = \delta(\gamma(u), v).$$

The constituent elements of a generative model are the generator γ and the transformation group δ.

The *generator* is usually a geometric object of dimension 1; that is, a parametric curve defined in the environment space

$$\gamma(u)\colon \mathbb{R} \to \mathbb{R}^3.$$

The *transformation group* defines a one-parameter family of transformations of the ambient space:

$$\delta(p, v) \colon \mathbb{R}^3 \times \mathbb{R} \to \mathbb{R}^3.$$

The shape of a generative object is the parametric surface $S(u, v)$ generated by the continuous transformation $\delta(\cdot, v)$ of the generator $\gamma(u)$. Notice that in this model the parameter space of S has a natural decomposition: the parameter u is relative to the generator, while v parameterizes the action of the transformation group.

A general and yet powerful transformation group is the affine transformation group of Euclidean space. This group is given by

$$h(p, v) = M_v(p) + T_v,$$

where $p = (x, y, z)$ is a point of Euclidean space, $M_v(p) : \mathbb{R}^3 \to \mathbb{R}^3$ is a linear transformation and $T_v \in \mathbb{R}^3$ is a 3D vector. Notice that both M_v and T_v depend on the parameter v.

9.3.1 Polygonal Approximation of Generative Models

Besides directly using the parametric description of a generative model, we can work with an approximate representation of its geometry. We choose a representation by decomposition corresponding to a piecewise linear approximation of the surface.

To generate the polygonal mesh that approximates the surface $S(u, v)$, given by a generative model (γ, δ), we discretize its parameter space $U = \{(u, v) : u \in [a, b], v \in [c, d]\}$.

The decomposition of U will be based on a regular sampling, and it corresponds to a grid of $N \times M$ points. Starting from the grid, we construct a simplicial mesh using the Coxeter-Freudenthal decomposition (see Figure 9.4).

Notice that in the horizontal direction we have a sampling of points along the curve $g(u)$ that was transformed by the function $h(\cdot, v)$ by a constant value of v.

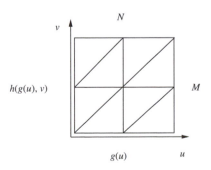

Figure 9.4. Mesh structure.

The routine `gener_affine` generates a polygonal mesh with resolution $N \times M$ that approximates the generative model given by g and h.

164a   ⟨*gener affine* 164a⟩≡

```
Poly *gener_affine(int n, Vector3 *g, int m, Matrix4 *h)
{
  int u, v;
  Poly *tl = NULL;
  Vector3 *a = NEWARRAY(n, Vector3);
  Vector3 *b = NEWARRAY(n, Vector3);
  for (v = 0; v < m; v++) {
    for (u = 0; u < n; u++) {
      b[u] = v3_m4mult(g[u], h[v]);
      if (u == 0|| v == 0)
        continue;
      tl = poly_insert(tl, poly3_make(a[u-1], a[u], b[u-1]));
      tl = poly_insert(tl, poly3_make(a[u], b[u], b[u-1]));
    }
    SWAP(a, b, Vector3 *);
  }
  free(a); free(b);
  return tl;
}
```

Defines:
  gener_affine, used in chunk 166a.

The routine `affine_group` calculates an array of matrices corresponding to a discretization of the transformation group given by the specification in t, which contains the code of the transformation, and p, which contains the value of the transformation parameter.

164b   ⟨*affine group* 164b⟩≡

```
Matrix4 *affine_group(int l, int m, char *t, Real **p)
{
  int v;
  Matrix4 *h = NEWARRAY(m, Matrix4);
  for (v = 0; v < m; v++)
    h[v] = m4_compxform(l, t, p, v);
  return h;
}
```

Defines:
  affine_group, used in chunk 166a.
Uses m4_compxform 164c.

The routine `m4_compxform` calculates a transformation matrix made up of the concatenation of basic transformations.

164c   ⟨*compxform* 164c⟩≡

```
Matrix4 m4_compxform(int k,  char *t, Real **h, int j)
```

```
{
  int i;
  Matrix4 m = m4_ident();

  for (i = 0; i < k; i++) {
    switch (t[i]) {
    case G_TX: m = m4_m4prod(m4_translate(h[i][j], 0, 0), m); break;
    case G_TY: m = m4_m4prod(m4_translate(0, h[i][j], 0), m); break;
    case G_TZ: m = m4_m4prod(m4_translate(0, 0, h[i][j]), m); break;
    case G_RX: m = m4_m4prod(m4_rotate('x', h[i][j]), m); break;
    case G_RY: m = m4_m4prod(m4_rotate('y', h[i][j]), m); break;
    case G_RZ: m = m4_m4prod(m4_rotate('z', h[i][j]), m); break;
    case G_SX: m = m4_m4prod(m4_scale(h[i][j], 1, 1), m); break;
    case G_SY: m = m4_m4prod(m4_scale(1, h[i][j], 1), m); break;
    case G_SZ: m = m4_m4prod(m4_scale(1, 1, h[i][j]), m); break;
    default:
    }
  }
  return m;
}
```
Defines:
  m4_compxform, used in chunk 164b.
Uses G_RX, G_RY, G_RZ, G_SX, G_SY, G_SZ, G_TX, G_TY, and G_TZ.

9.3.2 Types of Generative Models

We can have several types of generative models. The most common ones are based on a single transformation group and on the combined action of two transformation groups:

□ Generative models with a transformation:

  - Extrusion: translation

  - Revolution: rotation

□ Generative models with two transformations:

  - Taper: translation, scale

  - Bend: translation, rotation

  - Twist: translation, rotation

Notice the generative models are not unique. For instance, we can generate a cylinder in two ways:

1. circle + extrusion

2. line + rotation

9.3.3   Surfaces of Revolution

We will demonstrate the implementation of generative models by giving a concrete example. Consider the family of surfaces of revolution. These surfaces are generated by the rotation of a planar curve around an axis contained in that plane.

The routine `rotsurf` generates the polygonal approximation of a surface of revolution by the rotation of 360 degrees of the curve g.

166a

⟨*rotsurf* 166a⟩≡

```
Poly *rotsurf(int n, Vector3 *g, int m)
{
  Matrix4 *h; Real *p[1]; Poly *s;
  char t[1] = {G_RY};
  p[0] = linear(0, PITIMES2, m);
  s = gener_affine(n, g, m, h = affine_group(1, m, t, p));
  efree(h);
  return s;
}
```

Defines:
  rotsurf, never used.
Uses **affine_group** 164b, **G_RY**, **gener_affine** 164a, and **linear** 166b.

The routine `linear` is an auxiliary routine that calculates a linear interpolation between the values v_0 and v_1.

166b

⟨*linear* 166b⟩≡

```
Real *linear(Real v0, Real v1, int n)
{
  int i;
  Real *x = NEWTARRAY(n, Real);
  Real incr = (v1 - v0) / (n -1);
  for (i = 0; i < n; i++)
    x[i] = v0 + (incr * i);
  return x;
}
```

Defines:
  linear, used in chunk 166a.

9.4   Comments and References

In this chapter we described the main modeling techniques and developed libraries for the implementation of those techniques.

9.4.1   Revision

The API of the CSG modeling library is made up of the following routines.

```
CsgNode *csg_parse();
CsgNode *csg_prim(Prim *p);
CsgNode *csg_link(int op, CsgNode *lft, CsgNode *rgt);

char *csg_opname(char c);
void csg_write(CsgNode *t, FILE *fd);

Val csg_union_parse(int c, Pval *p);
Val csg_inter_parse(int c, Pval *p);
Val csg_diff_parse(int c, Pval *p);
Val csg_prim_parse(int c, Pval *p);
```

The API of the Generative modeling libraries is made up of the routines below.

```
Poly *rotsurf(int n, Vector3 *g, int m);
Poly *gener_affine(int n, Vector3 *g, int m, Matrix4 *h);
Matrix4 m4_compxform(int k,  char *t, Real **h, int j);
Matrix4 *affine_group(int l, int m, char *t, Real **p);

Real *linear(Real v0, Real v1, int n);
```

Exercises

1. Using the CSG library, write a program to create constructive solid models. The program should accept definitions of geometric primitives in the format (D = def), where D is a capital letter and def is the definition of the primitive. For example,

    ```
    A = s {1, 1, 1, 4};
    B = s {3, 2, 1, 10};

    (A| (B & A))
    ```

2. Implement the operation csg_classify to perform the point membership classification in relation to a CSG model.

3. Using the library GENER, write a program to create a rotation surface. The program should read a 2D curve and have as parameters the rotation axis, the total rotation angle, and the mesh discretization.

4. Implement, in the CSG representation, the operation of geometric transformation. For this, define the CSG Node of the type CSG_TRANSFORM.

5. Using the GP and CSG libraries, write an interactive program to create CSG objects. The program should support primitives, groups, transformations (translation, rotation, and scale), and point membership operations (union, difference, complement, intersection).

6. Write a program to calculate the approximate volume of a CSG model.

7. Using the GP and GENER libraries, write an interactive program to create rotation surfaces. The program must support the input and editing of curves and the drawing of the surface.

8. Implement the generative model based on extrusion.

9. Write two programs to create a cylinder: (1) using the model of rotation surfaces and (2) using the model of extrusion surfaces.

10. Implement the generative models TAPER, TWIST, and BEND, and write a program to create surfaces based on those models.

10 Hierarchies and Articulated Objects

In a 3D scene, sets of objects generally maintain some physical relation that implies a geometric linkage between them. This relation can be functional, as in the case of the chairs of an auditorium that are organized in numbered rows; or it can be a structural, as in the case of a door that it fastened by a hinge. In this chapter we will study the use of geometric linkages for structuring sets of elements.

10.1 Geometric Links

A geometric transformation establishes an spatial link between two sets of objects. In a 3D scene, we have a coordinate system common to every object called a *global (or scene) coordinate system*. In Chapter 8 we saw that primitive objects have a canonical coordinate system called the *local coordinate system* of the primitive.

We can think of a transformation as a change between coordinate systems. In this sense, transformations can be associated to a set of objects to define specific coordinate systems. We will use transformations to define geometric links common to a set of objects. Objects that share this link are subject to the same transformation.

Depending on the type of link, we have different forms of structuring. The most common are

□ **Groups of objects.** The transformations are used to position objects in space in relation to each other. A particular case is that of *composed objects*, constituted by the union of subobjects with fixed transformations between them.

□ **Articulated structures.** Formed by rigid bodies (parts) linked by geometric links (joints). Transformations act in two ways: fixed transformation operate between the coordinate systems of articulations; variable transformation correspond to the degrees of freedom of the articulation.

Later in this chapter we will study these two types of structures in detail.

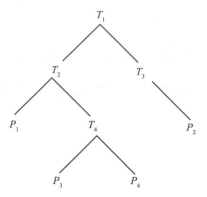

Figure 10.1. Object hierarchy.

10.1.1   Hierarchies

Some sets of objects are naturally constituted by subsets of objects. We therefore have a hierarchical structuring of those objects. This structure can be represented by a tree, with the leaves corresponding to individual objects P_k and the internal nodes corresponding to subsets of objects C_i. Geometric link relations generally reflect spatial properties of such structuring, and for this reason they are part of this hierarchical representation. We associate, to each subset C_i, a transformation T_i (see Figure 10.1).

In this case, the transformations T_i are recursively applied according to the tree structure. In other words, transformations affect the elements of the set and spread to their descendants. The result is that a transformation T_{P_k} corresponds to each individual object P_k, given by the composition of transformations to which the object is subordinated.

In many computer graphics applications, such as viewing methods, it is convenient to work with a nonhierarchical representation of the scene objects. For this, it is necessary to convert the tree structure into a list. This conversion is called *flattening*.

The nonhierarchical representation is a list of pairs (P_k, T_{P_k}) of the objects and their transformations. To create this representation, we calculate their composed transformations T_{P_k} that concatenate the transformation matrices associated with each level of the hierarchy. This procedure can be established by an in-depth traversal of the tree.

For instance, the tree in Figure 10.1 corresponds to the following list:

$$((P1, T_{P_1}), (P2, T_{P_2}), (P3, T_{P_3}), (P4, T_{P_4})),$$

where the composed transformations are given by

$$\begin{aligned}
T_{P_1}(P_1) &= T_1(T_2(P_1)), \\
T_{P_2}(P_2) &= T_1(T_2(T4(P_3))), \\
T_{P_3}(P_3) &= T_1(T_2(T4(P_4))), \\
T_{P_4}(P_4) &= T_1(T_3(P_1)).
\end{aligned}$$

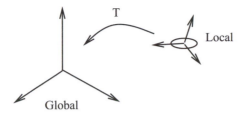

Figure 10.2. Transformation between the global coordinate system (of the scene) and the local coordinate system (of the object).

10.1.2 Transforming the Geometry

The use of transformations associated with objects requires a mapping between the global coordinate system of the 3D scene and the local coordinate system of the object P_k, which is given by the transformation T_k (see Figure 10.2).

In Chapter 4 we saw that, for objects described parametrically, we use the transformation T directly, while for objects described in implicitly, we use the inverse T^{-1} of the transformation.

10.1.3 Affine Invariance

We will choose the class of affine transformations to implement the geometric links in the clusterings and hierarchies. The main reason for this choice is that, besides including practically all the important transformations, this class allows the efficient use of transformations in the modeling and viewing processes.

In this context, it's desirable for the class of geometric transformations to have *affine invariance*. This property guarantees that, given a discretization $D_\mathcal{O}$ of a graphic object $\mathcal{O}$ and a transformation T, the result of applying T to the elements of $D_\mathcal{O}$ is the same as that of reconstructing $\mathcal{O}$ and later applying T. This property is indicated by the commutative diagrams below, where R is reconstruction operator:

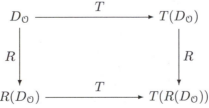

The importance of this property can be better understood by a concrete example.

Example 10.1 (Straight line). Consider a segment of straight line $\overline{p_0 p_1}$ given by its parametric representation $g : [0, 1] \to \mathbb{R}^3$, where $g(u) = up_0 + (1 - u)p_1$, with $p_0, p_1 \in \mathbb{R}^3$. In this case, the reconstruction operator is $R(p_0, p_1) \equiv g$.

Figure 10.3. Affine invariance and transformation.

If T is a affine transformation, then

$$T(R(p_0, p_1)(u)) = R(T(p_0), T(p_1))(u),$$

or

$$T(g(u)) = uT(p_0) + (1 - u)T(p_1).$$

The great advantage of having this property is that to transform the straight line segment, it is enough to apply T to the ends p_0 and p_1 (see Figure 10.3). □

The result of the above example is valid for the majority of geometric descriptions of graphic objects.

- □ Straight line and polygons

    - Vertices

- □ Curves and parametric surfaces[1]

    - Control points

- □ Implicit surfaces

    - Geometric elements

10.2   Hierarchies and Transformations

In this section we will present the implementation for calculating transformations associated with objects of a hierarchical structure. The operation consists essentially of an in-depth visit to the tree nodes representing the hierarchy. Composition of the transformations is performed at each internal node along the descent path, from the tree root toward its leaves. In each leaf, the composed transformation is applied to the corresponding object. This procedure can be implemented in a recursive mode. Notice that is necessary to keep the intermediate results of the composed transformations at each node of the tree.

An appropriate data structure for implementing this operation is the *stack* structure, which allows us to efficiently store the partial data of this calculation. The transformations

---

[1]Remember that NURBS (nonuniform rational B-splines) also have projective invariance.

are represented by a 4×4 matrix. A *current transformation matrix*, or *CTM*, corresponds to the top of the stack at each step of the process. To implement the stack engine, we will define the operations of *push* and *pop*, allowing access to the data structure. We will also define operations with the current transformation (*CTM*).

10.2.1   Stack Operations

The structure Stack4 represents a stack. It contains the maximum (size) and arrays with the direct and inverse (mbot and ibot) transformations. The pointers mtop and itop point to the top of the stack.

173a   ⟨*stack 4* 173a⟩≡
```
typedef struct Stack4 {
  int size;
  Matrix4
    *mbot, *mtop,
    *ibot, *itop;
} Stack4;
```
Defines:
  Stack4, used in chunks 173–76.

The routine s4_initstack is the stack constructor.

173b   ⟨*init stack* 173b⟩≡
```
Stack4 *s4_initstack(int size)
{
  int i;
  Matrix4 *m;
  Stack4 *s  = (Stack4 *) emalloc(sizeof (Stack4));
  s->size = size;
  s->mbot = ( Matrix4 * ) emalloc( size * sizeof(Matrix4));
  s->ibot = ( Matrix4 * ) emalloc( size * sizeof(Matrix4));

  for (m = s->mbot, i = 0; i < s->size; i++)
    *m++ = m4_ident();
  for (m = s->ibot, i = 0; i < s->size; i++)
    *m++ = m4_ident();

  s->mtop = s->mbot;
  s->itop = s->ibot;

  return s;
}
```
Defines:
  s4_initstack, used in chunk 179a.
Uses Stack4 173a.

The routine s4_push pushes the current transformation onto the stack.

174a   ⟨*push* 174a⟩≡
```
void s4_push(Stack4 *s)
{
  Matrix4 *m;
  if ((s->mtop - s->mbot) >= (s->size - 1))
    error("(s4_push): stack overflow");
  m = s->mtop;
  s->mtop++;
  *s->mtop = *m;
  m = s->itop;
  s->itop++;
  *s->itop = *m;
}
```
Defines:
  s4_push, used in chunk 179a.
Uses Stack4 173a.

The routine s4_pop pops the current transformation off the stack.

174b   ⟨*pop* 174b⟩≡
```
void s4_pop(Stack4 *s)
{
  if (s->mtop <= s->mbot)
    error("(s4_pop()) stack underflow\n");
  s->mtop--;
  s->itop--;
}
```
Defines:
  s4_pop, used in chunk 179a.
Uses Stack4 173a.

10.2.2 Transformations

We will construct affine transformations that compose the basic transformations of translation, rotation, and scaling.

The routine s4_translate concatenates the translation matrix with the top of the stack.

174c   ⟨*stranslate* 174c⟩≡
```
void s4_translate(Stack4 *s, Vector3 t)
{
  *s->mtop = m4_m4prod(*s->mtop, m4_translate( t.x, t.y, t.z));
  *s->itop = m4_m4prod(m4_translate(-t.x,-t.y,-t.z), *s->itop);
}
```
Defines:
  s4_translate, used in chunk 179b.
Uses Stack4 173a.

The routine `s4_scale` concatenaties the scaling matrix with the top of the stack.

175a ⟨*sscale* 175a⟩ ≡
```
void s4_scale(Stack4 *s, Vector3 v)
{
  *s->mtop = m4_m4prod(*s->mtop, m4_scale(v.x, v.y, v.z));

  if (REL_EQ(v.x, 0.0)|| REL_EQ(v.y,0.0)|| REL_EQ(v.z,0.0))
    fprintf(stderr,"(s4_scale()) unable to invert scale matrix\n");
  else
    *s->itop = m4_m4prod(m4_scale(1./v.x,1./v.y,1./v.z), *s->itop);
}
```
Defines:
  s4_scale, used in chunk 180a.
Uses Stack4 173a.

The routine `s4_rotate` concatenates the rotation matrix with the top of the stack.

175b ⟨*srotate* 175b⟩ ≡
```
void s4_rotate(Stack4 *s, char axis, Real angle)
{
  *s->mtop = m4_m4prod(*s->mtop, m4_rotate(axis,angle));
  *s->itop = m4_m4prod(m4_rotate(axis,-angle), *s->itop);
}
```
Defines:
  s4_rotate, used in chunk 180b.
Uses Stack4 173a.

The routines `s4_v3xform` and `s4_n3xform` apply the current transformation to geometric elements. The routine `s4_v3xform` transforms a vector.

175c ⟨*v3xform* 175c⟩ ≡
```
Vector3 s4_v3xform(Stack4 *s, Vector3 v)
{
  return v3_m4mult(v, *s->mtop);
}
```
Defines:
  s4_v3xform, never used.
Uses Stack4 173a.

The routine `s4_v3xform` transforms the normal direction of a tangent plane.

175d ⟨*n3xform* 175d⟩ ≡
```
Vector3 s4_n3xform(Stack4 *s, Vector3 nv)
{
  return v3_m4mult(nv, m4_transpose(*s->itop));
}
```
Defines:
  s4_n3xform, never used.
Uses Stack4 173a.

The routines `s4_getmat` and `s4_getimat` return, respectively, the direct and inverse current transformations.

176a   ⟨*getmat* 176a⟩≡
```
Matrix4 s4_getmat(Stack4 *s)
{
  return *s->mtop;
}
```
Defines:
  `s4_getmat`, used in chunk 181a.
Uses `Stack4` 173a.

176b   ⟨*getimat* 176b⟩≡
```
Matrix4 s4_getimat(Stack4 *s)
{
  return *s->itop;
}
```
Defines:
  `s4_getimat`, used in chunk 181a.
Uses `Stack4` 173a.

The routine `s4_loadmat` allows us to modify the current transformation matrix.

176c   ⟨*loadmat* 176c⟩≡
```
void s4_loadmat(Stack4 *s, Matrix4 *md, Matrix4 *im)
{
  *s->mtop = *md;
  *s->itop = (im == (Matrix4 *)0)? m4_inverse(*md) : *im;
}
```
Defines:
  `s4_loadmat`, never used.
Uses `m4_inverse` and `Stack4` 173a.

The routine `s4_concmat` allows us to concatenate a matrix with the current transformation.

176d   ⟨*concmat* 176d⟩≡
```
void s4_concmat(Stack4 *s, Matrix4 *md, Matrix4 *im)
{
  *s->mtop = m4_m4prod(*md, *s->mtop );
  if ( im == (Matrix4 *)0)
    *s->itop = m4_m4prod(*s->itop, m4_inverse(*md));
  else
    *s->itop = m4_m4prod(*s->itop, *im);
}
```
Defines:
  `s4_concmat`, never used.
Uses `m4_inverse` and `Stack4` 173a.

10.3 Groups of Objects

In this section we will show the implementation of a 3D scene description language for hierarchical groups of objects. This description will serve for both composed and articulated objects.

10.3.1 Hierarchy Description

The format adopted for object hierarchies is based on the group construction containing transformations (translate, rotate, and scale) and subgroups of objects (children).

177a

```
⟨group scn 177a⟩≡
    group{
          transform = { translate {v = {0, .0, 0}}, rotate {z = 0 }},
          children = group {
                          transform = { translate {v = {.1, 0, 0}}},
                          children = primobj{ shape = sphere{radius = .1 }}
                    },
          transform = { translate {v = {.2, 0, 0}}, rotate {z = 0 }},
          children = group {
                          transform = { translate {v = {.2, 0, 0}}},
                          children = primobj{ shape = sphere{radius = .1}}
                    }
    };
```

10.3.2 Objects

In the previous chapters on modeling we discussed several representation schema for geometric objects. Before defining groups of objects, we must more precisely define the notion of an object in our system: an *object* will be represented by the structure Object consisting of its geometric support (shape) and its attributes, such as material type.

177b

```
⟨object struct 177b⟩≡
    typedef struct Object {
      struct Object   *next;
      struct Material *mat;
      int   type; /* shape */
      union {
        struct Poly     *pols;
        struct Prim     *prim;
        struct CsgNode *tcsg;
      } u;
    } Object;
```
Defines:
  Object, used in chunks 178, 181, 182, and 187a.

Notice this structure has the purpose of encapsulating, in a single computational entity, the different geometric representation schema applied to the system. In this way, the form of the object can use representation by primitives, by decomposition schema (polygonal meshes), and constructive schema (CSG).

```
#define V_CSG_NODE  901
#define V_PRIM      902
#define V_POLYLIST  903
```

Note that the structure Object was designed as an element of a single linked list of objects. This fact will be used to represent sets of objects.

The routine obj_new is the object constructor. It allocates the structure and initializes the fields corresponding to the geometry of the object. The macro SET_MAT_DEFAULT will be defined later.

178a   ⟨*obj new* 178a⟩≡
```
Object *obj_new(int type, void *v)
{
  Object *o = NEWSTRUCT(Object);
  o->next = NULL;
  SET_MAT_DEFAULT(o);
  switch (o->type = type) {
  case V_CSG_NODE: o->u.tcsg = v; break;
  case V_PRIM: o->u.prim = v; break;
  case V_POLYLIST: o->u.pols = v; break;
  default: error("(newobj) wrong type");
  }
  return o;
}
```
Defines:
   obj_new, never used.
Uses Object 177b and SET_MAT_DEFAULT.

The routine obj_free is the object destructor.

178b   ⟨*obj free* 178b⟩≡
```
void obj_free(Object *o)
{
  switch (o->type) {
  case V_PRIM: prim_destroy(o->u.prim); break;
  case V_CSG_NODE: csg_destroy(o->u.tcsg); break;
  case V_POLYLIST: plist_free(o->u.pols); break;
  }
  efree(o->mat->tinfo); efree(o->mat);
  efree(o);
}
```
Defines:
   obj_free, used in chunk 182c.
Uses Object 177b.

10.3.3   Groups and Lists of Objects

We will adopt two description types for objects with links. Externally, we will adopt the hierarchical description specified in Section 10.3.1. Internally, we will adopt the equivalent nonhierarchical description by list of objects.

Conversion between the external and internal representations will be performed by the operators of the 3D scene description language, described next. Routines for processing the hierarchy are based in the stack engine. They use the static structure `Stack4`.

```
static Stack4 *stk = NULL;
```

The routine `group_parse` performs an in-depth visit to the hierarchy tree. This routine implements the semantics of the operator `group` of the 3D scene description language. It pushes the current transformation onto the descent direction toward the leaves of the tree and pops the transformation up along the ascent direction toward the root of the tree. At each node, it executes the object transformation at that level of the hierarchy, calling the routine `transform_objects`, and it creates a list containing the objects of that subtree using the routine `collect_objects`. We will present these two routines next.

179a

⟨*group parse* 179a⟩≡
```
Val group_parse(int pass, Pval *pl)
{
  Val v = {V_NULL, 0};
  switch (pass) {
  case T_PREP:
    if (stk == NULL) stk = s4_initstack(MAX_STK_DEPTH);
    s4_push(stk);
    break;
  case T_EXEC:
    transform_objects(pl);
    s4_pop(stk);
    v.u.v = collect_objects(pl); v.type = V_GROUP;
    break;
  }
  return v;
}
```
Defines:
  group_parse, never used.
Uses collect_objects 181c, MAX_STK_DEPTH, s4_initstack 173b, s4_pop 174b, s4_push 174a,
  stk, and transform_objects 181a.

The routines `translate_parse`, `scale_parse`, and `rotate_parse` implement the semantics of the transformation operators of the language. They perform the concatenation of the specified transformations with the current transformation matrix.

179b

⟨*translate parse* 179b⟩≡
```
Val translate_parse(int pass, Pval *p)
{
```

```
      Val v = {V_NULL, 0};
      if (pass == T_EXEC) {
        if (p->val.type == V_PVL)
          s4_translate(stk, pvl_to_v3(p->val.u.v));
        else
          error("(translate) wrong argument");
      }
      return v;
    }
```
Defines:
  translate_parse, never used.
Uses s4_translate 174c and stk.

180a   ⟨*scale parse* 180a⟩≡
```
      Val scale_parse(int pass, Pval *p)
      {
        Val v = {V_NULL, 0};
        if (pass == T_EXEC) {
          if (p->val.type == V_PVL)
            s4_scale(stk, pvl_to_v3(p->val.u.v));
          else
            error("(scale) wrong argument");
        }
        return v;
      }
```
Defines:
  scale_parse, never used.
Uses s4_scale 175a and stk.

180b   ⟨*rotate parse* 180b⟩≡
```
      Val rotate_parse(int pass, Pval *p)
      {
        Val v = {V_NULL, 0};
        if (pass == T_EXEC) {
          if (strcmp(p->name, "x") == 0 && p->val.type == V_NUM )
            s4_rotate(stk, 'x', p->val.u.d);
          else if (strcmp(p->name, "y") == 0 && p->val.type == V_NUM )
            s4_rotate(stk, 'y', p->val.u.d);
          else if (strcmp(p->name, "z") == 0 && p->val.type == V_NUM )
            s4_rotate(stk, 'z', p->val.u.d);
          else
            error("(rotate) wrong argument");
        }
        return v;
      }
```
Defines:
  rotate_parse, never used.
Uses s4_rotate 175b and stk.

10.3.4 Object Transformation

The routine `transform_objects` traverses the list of objects subordinate to a group and applies the current transformation to each of them.

181a

⟨*transform objects* 181a⟩≡

```
static void transform_objects(Pval *pl)
{
  Pval *p;
  for (p = pl; p != NULL; p = p->next)
    if (p->val.type == V_OBJECT)
      obj_transform(p->val.u.v, s4_getmat(stk), s4_getimat(stk));
}
```

Defines:
  transform_objects, used in chunk 179a.
Uses obj_transform 181b, s4_getimat 176b, s4_getmat 176a, and stk.

The routine `obj_transform` transforms an object based on its type.

181b

⟨*obj xform* 181b⟩≡

```
void obj_transform(Object *o, Matrix4 m, Matrix4 mi)
{
  switch (o->type) {
  case V_PRIM: prim_transform(o->u.prim, m, mi); break;
  case V_CSG_NODE: csg_transform(o->u.tcsg, m, mi); break;
  case V_POLYLIST: plist_transform(o->u.pols, m); break;
  }
}
```

Defines:
  obj_transform, used in chunk 181a.
Uses Object 177b.

10.3.5 Collecting Objects in a List

The routine `group_parse` receives as an argument a list that can contain individual objects and lists of objects. The objects are primitives defined within the scope of the group. The lists of objects are subgroups of this group of objects.

The routine `collect_objects` creates a collection with all the subordinate objects to a group. In other words, it places in a single list the elements of the subtree of a specific node in the hierarchy.

181c

⟨*collect objects* 181c⟩≡

```
static Object *collect_objects(Pval *pl)
{
  Pval *p; Object *olist = NULL;
  for (p = pl; p != NULL; p = p->next) {
    if (p->val.type == V_OBJECT)
      olist = obj_insert(olist, p->val.u.v);
```

```
        else if (p->val.type == V_GROUP)
            olist = obj_list_insert(olist, p->val.u.v);
    }
    return olist;
}
```

Defines:
  collect_objects, used in chunk 179a.
Uses obj_insert 182a, obj_list_insert 182b, and Object 177b.

The routine obj_insert inserts an object in the list.

182a   ⟨*obj insert* 182a⟩≡
```
    Object *obj_insert(Object *olist, Object *o)
    {
        o->next = olist;
        return o;
    }
```

Defines:
  obj_insert, used in chunks 181c and 182b.
Uses Object 177b.

The routine obj_list_insert inserts a list of objects in the list.

182b   ⟨*obj list insert* 182b⟩≡
```
    Object *obj_list_insert(Object *olist, Object *l)
    {
        Object *t, *o = l;
        while (o != NULL) {
            t = o; o = o->next;
            olist = obj_insert(olist, t);
        }
        return olist;
    }
```

Defines:
  obj_list_insert, used in chunk 181c.
Uses obj_insert 182a and Object 177b.

The routine obj_list_free frees the memory allocated for a list of objects.

182c   ⟨*obj list free* 182c⟩≡
```
    void obj_list_free(Object *ol)
    {
        Object *t, *o = ol;
        while (o != NULL) {
            t = o; o = o->next;
            obj_free(t);
        }
    }
```

Defines:
  obj_list_free, used in chunk 188b.
Uses obj_free 178b and Object 177b.

10.3.6 Parameterized Links

Articulated structures are composed of variable geometric links, defined by a dependency graph. The elements of this graph are

□ **Links.** Mapping between coordinate systems,

□ **Joints.** Variable transformations (degrees of freedom),

□ **Objects.** Local geometry.

Example 10.2 (Articulated Arm).

183a   ⟨*arm* 183a⟩≡
```
group {
  transform = { translate {v = {0, 0, 0}},
                    rotate {z = arg{ r1 = 0 }}},
  children = group { children = primobj{ shape = cylinder { height = 1 }}},
  transform = { translate {v = {1, 0, 0}},
                    rotate {z = motor{ arg{ r2 = 0 }}}},
  children = group { children = primobj{ shape = cylinder { height = 1 }}},
}
```

□

The transformation values associated with the degrees of freedom of the articulated structure can be obtained in several ways. One, the implementation of which we will describe next, is through the use of variables defined in the command line of the interpreter of the 3D scene description language.

The routine `arg_init` initializes the local structures with the list of arguments from the program's command line.

```
static int m_argc;
static char **m_argv;
```

183b   ⟨*arg init* 183b⟩≡
```
  void arg_init(int ac, char **av)
  {
      m_argc = ac; m_argv = av;
  }
```
Defines:
   arg_init, never used.
Uses m_argc and m_argv.

The routine `arg_parse` implements the operator `arg` of the 3D scene description language.

183c   ⟨*arg parse* 183c⟩≡
```
  Val arg_parse(int pass, Pval *p)
  {
```

```
    Val v = {V_NULL, 0};
    switch (pass) {
    case T_EXEC:
      if (p != NULL && p->val.type == V_NUM)
        v.u.d = arg_get_dval(p->name, p->val.u.d);
      else
        fprintf(stderr, "error: arg parse %lx\n",p);
      v.type = V_NUM;
      break;
    }
    return v;
  }
```

Defines:
  arg_parse, never used.
Uses arg_get_dval 184.

The routine `arg_get_dval` seeks in the list of arguments a pair of the type -name value. If the pair is found, it returns the value; otherwise it returns defval.

184   ⟨arg get dval 184⟩≡
```
    double arg_get_dval(char *s, Real defval)
    {
      int i;
      for (i = 1; i < m_argc; i++)
        if (m_argv[i][0] == '-' && strcmp(m_argv[i]+1, s) == 0 && i+1 < m_argc)
          return atof(m_argv[i+1]);
      return defval;
    }
```

Defines:
  arg_get_dval, used in chunk 183c.
Uses m_argc and m_argv.

Notice that these routines can be used in several contexts.

10.4   Animation

In this section we will develop a computational schema to support procedural constructions of animations in general, and in particular of articulated objects.

10.4.1   Animation Clock

To implement procedural animation, we have to define routines to control the clock. The current time of the animation is represented by the variable time. The Boolean variable stop indicates whether the clock has stopped or not.

```
static Real time = 0;
static Boolean stop = FALSE;
```

The routine `time_reset` restarts the clock.

185a
```
⟨time reset 185a⟩≡
  void time_reset(Real t)
  {
    time = t;
    stop = FALSE;
  }
```
Defines:
  time_reset, used in chunk 187b.
Uses stop and time.

The routine `time_done` indicates whether the animation time has finished.

185b
```
⟨time done 185b⟩≡
  Boolean time_done(Real tlimit)
  {
    return (time > tlimit|| stop == TRUE);
  }
```
Defines:
  time_done, used in chunk 187b.
Uses stop and time.

The routine `time_incr` advances the clock.

185c
```
⟨time incr 185c⟩≡
  Real time_incr(Real tincr)
  {
    if (!stop)
      time += tincr;
    return time;
  }
```
Defines:
  time_incr, used in chunk 187b.
Uses stop and time.

The routine `time_get` returns the current time.

185d
```
⟨time get 185d⟩≡
  Real time_get()
  {
    return time;
  }
```
Defines:
  time_get, used in chunk 186.
Uses time.

The routine `time_end` stops the clock, terminating the animation.

185e
```
⟨time end 185e⟩≡
  Real time_end()
  {
```

```
        stop = TRUE;
        return time;
    }
```

Defines:
  time_end, never used.
Uses stop and time.

10.4.2   Constructions for Procedural Animation

We will give the example of a procedural construction for animation.

Example 10.3 (engine). This animation operator implements an engine with constant speed. Its syntax is engine {IN A}.   □

An engine could be used to create a variable transformation in time:

```
transform = { rotate { z = motor{.2 }}}
```

The routine motor_parse implements the operator engine. It calculates the value at the current time.

186   ⟨motor parse 186⟩≡
```
    Val motor_parse(int pass, Pval *p)
    {
      Val v = {V_NULL, 0};
      switch (pass) {
      case T_EXEC:
        if (p != NULL && p->val.type == V_NUM)
          v.u.d = time_get() * p->val.u.d;
        else
          fprintf(stderr, "error: motor parse\n");
        v.type = V_NUM;
        pvl_free(p);
        break;
      }
      return v;
    }
```

Defines:
  motor_parse, never used.
Uses time_get 185d.

10.4.3   Execution of the Animation

Using the procedural animation constructions, we have a way to determine the values of several parameters that vary along time associated with objects in a 3D scene.

We will define a new data structure, Scene, containing the list of all scene objects. Later we will include other elements in this structure.

187a ⟨*scene structure* 187a⟩≡
```
typedef struct Scene {
  struct Object *objs;
} Scene;
```
Defines:
  Scene, used in chunks 187 and 188.
Uses Object 177b and objs.

To visualize the animation, we have to produce a sequence of images of the scene at different moments of time.

The program below implements the generation of a sequence of frames of an animation.

187b ⟨*anim* 187b⟩≡
```
int main(int argc, char **argv)
{
  Scene *s;
  init_scene();
  time_reset(0);
  s = scene_eval(scene_read());
  while (!time_done(timeoff)) {
    render_frame(s, get_time());
    scene_free(s);
    s = scene_eval();
    time_incr(1);
  }
}
```
Defines:
  main, used in chunks 313, 317, and 318c.
Uses Scene 187a, scene_eval 188a, scene_free 188b, scene_read 187c, time_done 185b,
  time_incr 185c, and time_reset 185a.

The routine scene_read reads the file with the 3D scene description and the animation constructions.

187c ⟨*scene read* 187c⟩≡
```
Scene *scene_read(void)
{
  if (lang_parse() == 0)
    return lang_ptree();
  else
    error("(scene read)");
}
```
Defines:
  scene_read, used in chunk 187b.
Uses Scene 187a.

The routine `scene_eval` interprets the description of the 3D scene and the animation constructions for the current time t. Notice the routine uses the nondestructive evaluation (`lang_nd_eval`) of the scene description.

188a   ⟨*scene eval* 188a⟩ ≡

```
Scene *scene_eval(void)
{
  Scene *s;
  Val v = lang_nd_eval();
  if (v.type != V_SCENE)
    error("(scene eval)");
  else
    s =  v.u.v;
  return s;
}
```

Defines:
  scene_eval, used in chunk 187b.
Uses Scene 187a.

The routine `scene_free` frees the memory allocated for the 3D scene at time t.

188b   ⟨*scene free* 188b⟩ ≡

```
void scene_free(Scene *s)
{
  if (s->objs)
    obj_list_free(s->objs);
  efree(s);
}
```

Defines:
  scene_free, used in chunk 187b.
Uses obj_list_free 182c, objs, and Scene 187a.

10.5   Comments and References

In this chapter we discussed hierarchies and their use in animation. We developed a library for hierarchies and another for procedural animation.

The API of the library of hierarchies consists of the following routines:

```
Stack4 *s4_initstack(int size);
void s4_push(Stack4 *s);
void s4_pop(Stack4 *s);

void s4_translate(Stack4 *s, Vector3 t);
void s4_scale(Stack4 *s, Vector3 v);
void s4_rotate(Stack4 *s, char axis, Real angle);

Vector3 s4_v3xform(Stack4 *s, Vector3 v);
```

```
Vector3 s4_n3xform(Stack4 *s, Vector3 nv);

Matrix4 s4_getmat(Stack4 *s);
Matrix4 s4_getimat(Stack4 *s);
void s4_loadmat(Stack4 *s, Matrix4 *md, Matrix4 *im);
void s4_concmat(Stack4 *s, Matrix4 *md, Matrix4 *im);
```

The routines implementing hierarchies in the scene description language are the following:

```
Val group_parse(int pass, Pval *pl);
Val translate_parse(int pass, Pval *p);
Val scale_parse(int pass, Pval *p);
Val rotate_parse(int pass, Pval *p);
```

The API of the animation library consists of the following routines:

```
void time_reset(Real t);
Boolean time_done(Real tlimit);
Real time_incr(Real tincr);
Real time_get();
Real time_end();

Val motor_parse(int pass, Pval *p);

void arg_init(int ac, char **av);
double arg_get_dval(char *s, Real defval);
Val arg_parse(int pass, Pval *p);
```

Exercises

1.   Write an interactive program to associate transformations to a primitive object.

2.   Write a program to interpret and to visualize a hierarchical object, composed of primitives and described in the SDL language. Use the command "arg" to pass parameters in the command line of the program.

3.   Modify the programs of Exercises 10.1 and 10.2 to work with CSG objects.

4.   Modify the programs of Exercises 10.1 and 10.2 to work with polygonal meshes.

5.   Write a program to show an analog clock in a window.

6.   Write a program to interactively create an articulated sequence.

7.   Write a program to scan an articulate sequence and animate it.

8.   Write the description, in the SDL language, of an articulated humanoid, and use the program from Exercise 10.7 to visualize it.

11 Viewing and Camera Transformations

Viewing a 3D scene requires converting the 3D data from world space to 2D information in the image. Camera transformations are one of the main components of this process. In earlier chapters we discussed the use of transformations for modeling 3D objects. In this chapter, we will study viewing transformations.

11.1 The Viewing Process

The viewing process consists of a sequence of operations that map 3D objects of the scene into their 2D projections on the image.

11.1.1 Viewing Operations and Reference Spaces

The viewing operations are the following:

- Camera mapping,

- Culling and clipping,

- Perspective transformation,

- Visibility calculation,

- Rasterization.

Each one of these operations has different characteristics. For this reason, they can be performed in a simpler and more efficient way if a proper coordinate system is selected. The viewing process (or *viewing pipeline*) corresponds to a sequence of transformations and operations through which the objects of a scene are successively mapped to reference spaces where each of the viewing operations is performed (see Figure 11.1). The reference

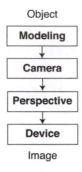

Figure 11.1. Sequence of viewing transformations.

spaces for the viewing operations are as follows:

- □ Object (or model) space,
- □ World (or scene) space,
- □ Camera space,
- □ Visibility space,
- □ Image space.

Object space. The object space uses the local coordinate system of the object. This space has the following characteristics: the origin corresponds to the center of mass of the object, and one of the main directions is aligned with the largest axis of the object. The dimensions are normalized. Modeling operations and geometric calculations with the object are performed in this space.

World space. The world space uses the global coordinate system of the application. It serves as a common frame for every object of the scene. Their dimensions are defined in application-dependent units. Illumination operations are performed in this space.

Camera space. The camera space uses the coordinate system of the observer, in which the viewing direction corresponds to the z-axis, and the plane of the image is parallel to the xy-plane. The viewing volume is mapped in the normalized pyramid. The clipping operation is performed in this space.

Visibility space. The visibility space uses a coordinate system resulting from the projective transformation, in which the center of projection is mapped onto an ideal point. In this way, the view volume becomes a parallelepiped. The calculation of the visible surfaces is performed in this space.

Image space. The image space uses the coordinate system of the graphics device. It has discrete coordinates. In this space, the rasterization is performed.

11.1.2 Virtual Camera and Viewing Parameters

The viewing specification is performed based on the model of a virtual camera. This model defines the necessary parameters to generate an image of the 3D scene. The viewing parameters include:

- □ Center of projection,

- □ Viewing direction,

- □ Vertical view up vector,

- □ View plane of the projection,

- □ Front and back planes,

- □ Center and dimensions of the image,

- □ Projection type.

The data structure `View` represents a view. It contains all the viewing parameters, as well as their corresponding transformations.

193   ⟨*view structure* 193⟩≡

```
typedef struct View {
    Vector3  center;        /* center of projection */
    Vector3  normal;        /* view plane normal vector */
    Vector3  up;            /* view up vector */

    Real     dist;          /* view plane distance from viewpoint*/
    Real     front;         /* front plane dist. from viewpoint */
    Real     back;          /* back plane dist. from viewpoint */

    UVpoint  c;             /* relative to view plane center */
    UVpoint  s;             /* window u,v half sizes */

    Box3d    sc;            /* current, in pix space */

    int      type;          /* projection type */

    Matrix4  V, Vinv;       /* view xform and inverse */
    Matrix4  C, Cinv;       /* clip space xform and inverse */
    Matrix4  P, Pinv;       /* perspective xforms and inverse */
    Matrix4  S, Sinv;       /* device xform and inverse */
} View;
```

Defines:
  View, used in chunks 194c, 195a, and 206–9.
Uses **perspective** 207b, **UVpoint** 194a, and **view**.

The projection type can be either perspective (conical) or orthographic (parallel).

```
#define PERSPECTIVE  1
#define ORTHOGRAPHIC 2
```

The structure UVpoint represents a vector on the image plane.

194a   ⟨*uv point* 194a⟩≡
```
typedef struct UVpoint {
  Real u,v;
} UVpoint;
```
Defines:
  UVpoint, used in chunk 193.

Some useful relations are given by the macros below:

194b   ⟨*view relations* 194b⟩≡
```
zmin = view.front / view.back
AspectRatio = view.s.u / view.s.v
fieldofView = 2 * arctan( view.s.u / view.dist ) n
PixelAspect = aspect * ((sc_upper.y - sc_lower.y +1) / (sc_upper.x -
                                                  sc_lower.x +1))
```
Uses view.

11.1.3   Specifying the Viewing Parameters

Access to the structure View will be done through a set of routines allowing us to specify the viewing parameters. These routines verify the consistency of the data, guaranteeing that the structure represents a valid view. The routines access a pointer to a view stored in the internal variable view.

```
static  View *view;
```

The routine setview initializes the variable view.

194c   ⟨*setview* 194c⟩≡
```
void setview(View *v)
{
  view = v;
}
```
Defines:
  setview, used in chunks 206–8.
Uses View 193 and view.

The routine `getview` returns the current view.

195a   ⟨*getview* 195a⟩≡

```
View *getview(void)
{
  return view;
}
```

Defines:
  getview, used in chunk 206a.
Uses View 193 and view.

The routine `setviewpoint` defines the viewing point.

195b   ⟨*setviewpoint* 195b⟩≡

```
void setviewpoint(Real x, Real y, Real z)
{
  view->center.x = x;
  view->center.y = y;
  view->center.z = z;
}
```

Defines:
  setviewpoint, used in chunks 197c, 206b, 207a, and 209.
Uses view.

The routine `setviewnormal` defines the viewing direction. Notice it normalizes this vector.

195c   ⟨*setviewnormal* 195c⟩≡

```
void setviewnormal(Real x, Real y, Real z)
{
  double d = sqrt(SQR(x)+SQR(y)+SQR(z));

  if (d < ROUNDOFF)
    error("invalid view plane normal");
  view->normal.x = x / d;
  view->normal.y = y / d;
  view->normal.z = z / d;
}
```

Defines:
  setviewnormal, used in chunks 197c, 206b, 207a, and 209.
Uses ROUNDOFF and view.

The routine `setviewup` defines the view up vector.

195d   ⟨*setviewup* 195d⟩≡

```
void setviewup(Real x, Real y, Real z)
{
  if (fabs(x) + fabs(y) + fabs(z) < ROUNDOFF)
    error("no view up direction");
  view->up.x = x;
  view->up.y = y;
```

```
    view->up.z = z;
  }
```

Defines:
  setviewup, used in chunks 197c, 206b, and 207a.
Uses ROUNDOFF and view.

The routine setviewdistance defines the projection plane, given by the distance starting from the center of projection along the viewing direction.

196a   ⟨*setviewdistance* 196a⟩≡
```
  void setviewdistance(Real d)
  {
    if (fabs(d) < ROUNDOFF)
      error("invalid view distance");
    view->dist = d;
  }
```

Defines:
  setviewdistance, used in chunks 197c, 207, and 208a.
Uses ROUNDOFF and view.

The routine setviewdepth defines the near and far planes of the clipping volume.

196b   ⟨*setviewdepth* 196b⟩≡
```
  void setviewdepth(Real front, Real back)
  {
    if (fabs(back - front) < ROUNDOFF|| fabs(back) < ROUNDOFF)
      error("invalid viewdepth");
    view->front = front;
    view->back = back;
  }
```

Defines:
  setviewdepth, used in chunks 197c, 207, and 208a.
Uses ROUNDOFF and view.

The routine setwindow defines the viewing window in the projection plane, given by its center and dimensions.

196c   ⟨*setwindow* 196c⟩≡
```
  void setwindow(Real cu, Real cv, Real su, Real sv)
  {
    if (fabs(su) < ROUNDOFF|| fabs(sv) < ROUNDOFF)
      error("invalid window size");
    view->c.u = cu; view->c.v = cv;
    view->s.u = su; view->s.v = sv;
  }
```

Defines:
  setwindow, used in chunks 197c, 207, and 208a.
Uses ROUNDOFF and view.

The routine `setprojection` defines the projection type.

197a   ⟨*setprojection* 197a⟩≡
```
void setprojection(int type)
{
  if (type != PERSPECTIVE && type != ORTHOGRAPHIC)
    error("invalid projection type");
  view->type = type;
}
```
Defines:
  `setprojection`, used in chunks 197c, 207, and 208a.
Uses `ORTHOGRAPHIC`, `PERSPECTIVE`, and `view`.

The routine `setviewport` defines the support region of the image in the device.

197b   ⟨*setviewport* 197b⟩≡
```
void setviewport(Real l, Real b, Real r, Real t, Real n, Real f)
{
  if(fabs(r-l) < ROUNDOFF|| fabs(t-b) < ROUNDOFF)
    error("invalid viewport");
  view->sc_min.x = l;   view->sc_max.x = r;
  view->sc_min.y = b;   view->sc_max.y = t;
  view->sc_min.z = n;   view->sc_max.z = f;
}
```
Defines:
  `setviewport`, used in chunks 197c and 208b.
Uses `ROUNDOFF`, `view`, and `viewport` 208b.

The routine `setviewdefaults` defines the default viewing parameters.

197c   ⟨*setviewdefaults* 197c⟩≡
```
void setviewdefaults(void)
{
  setviewpoint(0.0,-5.0,0.0);
  setviewnormal(0.0,1.0,0.0);
  setviewup(0.0,0.0,1.0);
  setviewdistance(1.0);
  setviewdepth(1.0,100000.0);
  setwindow(0.0,0.0,0.41421356,0.31066017);
  setprojection(PERSPECTIVE);
  setviewport(0.,0.,320.,240.,-32768.,32767.);
}
```
Defines:
  `setviewdefaults`, used in chunk 206a.
Uses `PERSPECTIVE`, `setprojection` 197a, `setviewdepth` 196b, `setviewdistance` 196a,
  `setviewnormal` 195c, `setviewpoint` 195b, `setviewport` 197b, `setviewup` 195d,
  and `setwindow` 196c.

11.2   Viewing Transformations

In this section we will describe the viewing transformations. We will show how to calculate the corresponding matrices starting from the definition of the reference spaces.

11.2.1   Camera Transformation

The camera transformation maps the coordinate system of the 3D scene into the coordinate system of the camera. First, a translation takes the center of projection to the origin:

$$A = \begin{pmatrix} I & -V \\ 0 & 1 \end{pmatrix}.$$

Then a rotation aligns the reference system of the camera $\{u, v, n\}$ with the canonical basis of the space $\{e_1, e_2, e_3\}$, formed by the vectors $e_1 = (1, 0, 0)$, $e_2 = (0, 1, 0)$, and $e_3 = (0, 0, 1)$.

To calculate the vectors of the reference system, we use the viewing direction n and the view up vector U. We project the vector U on the camera plane, which is orthogonal to n,

$$v = \frac{U - (U \cdot n)n}{|U - (U \cdot n)n|},$$

and we normalize it. Next, we obtain a unit vector u, perpendicular to n and v, using the cross product $u = n \times v$. Notice the camera system's orientation is opposite the orientation of the scene system $\{e_1, e_2, e_3\}$. This is reflected in the order we used to compute the cross product.

The orthonormal matrix below is a rotation matrix that maps the frame $\{e_1, e_2, e_3\}$ into the frame $\{u, v, n\}$:

$$B = \begin{pmatrix} u^T & 0 \\ v^T & 0 \\ n^T & 0 \\ 0 & 1 \end{pmatrix}.$$

The camera transformation is given by the matrix $V = BA$, resulting from the concatenation of the matrices above:

$$V = \begin{pmatrix} u_x & u_x & u_x & -u.V_p \\ v_y & v_y & v_y & -v.V_p \\ n_z & n_z & n_z & -n.V_p \\ 0 & 0 & 0 & 1 \end{pmatrix}.$$

The routine `makeviewV` calculates the matrix V using the viewing parameters.

198   ⟨*make view v* 198⟩≡
```
void makeviewV(void)
{
```

```
    Vector3 n,u,v,t;

    n = view->normal;
    v = v3_sub(view->up, v3_scale(v3_dot(view->up, n), n));
    if (v3_norm(v) < ROUNDOFF)
      error("view up parallel to view normal");
    v = v3_unit(v);
    u = v3_cross(n, v);
    t.x = v3_dot(view->center, u);
    t.y = v3_dot(view->center, v);
    t.z = v3_dot(view->center, n);
    view->V = m4_ident();
    view->V.r1.x =  u.x; view->V.r2.x =  v.x; view->V.r3.x =  n.x;
    view->V.r1.y =  u.y; view->V.r2.y =  v.y; view->V.r3.y =  n.y;
    view->V.r1.z =  u.z; view->V.r2.z =  v.z; view->V.r3.z =  n.z;
    view->V.r1.w = -t.x; view->V.r2.w = -t.y; view->V.r3.w = -t.z;
    makeviewVi();
  }
```

Defines:
  makeviewV, used in chunks 206, 207a, and 209.
Uses makeviewVi 199, ROUNDOFF, and view.

The routine makeviewVi calculates the inverse of the camera transformation.

199 ⟨*make view vi* 199⟩≡
```
    void makeviewVi(void)
    {
      Vector3 n,u,v,t;
      view->Vinv = m4_ident();
      n = view->normal;
      v = v3_sub(view->up, v3_scale(v3_dot(view->up, n), n));
      if (v3_norm(v) < ROUNDOFF)
        error("view up parallel to view normal");
      v = v3_unit(v);
      u = v3_cross(n, v);
      t = view->center;
      view->Vinv = m4_ident();
      view->Vinv.r1.x = u.x; view->Vinv.r2.x = u.y; view->Vinv.r3.x = u.z;
      view->Vinv.r1.y = v.x; view->Vinv.r2.y = v.y; view->Vinv.r3.y = v.z;
      view->Vinv.r1.z = n.x; view->Vinv.r2.z = n.y; view->Vinv.r3.z = n.z;
      view->Vinv.r1.w = t.x; view->Vinv.r2.w = t.y; view->Vinv.r3.w = t.z;
    }
```

Defines:
  makeviewVi, used in chunk 198.
Uses ROUNDOFF and view.

11.2.2   Clipping Transformation

The clipping transformation maps the coordinate system of the camera into a normalized system, where the viewing volume is a rectangular pyramid with the apex at the origin and basis on the plane $z = 1$.

First we do a shearing to align the center of the image with axis z. Notice this is necessary because the image window cannot be centralized:

$$D = \begin{pmatrix} 1 & 0 & -c_u/d & 0 \\ 0 & 1 & -c_v/d & 0 \\ 0 & 0 & 1 & 0 \\ 0 & 0 & 0 & 1 \end{pmatrix}.$$

Then we perform a scaling such that the basis of the viewing pyramid is mapped into the unit square on the plane $z = 1$:

$$R = \begin{pmatrix} d/(s_u f) & 0 & 0 & 0 \\ 0 & d/(s_v f) & 0 & 0 \\ 0 & 0 & 1/f & 0 \\ 0 & 0 & 0 & 1 \end{pmatrix}.$$

The clipping transformation is given by the matrix $C = RD$, resulting from the concatenation of the matrices above:

$$C = \begin{pmatrix} d/(s_u f) & 0 & -c_u/(s_u f) & 0 \\ 0 & d/(s_v f) & -c_v/(s_v f) & 0 \\ 0 & 0 & 1/f & 0 \\ 0 & 0 & 0 & 1 \end{pmatrix}.$$

The routine `makeviewC` computes the matrix C.

200        $\langle make\ view\ c\ 200 \rangle \equiv$
```
void makeviewC(void)
{
  view->C = m4_ident();
  view->C.r1.x = view->dist / (view->s.u * view->back);
  view->C.r2.y = view->dist / (view->s.v * view->back);
  view->C.r3.z = 1 / view->back;
  view->C.r1.z = - view->c.u / (view->s.u * view->back);
  view->C.r2.z = - view->c.v / (view->s.v * view->back);
  makeviewCi();
}
```
Defines:
  `makeviewC`, used in chunks 206–8.
Uses `makeviewCi` 201 and `view`.

The routine `makeviewCi` computes the inverse of the matrix C.

201 ⟨*make view ci* 201⟩≡
```
void makeviewCi(void)
{
  view->Cinv = m4_ident();
  view->Cinv.r1.x = (view->s.u * view->back) / view->dist;
  view->Cinv.r2.y = (view->s.v * view->back) / view->dist;
  view->Cinv.r3.z = view->back;
  view->Cinv.r1.z = (view->c.u * view->back) / view->dist;
  view->Cinv.r2.z = (view->c.v * view->back) / view->dist;
}
```
Defines:
   `makeviewCi`, used in chunk 200.
Uses `view`.

11.2.3 Perspective Transformation

The perspective transformation maps the normalized viewing pyramid given by the planes

$$x = \pm z, \quad y = \pm z, \quad z = z_{\min}, \quad z = 1$$

in the parallelepiped

$$-1 \le x \le 1, \quad -1 \le y \le 1, \quad 0 \le z \le 1,$$

where $z_{\min} = n/f$. This change of coordinates consists of a projective transformation, which takes the center of projection at the ideal point corresponding to the straight projection line. First, a translation is performed, taking $z_{\min}$ to the origin of the projective space $\mathbb{RP}^3$:

$$E = \begin{pmatrix} 1 & 0 & 0 & 0 \\ 0 & 1 & 0 & 0 \\ 0 & 0 & 1 & -z_{\min} \\ 0 & 0 & 0 & 1 \end{pmatrix}.$$

Then a scaling is performed to map the interval along the direction z $[z_{\min}, 1]$ in $[0, 1]$:

$$F = \begin{pmatrix} 1 & 0 & 0 & 0 \\ 0 & 1 & 0 & 0 \\ 0 & 0 & 1/(1 - z_{\min}) & 0 \\ 0 & 0 & 0 & 1 \end{pmatrix}.$$

Finally, the projective transformation is applied:

$$G = \begin{pmatrix} 1 & 0 & 0 & 0 \\ 0 & 1 & 0 & 0 \\ 0 & 0 & 1 & 0 \\ 0 & 0 & (1 - z_{min})/z_{min} & 1 \end{pmatrix}.$$

The perspective transformation is given by the matrix $P = GFE$:

$$P = \begin{pmatrix} 1 & 0 & 0 & 0 \\ 0 & 1 & 0 & 0 \\ 0 & 0 & 1/(1 - z_{\min}) & -z_{\min}/(1 - z_{\min}) \\ 0 & 0 & 1 & 0 \end{pmatrix}.$$

Remember that after applying the projective transformation, it is necessary to perform the homogeneous division by w.

The routine `makeviewP` computes the matrix P.

202a   ⟨*make view p* 202a⟩≡
```
void makeviewP(void)
{
    view->P = m4_ident();
    view->P.r3.z = view->back / (view->back - view->front);
    view->P.r3.w = -view->front / (view->back - view->front);
    view->P.r4.z = 1;
    view->P.r4.w = 0;
    makeviewPi();
}
```
Defines:
  `makeviewP`, used in chunks 206 and 207.
Uses `makeviewPi` 202b and `view`.

The routine `makeviewPi` computes the inverse of the matrix P.

202b   ⟨*make view pi* 202b⟩≡
```
void makeviewPi(void)
{
    view->Pinv = m4_ident();
    view->Pinv.r3.z = 0;
    view->Pinv.r4.z = - (view->back - view->front) / view->front;
    view->Pinv.r4.w = view->back / view->front;
    view->Pinv.r3.w = 1;
    view->Pinv.r4.w = 0;
}
```
Defines:
  `makeviewPi`, used in chunk 202a.
Uses `view`.

Calculation of the transformation corresponding to the orthogonal projection is analogous to the perspective projection, except that it does not involve a projective transformation. We will not show the details of this calculation. The matrix O of the orthogonal projection is

$$O = \begin{pmatrix} 1/s_u & 0 & 0 & -c_u/s_u \\ 0 & 1/s_v & 0 & -c_v/s_v \\ 0 & 0 & 1/(f - n) & -n/(f - n) \\ 0 & 0 & 1 & 0 \end{pmatrix}.$$

The routine `makeview0` computes the matrix O.

203a   ⟨*make view o* 203a⟩≡

```
void makeview0(void)
{
  view->C = m4_ident();
  view->C.r1.x = 1 / view->s.u;
  view->C.r2.y = 1 / view->s.v;
  view->C.r3.z = 1 / (view->back - view->front);
  view->C.r1.w = - view->c.u / view->s.u;
  view->C.r2.w = - view->c.v / view->s.v;
  view->C.r3.w = - view->front / (view->back - view->front);
  view->P = m4_ident();
  makeview0i();
}
```

Defines:
  `makeview0`, used in chunk 208a.
Uses `makeview0i` 203b and `view`.

The routine `makeview0i` computes the inverse of the matrix O.

203b   ⟨*make view oi* 203b⟩≡

```
void makeview0i(void)
{
  view->Cinv = m4_ident();
  view->Cinv.r1.x = view->s.u;
  view->Cinv.r2.y = view->s.v;
  view->Cinv.r3.z = (view->back - view->front);
  view->Cinv.r1.w = view->c.u;
  view->Cinv.r2.w = view->c.v;
  view->Cinv.r3.w = view->front;
  view->Pinv = m4_ident();
}
```

Defines:
  `makeview0i`, used in chunk 203a.
Uses `view`.

11.2.4   Device Transformation

The device transformation maps the normalized visibility volume onto the support volume of the image on the graphics hardware. Notice that we are including the depth information, given it is supported by many devices (i.e., Z-buffer).

First, a translation is performed so the vertex $(-1, -1, 0)$ can be mapped at the origin. A scaling of $1/2$ is applied at x and y. This produces the normalized device coordinates

(*NDC*) volume:

$$K = \begin{pmatrix} 0.5 & 0 & 0 & 0.5 \\ 0 & 0.5 & 0 & 0.5 \\ 0 & 0 & 1 & 0 \\ 0 & 0 & 0 & 1 \end{pmatrix}.$$

Then the *NDC* volume is mapped to the scale of the device:

$$L = \begin{pmatrix} \Delta_X & 0 & 0 & X_{\min} \\ 0 & \Delta_Y & 0 & Y_{\min} \\ 0 & 0 & \Delta_Z & Z_{\min} \\ 0 & 0 & 0 & 1 \end{pmatrix},$$

where $\Delta_i = (i_{max} - i_{min})$ are the dimensions of the 3D frame of the image.

Finally, a rounding to the closest integer coordinate is performed, using the matrix below and the function floor:

$$M = \begin{pmatrix} 1 & 0 & 0 & 0.5 \\ 0 & 1 & 0 & 0.5 \\ 0 & 0 & 1 & 0.5 \\ 0 & 0 & 0 & 1 \end{pmatrix} \quad \text{floor}(x, y, z).$$

The device transformation is given by the matrix $S = KLM$:

$$S = \begin{pmatrix} \Delta_x/2 & 0 & 0 & (\nabla_x + 1)/2 \\ 0 & \Delta_y/2 & 0 & (\nabla_y + 1)/2 \\ 0 & 0 & \Delta_z & Z_{min} + 0.5 \\ 0 & 0 & 0 & 1 \end{pmatrix},$$

where $\Delta_i = (i_{max} - i_{min})$ and $\nabla_i = (i_{max} + i_{min})$.

The routine makeviewS calculates the matrix S.

204   ⟨*make view s* 204⟩≡

```
void makeviewS(void)
{
  view->S = m4_ident();
  view->S.r1.x = (view->sc.ur.x - view->sc.ll.x) / 2;
  view->S.r2.y = (view->sc.ur.y - view->sc.ll.y) / 2;
  view->S.r3.z =  view->sc.ur.z - view->sc.ll.z;
  view->S.r1.w = (view->sc.ur.x + view->sc.ll.x +1) / 2;
  view->S.r2.w = (view->sc.ur.y + view->sc.ll.y +1) / 2;
  view->S.r3.w =  view->sc.ll.z + 0.5;
  makeviewSi();
}
```

Defines:
  makeviewS, used in chunks 206a and 208b.
Uses makeviewSi 205 and view.

The routine `makeviewSi` calculates the inverse of the matrix S.

205   ⟨*make view si 205*⟩≡

```
void makeviewSi(void)
{
  view->Sinv = m4_ident();
  view->Sinv.r1.x = 2 / (view->sc.ur.x - view->sc.ll.x);
  view->Sinv.r2.y = 2 / (view->sc.ur.y - view->sc.ll.y);
  view->Sinv.r3.z = 1 / (view->sc.ur.z - view->sc.ll.z);
  view->Sinv.r1.w = - (view->sc.ur.x + view->sc.ll.x +1) /
                    (view->sc.ur.x - view->sc.ll.x);
  view->Sinv.r2.w = - (view->sc.ur.y + view->sc.ll.y +1) /
                    (view->sc.ur.y - view->sc.ll.y);
  view->Sinv.r3.w = - (view->sc.ll.z + 0.5) /
                    (view->sc.ur.z - view->sc.ll.z);
}
```

Defines:
  `makeviewSi`, used in chunk 204.
Uses `view`.

11.2.5 Transformation Sequence

The viewing transformations presented in this section are applied in sequence to the objects of the 3D scene. This application depends on the geometric description of the objects.

If objects are described in the parametric form, the direct transformations are used in the order below.

$$3\text{D Scene} \to \boxed{V} \to \boxed{C} \to \boxed{P} \to \boxed{S} \to \text{Image}$$

If objects are described in the implicit form, the inverse transformations are used in the order below.

$$\text{Image} \to \boxed{S^{-1}} \to \boxed{P^{-1}} \to \boxed{C^{-1}} \to \boxed{V^{-1}} \to 3\text{D Scene}$$

These two sequences of transformations configure two different strategies for organizing the operations in a viewing system. The first, defined by transformations in the direct order, corresponds to the *scene-centered* methods (see Figure 11.2). The second, defined by transformations in the inverse order, corresponds to the *image-centered* methods (see Figure 11.3).

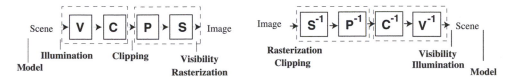

Figure 11.2. Object-centered viewing.   Figure 11.3. Image-centered viewing.

11.3　Viewing Specification

The viewing specification is performed by higher-level routines that define groups of parameters related to each of the viewing transformations.

11.3.1　Initialization

The routine initview initializes the viewing parameters and calculates the transformation matrices.

206a

⟨*initview* 206a⟩≡

```
View* initview(void)
{
  setview(NEWSTRUCT(View));
  setviewdefaults();
  makeviewV();
  makeviewC();
  makeviewP();
  makeviewS();
  return getview();
}
```

Defines:
  initview, used in chunk 209.
Uses getview 195a, makeviewC 200, makeviewP 202a, makeviewS 204, makeviewV 198,
  setview 194c, setviewdefaults 197c, and View 193.

11.3.2　Camera

The routines lookat and camera define the parameters of the camera transformation.

206b

⟨*lookat* 206b⟩≡

```
void lookat(View *v, Real vx, Real vy, Real vz,
            Real px, Real py, Real pz, Real ux, Real uy, Real uz)
{
  setview(v);
  setviewpoint(vx, vy, vz);
  setviewnormal(px - vx ,py - vy, pz - vz);
  setviewup(ux, uy, uz);
  makeviewV();
}
```

Defines:
  lookat, used in chunk 209.
Uses makeviewV 198, setview 194c, setviewnormal 195c, setviewpoint 195b,
  setviewup 195d, and View 193.

207a ⟨*camera* 207a⟩≡
```
void camera(View *v, Real rx, Real ry, Real rz, Real nx, Real ny, Real nz
    , Real ux, Real uy, Real uz, Real deye)
{
  setview(v);
  setviewup(ux,uy,uz);
  setviewnormal(nx,ny,nz);
  setviewpoint(rx - (v->normal.x*deye),
               ry - (v->normal.y*deye),
               rz - (v->normal.z*deye));
  makeviewV();
}
```
Defines:
  camera, never used.
Uses makeviewV 198, setview 194c, setviewnormal 195c, setviewpoint 195b,
  setviewup 195d, and View 193.

11.3.3 Perspective

The routines perspective and frustum define the parameters related to the clipping
and perspective projection transformations.

207b ⟨*perspective* 207b⟩≡
```
void perspective(View *v, Real fov, Real ar, Real near, Real far)
{
  setview(v);
  setprojection(PERSPECTIVE);
  setviewdistance(near);
  setviewdepth(near,far);
  if (ar < ROUNDOFF)
    error("illegal aspect ratio");
  setwindow(0, 0, tan(fov/2) * near, (tan(fov/2) * near)/ar);
  makeviewC();
  makeviewP();
}
```
Defines:
  perspective, used in chunks 193 and 209.
Uses makeviewC 200, makeviewP 202a, PERSPECTIVE, ROUNDOFF, setprojection 197a,
  setview 194c, setviewdepth 196b, setviewdistance 196a, setwindow 196c,
  and View 193.

207c ⟨*frusntrum* 207c⟩≡
```
void frustum(View *v, Real l, Real b, Real r, Real t, Real near, Real far)
{
  setview(v);
  setprojection(PERSPECTIVE);
  setviewdistance(near);
```

```
      setviewdepth(near,far);
      setwindow((l+r)/2, (b+t)/2, (r-l)/2, (t-b)/2);
      makeviewC();
      makeviewP();
    }
```

Defines:
   frustum, never used.
Uses makeviewC 200, makeviewP 202a, PERSPECTIVE, setprojection 197a, setview 194c,
   setviewdepth 196b, setviewdistance 196a, setwindow 196c, and View 193.

   The routine orthographic defines the parameters related to the clipping and orthographic projection transformations.

208a   ⟨orthographic 208a⟩ ≡
```
      void orthographic(View *v, Real l, Real b, Real r, Real t, Real near,
                        Real far)
      {
        setview(v);
        setprojection(ORTHOGRAPHIC);
        setviewdistance(near);
        setviewdepth(near,far);
        setwindow((l+r)/2, (b+t)/2, (r-l)/2, (t-b)/2);
        makeviewC();
        makeviewO();
      }
```

Defines:
   orthographic, never used.
Uses makeviewC 200, makeviewO 203a, ORTHOGRAPHIC, setprojection 197a, setview 194c,
   setviewdepth 196b, setviewdistance 196a, setwindow 196c, and View 193.

11.3.4   Device

The routine viewport defines the parameters related to the device transformation.

208b   ⟨viewport 208b⟩ ≡
```
      void viewport(View *v, Real l, Real b, Real w, Real h)
      {
        setview(v);
        setviewport(l,b,l+w,b+h,-32767.,32767.);
        makeviewS();
      }
```

Defines:
   viewport, used in chunks 197b and 209.
Uses makeviewS 204, setview 194c, setviewport 197b, and View 193.

11.3.5   Specifying a View in the 3D Scene Description Language

The routine `view_parse` implements the command for specifying a view in the 3D scene description language.

209   ⟨*parse view* 209⟩≡

```
Val view_parse(int pass, Pval *pl)
{
  Val v;
  if (pass == T_EXEC) {
    View *view = initview();
    Vector3 ref = pvl_get_v3(pl, "from", v3_make(0,-5,0));
    Vector3 at = pvl_get_v3(pl, "at", v3_make(0,0,0));
    Vector3 up = pvl_get_v3(pl, p", v3_make(0,0,1));
    double fov = pvl_get_num(pl, "fov", 90);
    double w = pvl_get_num(pl, "imgw", 320);
    double h = pvl_get_num(pl, "imgh", 240);
    lookat(view, ref.x, ref.y, ref.z, at.x, at.y, at.z, up.x, up.y, up.z);
    setviewpoint(ref.x, ref.y, ref.z);
    setviewnormal(at.x - ref.x ,at.y - ref.y, at.z - ref.z);
    makeviewV();
    perspective(view, fov * DTOR, w/h, 1.0, 100000.0);
    viewport(view, 0.,0., w, h);
    v.type = CAMERA;
    v.u.v = view;
  }
  return v;
}
```

Defines:
  view_parse, never used.
Uses initview 206a, lookat 206b, makeviewV 198, perspective 207b, setviewnormal 195c,
  setviewpoint 195b, View 193, view, and viewport 208b.

11.4   Comments and References

In this chapter we presented the viewing transformation and its specification through a virtual camera.

The API of the library VIEW includes the following routines:

```
View* initview(void);
void lookat(View *v,Real vx, Real vy, Real vz, Real px, Real py, Real pz,
            Real ux, Real uy, Real uz);
void camera(View *v, Real rx, Real ry, Real rz,
            Real nx, Real ny, Real nz, Real ux, Real uy, Real uz, Real deye);
void perspective(View *v, Real fov, Real ar, Real near, Real far);
void orthographic(View *v, Real l, Real b, Real r, Real t, Real near,
                  Real far);
```

```
void frustum(View *v, Real l, Real b, Real r, Real t, Real near, Real far);
void viewport(View *v, Real l, Real b, Real w, Real h);

void setview(View *v);
View *getview(void);
void setviewpoint(Real x, Real y, Real z);
void setviewnormal(Real x, Real y, Real z);
void setviewup(Real x, Real y, Real z);
void setviewdistance(Real d);
void setviewdepth(Real front, Real back);
void setwindow(Real cu, Real cv, Real su, Real sv);
void setprojection(int type);
void setviewport(Real l, Real b, Real r, Real t, Real n, Real f);
void setviewdefaults(void);

void makeviewV(void);
void makeviewC(void);
void makeviewO(void);
void makeviewP(void);
void makeviewS(void);
void makeviewVi(void);
void makeviewCi(void);
void makeviewOi(void);
void makeviewPi(void);
void makeviewSi(void);
```

Exercise

1. Write a program using the VIEW library to draw a wireframe image of a 3D scene. Input to the program should be in the scene description language, specifying the virtual camera and one or more objects.

12 | Surface Clipping for Viewing

The clipping operation is one of the basic geometric tools in computer graphics. It plays an important role in solving geometric modeling and viewing problems. In this chapter we will study the surface clipping operation in the viewing process.

12.1 Foundations of the Clipping Operation

We call the operation that determines the set of points of a graphic object contained in a region of the environment space *clipping*.

12.1.1 Space Splitting

Given a closed and connected surface $M \subset \mathbb{R}^n$ of dimension $n - 1$, M divides the space into two regions A and B, in which M is the common boundary. The *clipping operation* of a subset S of $\mathbb{R}^n$ consists of determining the subsets $S \cap A$ and $S \cap B$. The surface M is called the *clipping surface*.

Notice that separability is a fundamental property of surface M for the clipping operation, which determines a partition of the environment space in two regions.

In general, the clipping operation involves the solution of three different problems:

□ **Intersection.** Determining the points of S that are at the boundary given by M.

□ **Classification.** Classifying points of S contained in regions A and B.

□ **Structuring.** Building a representation of the sets $S \cap A$ and $S \cap B$ using the results of the above stages.

The clipping calculation depends on the dimension of the subset S, as well as of its geometric representation. In $\mathbb{R}^3$, S can be a point, a curve, a surface, or a solid. The representation of S can be given by a primitive, by a constructive schema, or by decomposition.

Another factor that influences the complexity of the clipping operation is the geometry of the clipping surface M. More specifically, if M is convex, the problem is considerably simplified.

12.1.2   Clipping and Viewing

In the viewing process, the clipping operation has the purpose of determining which objects are inside the virtual camera's field of view. Those objects will be processed and others will be discarded. Clipping in the viewing process is necessary for two reasons. First, clipping prevents points in the opposite viewing direction being improperly projected on the image plane. Second, clipping increases efficiency by keeping objects that will not appear in the image from being processed.

As we saw in the previous chapter, the clipping viewing volume is called the viewing frustum, which corresponds to a truncated pyramid. The normalized clipping volume is carefully chosen in a way to make the solution of the problem simpler. In this way, the viewing frustum is given by the intersection of the semispaces

$$-x \leq z \leq x, \quad -y \leq z \leq z, \quad z_{\min} \leq z \leq 1. \tag{12.1}$$

This choice greatly simplifies the calculation of intersections. What is more, since the viewing frustum is convex, the classification operation is reduced to determining the position of points in relation to the six semispaces in Equation (12.1).

Another important observation is that the clipping problem can be trivially solved when the subset S is totally contained in region A or B. This case can be solely determined through point classification, and it does not require the intersection calculation or structuring.

The computational strategies described above are used together in the clipping algorithms. First, the problem is reduced to a canonical situation with the use of a proper coordinate system. Second, trivial cases with immediate solution are checked. Finally, the more complex cases are resolved.

12.2   Clipping Trivial Cases

The trivial cases in clipping happen when the subset S is entirely contained in one of the delimited regions by the clipping surface M. There are two cases: S is outside the viewing volume and should be eliminated from processing and S is inside of the viewing volume and can be projected on the virtual screen.

12.2.1   Trivial Reject

To detect whether a polygon is completely contained in the region external to the clipping volume, a classification of the polygon vertices is performed in relation to the semispaces determined by the support planes of the viewing frustum faces. These planes divide the space into 27 regions. A 6-bit code is attributed to each vertex, indicating the region in which it is located. The code indicates the relation between the region and each one of the semispaces (1 means the region is not in the same semispace of the clipping pyramid).

The routine `clipcode` calculates the vertex code.

213a   ⟨*clipcode* 213a⟩≡
```
int clipcode(Real h, Vector3 v)
{
  int c = 0;
  if (v.y >   v.z) c|=  01;
  if (v.y < -v.z) c|=  02;
  if (v.x >   v.z) c|=  04;
  if (v.x < -v.z) c|= 010;
  if (v.z >   1 ) c|= 020;
  if (v.z <   h ) c|= 040;
  return(c);
}
```
Defines:
  clipcode, used in chunk 213.

The routine `cull_poly3` determines if a triangle is in the region external to the clipping region. It applies the classification to each of the vertices. If all are contained in a semispace external to the viewing frustum, the triangle can then be rejected.

213b   ⟨*cull poly3* 213b⟩≡
```
int cull_poly3(Real h, Poly *p)
{
  int i, c[3];
  for (i = 0; i < p->n; i++)
    c[i] = clipcode(h, p->v[i]);
  return (c[0] & c[1] & c[2]);
}
```
Defines:
  cull_poly3, used in chunk 215.
Uses clipcode 213a.

12.2.2 Trivial Accept

The routine `inside_frustum` determines if a point is inside the viewing frustum. It can be used to perform the trivial accept test of convex objects, such as triangles or the bounding box of complex objects.

213c   ⟨*inside frustum* 213c⟩≡
```
int inside_frustum(Real h, Vector3 v)
{
  return  (clipcode(h, v) == 0);
}
```
Defines:
  inside_frustum, never used.
Uses clipcode 213a.

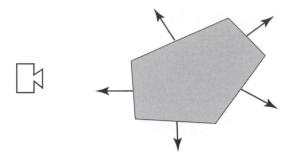

Figure 12.1. Camera and object with normals.

12.2.3   Faces with Opposite Orientation

In a solid object, the boundary faces with an orientation opposite to the the viewing direction are not visible and can be removed.

In surfaces with a boundary, the faces with opposite orientation can be visible, but this fact is generally taken into account in the illumination calculation.

The routine `is_backfacing` determines whether the orientation of a polygon is opposite the viewing direction. The calculation is performed from the inner product between the normal to the polygon and the viewing direction. (See Figure 12.1.)

214   ⟨*is backfacing* 214⟩≡

```
int is_backfacing(Poly *p, Vector3 v)
{
  Vector3 n = poly_normal(p);
  return (v3_dot(n, v) < 0)? TRUE : FALSE;
}
```

Defines:
  `is_backfacing`, never used.

12.3   Two-Step Clipping

A simple method of implementing polygon clipping consists of decomposing the operation into two steps: in the first step a 3D clipping is performed, and in the second step a 2D clipping takes place. The problem is organized in the following way:

□ **3D part.** Clip the polygons in relation to the front face of the viewing pyramid. This operation has to be performed in the 3D space before the projective transformation, in order to avoid projecting vertices located behind the camera onto the image plane.

□ **2D part.** Clip the polygons already projected in relation to the rectangle of the image. This operation can be performed analytically before the rasterization, or in an approximate way during the rasterization.

Therefore, the far plane clipping algorithm consists of the following steps:

1. Analysis of trivial cases,

2. 3D clipping by the front plane,

3. 2D clipping by the image rectangle.

The routine `hither_clip` implements steps (1) and (2), and step (3) is performed by the routine `render`.

215   ⟨*hither clip* 215⟩≡
```
    int hither_clip(Real h, Poly *p, void (*render)(), void (*plfree)())
    {
      if (cull_poly3(h, p)) {
        plfree(p); return FALSE;
      } else {
        return hclip(h, p, render, plfree);
      }
    }
```
Defines:
  hither_clip, never used.
Uses cull_poly3 213b and hclip 216a.

Step (1) (analysis of the trivial cases) is optional. This pre-processing has the purpose of increasing the efficiency of the algorithm and is implemented by the routine `cull_poly3`. In this way, polygons totally contained in the exterior of the clipping volume are eliminated.

12.3.1   3D Clipping by Subdivision

The method we describe next has several important characteristics. The routine `hclip` implements a recursive algorithm that performs an analytical clipping by a binary subdivision of triangles. The algorithm performs the clipping of a list of triangles, where the first triangle of the list contains geometric and attribute information.

The general structure of the algorithm is as follows: First, the triangle vertices are classified in relation to the front plane. This is determined by the number of vertices, n on the positive side of the front plane. Three cases exist:

☐ $n = 0$. the entire triangle is on the negative side of the plane and can be trivially rejected,

☐ $n = 3$. the entire triangle is on the positive side of the plane and it can be visualized (trivially accepted),

☐ $n = 1$ or $n = 2$. the triangle intersects the plane and clipping must be performed.

The routine `classify_vert` calculates n.

216a   ⟨*hclip* 216a⟩≡

```
int hclip(Real h, Poly *p, void (*render)(), void (*plfree)())
{
  Poly *pa, *pb, *a, *b;
  int n, i0, i1, i2;
  double t;

  switch (classify_vert(p, h)) {
  case 0: plfree(p); return FALSE;
  case 3: render(p); return TRUE;
  case 2:   case 1:
    if (EDGE_CROSS_Z(p, 0, 1, h)) {
      i0 = 0; i1 = 1; i2 = 2;
    } else if (EDGE_CROSS_Z(p, 1, 2, h)) {
      i0 = 1; i1 = 2; i2 = 0;
    } else if (EDGE_CROSS_Z(p, 2, 0, h)) {
      i0 = 2; i1 = 0; i2 = 1;
    }
  }
  t = (p->v[i1].z - h) / (p->v[i1].z - p->v[i0].z);

  a = pa = plist_alloc(n = plist_lenght(p), 3);
  b = pb = plist_alloc(n, 3);
  while (p != NULL) {
    poly_split(p, i0, i1, i2, t, pa, pb);
    p = p->next; pa = pa->next; pb = pb->next;
  }
  return hclip(h, a, render, plfree)| hclip(h, b, render, plfree);
}
```

Defines:
  hclip, used in chunk 215.
Uses classify_vert 218, EDGE_CROSS_Z 216b, and poly_split 217.

In the last case, the triangle is subdivided in two, and each of the resulting triangles is recursively submitted to the algorithm.

To perform the subdivision, one of the edges intersecting the front plane is chosen. The edge is subdivided at the intersection point with the plane, as shown in Figure 12.2.

The macro `EDGE_CROSS_Z` determines whether the edge (v_0, v_1) crosses the plane $z = h$.

216b   ⟨*edge cross z* 216b⟩≡

```
#define EDGE_CROSS_Z(P, V0, V1, H) \
               ((REL_GT((P)->v[V0].z, H) && REL_LT((P)->v[V1].z, H)) \
            || (REL_LT((P)->v[V0].z, H) && REL_GT((P)->v[V1].z, H)))
```

Defines:
  EDGE_CROSS_Z, used in chunk 216a.

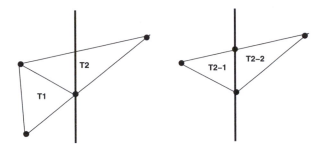

Figure 12.2. Subdivision in relation to the plane.

The routine `poly_split` subdivides the triangle.

⟨*poly split* 217⟩≡

```
void poly_split(Poly *p, int i0, int i1, int i2, Real t, Poly *pa,
                Poly *pb)
{
  Vector3 vm = v3_add(p->v[i1], v3_scale(t, v3_sub(p->v[i0], p->v[i1])));

  pa->v[0] = p->v[i1]; pa->v[1] = p->v[i2];
  pa->v[2] = pb->v[0] = vm;
  pb->v[1] = p->v[i2]; pb->v[2] = p->v[i0];
}
```

Defines:
  poly_split, used in chunk 216a.

Notice that, in the last case, when the two triangles resulting from the subdivision are processed by the algorithm recursion, one will be rejected and the other will be subdivided one last time (see Figure 12.3).

Finally, the polygons accepted in the second case move on to the last part of the method and are clipped out in 2D in relation to the image rectangle.

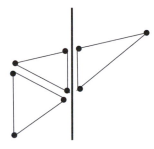

Figure 12.3. Result of the recursive subdivision in relation to the plane.

The routine `classify_vert`, calculates the number of vertices on the positive side of the plane $z = h$.

218   ⟨*classify vert* 218⟩≡

```
static int classify_vert(Poly *p, Real h)
{
  int i, k = 0;
  for (i = 0; i < 3; i++)
    if (REL_GT(p->v[i].z, h))  k++;
  for (i = 0; i < 3; i++)
     if (k > 0 && REL_EQ(p->v[i].z, h))  k++;
  return k;
}
```

Defines:
  `classify_vert`, used in chunk 216a.

An important observation about this algorithm is that special care must be taken during the vertex classification in relation to the plane $z = h$. The recursive algorithm results in vertices that are not in a generic position. This happens because the subdivision of an edge produces vertices exactly located on the clipping plane. In the algorithm recursion, vertex classification should take into account this possibility. This is done both in the routine `classify_vert` and in the macro `EDGE_CROSS_Z`. In this way, we avoid inconsistencies between the geometry and topology of the model.

12.4   Sequential Clipping

The clipping by subdivision algorithm described in the previous section simplifies the structuring problem by making a bisection of triangles. In this section we present an algorithm for general polygons with n sides. This clipping will be performed entirely in 3D in relation to the viewing frustum.

The strategy used in this algorithm consists of clipping the polygon sequentially, in relation to each of the semispaces determined by the faces of the viewing frustum. In each stage, the part of the polygon on the positive side of the current clipping plane is calculated and passed on to the next stage. Because the clipping volume is convex, at the end of the process, the resulting polygon is the intersection of the original polygon with the clipping volume.

This algorithm, with small modifications, can be used for clipping any convex volume.

12.4.1   The Sutherland-Hodgman Algorithm

This clipping algorithm uses the code below to identify the planes of the viewing frustum.

```
#define LFT 0
#define RGT 1
#define TOP 2
```

```
#define BOT 3
#define BAK 4
#define FRT 5
```

The routine `poly_clip` performs the Sutherland-Hodgman clipping algorithm [Sutherland and Hodgman 74] to a list of polygons, where the first polygon of the list contains the geometry information (i.e., vertex positions) and the other polygons contain attribute values (i.e., color, texture coordinates, normals, etc.). The strategy is first to compute distances to clipping planes based on the geometry information and subsequently to use this information to perform the clipping, both to the geometry and the attributes. The distance information is stored in the internal array dd. In this way, `poly_clip` first calls the routine `pclip_store` to compute the sequence of clip operations and then calls the routine `clip_copy` to transfer the operations to the output polygon. In the case that the polygon list has other attribute polygons, the clipping is also applied to the tail of the polygon list by the routine `pclip_apply` and `clip_copy`.

219   ⟨*poly clip* 219⟩≡
```
int poly_clip(Real h, Poly *p, void (*dispose)(), int chain)
{
  double dd[MAXD];
  Poly *a;
  int n;

  if (p->n > MAXV)
    error("(poly clip) too many vertices");

  n = clip_copy(pclip_store, p, h, dispose, dd);
  if (!chain)
    return n;
  for (a = p->next; a != NULL; a = a->next)
    n = clip_copy(pclip_apply, a, h, dispose, dd);

  return n;
}
```
Defines:
  `poly_clip`, never used.
Uses `clip_copy` 222b, `MAXD` 222a, `MAXV` 222a, `pclip_apply` 221c, and `pclip_store` 220a.

The routine `pclip_store` performs the clipping of a polygon by one clipping plane. It processes the edges of the input polygon performing the classification, intersection, and structuring. The current edge is given by k0 and k1, which are the indices of their initial and final vertices, respectively.

The vertices are classified based on their signed distance to the clipping plane, which is stored in the array dd. If the edge crosses the plane, its intersection point with the plane is calculated and inserted in the vertex list of the output polygon. If the final vertex of the edge is on the positive side of the plane, it is also inserted in the vertex list of the output polygon. Notice the first vertex of the input polygon will be processed last, because to close the cycle, the last edge corresponds to (v_{n-1}, v_0).

Also notice the routine pclip performs the sequencing of the clipping, increasing the code of the clipping plane and swapping the input buffer with the output one.

220a   ⟨*pclip store* 220a⟩≡

```
int pclip_store(int plane, Poly *s, Poly *d, Real h, double *dd)
{
  int i, k0, k1;
  double d0, d1;

  for (d->n = k1 = i = 0; i <= s->n ; i++,  k1 = (i == s->n)? 0 : i) {
    d1 = plane_point_dist(plane, s->v[k1], h);
    DA(dd, i, plane) = d1;
    if (i != 0) {
      if (PLANE_CROSS(d0, d1))
        d->v[d->n++] = v3_add(s->v[k1], v3_scale(d1/(d1-d0),
          v3_sub(s->v[k0], s->v[k1])));
      if (ON_POSITIVE_SIDE(d1))
        d->v[d->n++] = s->v[k1];
    }
    d0 = d1;
    k0 = k1;
  }
  return (plane++ == FRT)? d->n : pclip_store(plane, d, s, h, dd);
}
```

Defines:
  pclip_store, used in chunk 219.
Uses DA 222a, FRT, ON_POSITIVE_SIDE, PLANE_CROSS 221a, and plane_point_dist 220b.

The routine plane_point_dist calculates the signed distance of a vertex to the plane.

220b   ⟨*plane point dist* 220b⟩≡

```
Real plane_point_dist(int plane, Vector3 v, Real h)
{
  switch (plane) {
  case LFT: return v.z + v.x;
  case RGT: return v.z - v.x;
  case TOP: return v.z + v.y;
  case BOT: return v.z - v.y;
  case BAK: return  1 - v.z;
  case FRT: return -h + v.z;
  }
}
```

Defines:
  plane_point_dist, used in chunk 220a.
Uses BAK, BOT, FRT, LFT, RGT, and TOP.

The macro PLANE_CROSS detects whether an edge crossed the clipping plane. This calculation is based on the signed distances of the edge vertices to the plane.

221a   ⟨*plane cross* 221a⟩≡
```
#define PLANE_CROSS(D0, D1) ((D0) * (D1) < 0)
```
Defines:
  PLANE_CROSS, used in chunks 220a and 221c.

The macro ON_POS_SIDE detects whether a vertex is on the positive side of the clipping plane, starting from its signed distance.

221b   ⟨*on postive side* 221b⟩≡
```
#define ON_POS_SIDE(D1) ((D1) >= 0)
```
Defines:
  ON_POS_SIDE, never used.

The routine pclip_apply uses the distances to clipping planes computed by the routine pclip_store that are in the array dd to apply the actual clipping to attribute polygons.

In this way, the geometric clipping computation can be repeated to polygons with attribute values in subsequent steps without the need of explicit geometric information.

221c   ⟨*pclip apply* 221c⟩≡
```
int pclip_apply(int plane, Poly *s, Poly *d, Real h, double *dd)
{
  int i, k0, k1;
  double d0, d1;

  for (d->n = k1 = i = 0; i <= s->n ; i++,  k1 = (i == s->n)? 0 : i) {
    d1 = DA(dd, i, plane);
    if (i != 0) {
      if (PLANE_CROSS(d0, d1))
        d->v[d->n++] = v3_add(s->v[k1], v3_scale(d1/(d1-d0),
          v3_sub(s->v[k0], s->v[k1])));
      if (ON_POSITIVE_SIDE(d1))
        d->v[d->n++] = s->v[k1];
    }
    d0 = d1;
    k0 = k1;
  }
  return (plane++ == FRT)? d->n : pclip_apply(plane, d, s, h, dd);
}
```
Defines:
  pclip_apply, used in chunk 219.
Uses DA 222a, FRT, ON_POSITIVE_SIDE, and PLANE_CROSS 221a.

The macros DA, MAXV and MAXD control access to the plane distances array dd.

222a

⟨*da* 222a⟩≡

```
#define MAXV 16
#define MAXD ((MAXV+1)*(FRT+1))

#define DA(dd, i, p) dd[(p*MAXV)+i]
```

Defines:
  DA, used in chunks 220a and 221c.
  MAXD, used in chunk 219.
  MAXV, used in chunks 219 and 222b.
Uses FRT.

The routine `clip_copy` is responsible for the memory management of the algorithm. It allocates two internal buffers which will be alternately used as input and output at each stage of the clipping process. This routine also determines if it is necessary to allocate new memory for a clipped polygon and copies the result of the operation to the appropriate data structure.

222b

⟨*clip copy* 222b⟩≡

```
int clip_copy(int (*clip_do)(), Poly *p, Real h, void (*dispose)(),
              double *dd)
{
  Vector3 vs[MAXV], vd[MAXV];
  Poly s = {NULL, 0, vs}, d = {NULL, 0, vd};

  poly_copy(p, &s);
  if (clip_do(0, &s, &d, h, dd) > p->n) {
    if (dispose != NULL)
      dispose(p->v);
    p->v = NEWARRAY(s.n, Vector3);
  }
  poly_copy(&s, p);
  return s.n;
}
```

Defines:
  clip_copy, used in chunk 219.
Uses MAXV 222a.

12.5   Comments of References

In this chapter we discussed the problem of clipping surfaces for viewing and we presented algorithms to solve this problem. Figure 12.4 shows an example of the programs that perform the clipping and draws the orthogonal projections.

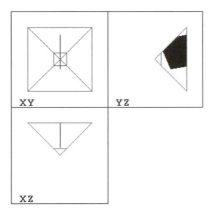

Figure 12.4. Clipping against the viewing pyramid (viewing frustum).

The API of the CLIP library consists of the following routines:

```
int is_backfacing(Poly *p);

int clip(Poly *s);

int clip_sub(Poly *p, void (*render)());
```

Exercises

1. Write a program to perform the clipping of a triangle against the front plane (far plane) using the subdivision algorithm. The result should be visualized using projections orthogonal to the z-axis.

2. Write a program to perform the clipping of a quadrilateral against the viewing pyramid (viewing frustum), using the Sutherland-Hodgman algorithm. The result should be visualized using projections orthogonal to the z-axis.

3. Modify the programs of the previous algorithms to also draw the projection planes.

13 Rasterization

The result of the viewing process is an image. In the case of viewing 3D scenes, objects in the field of view of the camera are projected on the plane of the image and discretized into elements of the image (or "pixels"). In this chapter, we will study the rasterization operation that performs this transformation.

13.1 Foundations of Rasterization

Consider a graphics object $\mathcal{O} = (S, f)$, with geometric support $S \subset R^n$ and attribute function $f : S \to R^k$, and a grid Δ of $\mathbb{R}^n$ with resolution $\Delta_1 \times \ldots \times \Delta_n$. The *rasterization* consists of determining the representation matrix of $\mathcal{O}$ induced by Δ.

The most common case is 2D rasterization, where $n = 2$ and S is a 2D subset of the plane. In this case, the representation matrix corresponds to a digital image (see Figure 13.1).

The rasterization process involves enumeration of the cells (C_i) of the grid Δ associated with the support S and also sampling of the attribute function f in each cell C_i.

The essence of the rasterization operation consists of determining whether a cell C_i of the grid Δ is part of the sequence of cells of the representation matrix of $\mathcal{O}$. This decision can be made based on the intersection between the cell and the set S. Notice that this process is closely related to that of the clipping operation discussed in Chapter 12.

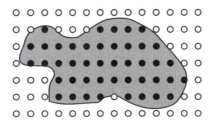

Figure 13.1. 2D rasterization.

In the context of viewing 3D scenes, objects are projected on the plane of the image and later rasterized. Depending on the dimension of S, the geometric support of S can be either a curve or a region of the plane.

The attribute function provides the color of the visual representation of the object on the image. For this reason it is called a *shading* (or *coloring*) function. The shading function results from the illumination simulation of the 3D scene. The illumination calculation, as well as the sampling of the shading function, will be discussed in other chapters.

The relation between the rasterization and the 3D viewing process is subtle due to the visibility problem. Ideally, we would rasterize only the surfaces visible to the virtual camera. In practice, three possibilities exist:

1. Rasterize after the visibility calculation,

2. Rasterize before the visibility calculation,

3. Calculate rasterization and visibility simultaneously.

We will treat the visibility problem in Chapter 14 and approach each of the above strategies. In this chapter we will discuss the rasterization algorithms without worrying about visibility.

13.1.1   Classification of Rasterization Methods

Rasterization essentially corresponds to a discretization of the geometric support of the graphics object O according to the grid Δ. We can classify the rasterization methods based on two criteria: the discretization strategy and the type of geometric description.

The discretization strategy is related to *how* to perform the rasterization. It can be incremental or by subdivision. *Incremental rasterization* uses an iterative process for discretizing the geometry, while *rasterization by subdivision* uses a recursive process. The incremental methods are generally more efficient. The methods by subdivision have the advantage of being adaptive.

The type of geometric description can be intrinsic or extrinsic, depending on which space the rasterization is based on. *Intrinsic rasterization* is based on the discretization of the graphics object, while the *extrinsic rasterization* is based on the discretization of the space. The intrinsic methods operate in the parameter space of the object. The extrinsic methods operate directly in the world space.

In the next sections we will discuss the rasterization methods using the above classification. We will see incremental methods, intrinsic and extrinsic, for polygonal regions; we will also see methods by subdivision, intrinsic and extrinsic, for straight line segments.

13.2   Incremental Methods

In this section we will present incremental methods for the rasterization of regions on the plane. The incremental rasterization algorithms are structured starting from two basic operations: initialization and traversal. The initialization determines an initial cell and calculates the incremental data. The traversal moves from the current cell to the next cell until all the cells are enumerated.

13.2.1   Intrinsic Incremental Rasterization

We will concentrate here on the case of triangle rasterization. This is the most important case for image synthesis. What is more, arbitrary polygonal regions can be triangular, and therefore they can be reduced to this case.

The routine `scan_poly` rasterizes a convex polygon. It decomposes the polygon into triangles, which are then rasterized by the routine `scan_spoly3`. The triangulation is performed by linking the first vertex of the polygon to the other vertices to form the triangles (v_0, v_{k-1}, v_k), $k = 2, \ldots n - 1$.

227a
⟨*scan poly* 227a⟩≡
```
void scan_poly(Poly *p, Paint *pfun, void *pdata)
{
  int k;
  for (k = 2; k < p->n; k++)
    scan_spoly3(p, k, pfun, pdata);
}
```
Defines:
  scan_poly, never used.
Uses scan_spoly3 227b.

The triangle rasterization method exploits the fact that the intersection of a convex polygonal region with a horizonal band of the grid is determined by a pair of edges (e_l, e_r). For each j, we have a sequence of cells $C_{i,j}$, with $x_l \leq i \leq x_r$, where $(x_l, j) \in e_l$ and $(x_r, j) \in e_r$. The interval $[x_l, x_r]$, called *span*, can be incrementally calculated starting from the parametric description of the triangle edges.

The routine `scan_spoly3` implements the rasterization of a triangle. The algorithm is made up of incremental processes nested in two levels: global (of the polygon) and local (of the edges).

At the global level, the initialization consists of determining the initial pair of edges. The traversal consists of enumerating the cells of each span, traversing the cycle of polygon edges. At the local level, the initialization consists of calculating the initial position and the increment value for an edge. The traversal consists of updating the current position along the edge.

227b
⟨*scan poly tri* 227b⟩≡
```
void scan_spoly3(Poly *p, int n, Paint *pfun, void *pdata)
{
  Edge *lft, *rgt, *seg, l, r, s;
  int lv, rv, tv = first_vertex(p->v, n);

  rgt = edge(p->v[tv], p->v[rv = NEXT(tv,n)], 'y', &r);
  lft = edge(p->v[tv], p->v[lv = PREV(tv,n)], 'y', &l);
```

```
    while (lft && rgt) {
      seg = edge(lft->p, rgt->p, 'x', &s);
      do
        pfun(seg->p, n, lv, lft->t, rv, rgt->t, seg->t, pdata);
      while (seg = increment(seg));
      if (!(rgt = increment(rgt))) { tv = rv;
        rgt = increment(edge(p->v[tv], p->v[rv = NEXT(rv,n)], 'y', &r));
      }
      if (!(lft = increment(lft))) { tv = lv;
        lft = increment(edge(p->v[tv], p->v[lv = PREV(lv,n)], 'y', &l));
      }
    }
  }
```

Defines:
scan_spoly3, used in chunk 227a.
Uses Edge 228b, edge 229a, first_vertex 228a, increment 229b, NEXT, and PREV.

The routine first_vertex calculates the vertex of lowest ordering, allowing us to determine the initial pair of edges of the rasterization.

228a   ⟨first vertex 228a⟩ ≡

```
    static int first_vertex(Vector3 v[], int n)
    {
      if (v[0].y < v[n-1].y)
        return ((v[0].y < v[n].y)? 0: n);
      else
        return ((v[n-1].y < v[n].y)? n-1: n);
    }
```

Defines:
first_vertex, used in chunk 227b.

The macros PREV and NEXT are used to traverse the cycle of edges in the negative and positive orientations, respectively.

```
#define PREV(K,N) ((K == N)? 0 : ((K == 0)? N - 1 : N))
#define NEXT(K,N) ((K == 0)? N : ((K == N)? N - 1 : 0))
```

The data structure Edge describes an edge. It contains the current position p, the increment of position i, the current parametric coordinate t, and the parametric increment d, besides the number of incremental steps n.

228b   ⟨edge structure 228b⟩ ≡

```
    typedef struct Edge {
      int n;
      Vector3 p, i;
      double t, d;
    } Edge;
```

Defines:
Edge, used in chunks 227b and 229.

The routine `edge` creates an edge (p_0, p_1) with increments along the x- or y-direction. Notice the increment in y performs a vertical scan, which traverses the boundary of the polygonal region. On the other hand, the increment in x performs a horizontal scan, which enumerates the cells of a span.

229a

⟨*edge* 229a⟩≡

```
static Edge *edge(Vector3 p0, Vector3 p1, char c, Edge *e)
{
  SNAP_XY(p0); SNAP_XY(p1);
  switch (c) {
  case 'x': e->n = ABS(p1.x - p0.x); break;
  case 'y': e->n = p1.y - p0.y; break;
  }
  e->t = 0;
  e->p = p0;
  e->d = (e->n < 1) ? 0.0 : 1.0 / e->n;
  e->i = v3_scale(e->d, v3_sub(p1, p0));
  return e;
}
```

Defines:
  edge, used in chunk 227b.
Uses Edge 228b and SNAP_XY.

The macro `SNAP_XY` restricts the coordinates (x, y) to the points of the integer grid $\mathbb{Z} \times \mathbb{Z}$.

```
#define SNAP_XY(V) {V.x = rint(V.x), V.y = rint(V.y);}
```

The routine `increment` updates the current position and parameter of the edge. It also tests the halting condition.

229b

⟨*increment* 229b⟩≡

```
static Edge *increment(Edge *e)
{
  e->p = v3_add(e->p, e->i);
  e->t += e->d;
  return (e->n-- > 0) ? e : (Edge *)0;
}
```

Defines:
  increment, used in chunk 227b.
Uses Edge 228b.

Each cell $C_{i,j}$, enumerated by the algorithm, is passed to the painting routine `pfun`, responsible for processing the corresponding pixel. The variable `pdata` stores the data used in this processing. In general, we have attributes of the graphics object that can be associated with the vertices of the polygon. The routine `pfun` calculates the values of the attributes in the cell by using bilinear interpolation.

The routine `seg_bilerp` implements the bilinear interpolation.

230a   ⟨*seg bilerp* 230a⟩≡

```
Vector3 seg_bilerp(Poly *p, int n, Real t, int lv, Real lt, int rv,
                   Real rt)
{
  return v3_bilerp(t, lt, p->v[NEXT(lv,n)], p->v[lv],
                   rt, p->v[PREV(rv,n)], p->v[rv]);
}
```

Defines:
  seg_bilerp, never used.
Uses NEXT and PREV.

13.2.2 Extrinsic Incremental Rasterization

The extrinsic incremental rasterization scans the cells of the integer grid on the image plane. The scan process is usually performed by lines and columns of the image matrix; in other words, the cells $C_{i,j}$ are visited by varying $i = 1, \ldots, n$, for $j = 0, \ldots, m$. A cell $C_{i,j}$ is part of the representation of a graphics object $\mathcal{O} = (S, f)$ if $(C_{i,j} \cap S) \neq \varnothing$. When S is a region of the plane, this determination can be performed in an approximate way by testing whether the center of the cell is contained in S.

The routine `scan_prim` performs the extrinsic rasterization of an implicit primitive. It performs the scan by line of the corresponding cells of the bounding box of the primitive. For each cell, the intersection between the surface and a ray, with origin in $(u, v, 0)$ and direction $(0, 0, 1)$, is calculated. If the intersection exists, the cell will then be processed by the routine `paint`.

230b   ⟨*scan prim* 230b⟩≡

```
void scan_prim(Prim *p, void (*paint)())
{
  Real u, v; Inode *l; Box3d bb = prim_bbox(p);

  for (v = bb.ll.y; v < bb.ur.y; v++)
    for (u = bb.ll.x; u < bb.ur.x; u++)
      if (l = prim_intersect(p, ray_make(v3_make(u,v,0), v3_make(0,0,1))))
        paint(u,v);
}
```

Defines:
  scan_prim, never used.

Notice that, as the implicit primitive is defined in the 3D space, the intersection with parallel rays corresponds to an orthogonal projection incorporated into the rasterization.

The process of rasterizing a 3D scene made up of several primitive objects requires, due to the visibility problem, the simultaneous rasterization of every object. In this case, the scan of the image cells is performed and, for each cell, the intersection between the corresponding ray and the objects of the 3D scene is calculated. If more than one object intersects the ray, it is necessary to determine which object is visible. This problem will be discussed in Chapter 14.

13.3   Rasterization by Subdivision

In this section we will discuss rasterization methods by subdivision for straight line segments. The rasterization algorithms by subdivision are made up of two basic operations: estimate and decomposition. The process begins with an initial configuration. At each level of recursion, an estimate is performed to determine whether a cell can be enumerated or whether a new decomposition is necessary. In the second case, a subdivision is performed and the algorithm is recursively applied to each part.

13.3.1   Intrinsic Subdivision

Rasterization by intrinsic subdivision of straight line segments is based on a test of the segment length. If its result is smaller than the diameter of the cell, the segment will be processed by the routine `paint`; otherwise, the segment will be subdivided at the middle point, thus establishing the recursion.

The routine `subdiv_line` implements the rasterization of a straight line segment.

231a

⟨*subdiv line* 231a⟩≡
```
void subdiv_line(Vector3 p, Vector3 q, void (*paint)())
{
  Box3d bb = bound(p, q);

  if ((bb.ur.x - bb.ll.x) <= 1 && (bb.ur.y - bb.ll.y) <= 1) {
    paint(bb.ll.x, bb.ll.y);
  } else {
    Vector3 m = v3_scale(0.5, v3_add(p,q));
    subdiv_line(p, m, paint);
    subdiv_line(m, q, paint);
  }
}
```
Defines:
  `subdiv_line`, never used.
Uses **bound** 231b.

The routine **bound** calculates the bounding box of a straight line segment.

231b

⟨*bound* 231b⟩≡
```
static Box3d bound(Vector3 p, Vector3 q)
{
  Box3d bb;
  bb.ll.x = MIN(p.x, q.x); bb.ll.y = MIN(p.y, q.y); bb.ll.z = MIN(p.z, q.z);
  bb.ur.x = MAX(p.x, q.x); bb.ur.y = MAX(p.y, q.y); bb.ur.z = MAX(p.z, q.z);
  return bb;
}
```
Defines:
  bound, used in chunk 231a.

This type of algorithm can be extended to perform the rasterization of polynomial patches, such as B-spline and Bézier surfaces. In those cases, there exist simple subdivision methods. The two greatest advantages are efficiency and adaptation.

13.3.2   Extrinsic Subdivision

Rasterization by extrinsic subdivision divides a rectangle contained on the image plane until it corresponds to a grid cell, or until it does not intersect the rasterized object.

The routine `subdiv_boxline` implements the rasterization for straight line segments.

232a   ⟨*subdiv boxline* 232a⟩≡

```
void subdiv_boxline(Box3d bb, Vector3 p, Vector3 q, void (*paint)())
{

  if (disjoint(p, q, bb))
    return;

  if ((bb.ur.x - bb.ll.x) <= 1 && (bb.ur.y - bb.ll.y) <= 1) {
    paint(bb.ll.x, bb.ll.y);
  } else {
    subdiv_boxline(b_split(bb, 1), p, q, paint);
    subdiv_boxline(b_split(bb, 2), p, q, paint);
    subdiv_boxline(b_split(bb, 3), p, q, paint);
    subdiv_boxline(b_split(bb, 4), p, q, paint);
  }
}
```

Defines:
  subdiv_boxline, never used.
Uses b_split 233b and disjoint 232b.

The routine `disjoint` calculates whether the segment $\overline{pq}$ has no intersection with the rectangle *bb*. First, it tests whether the segment is totally contained in the negative semiplanes determined by the edges of the rectangle. Then it tests if the rectangle is totally located in one of the semiplanes determined by the segment.

232b   ⟨*disjoint* 232b⟩≡

```
static int disjoint(Vector3 p, Vector3 q, Box3d bb)
{
  if (((p.x < bb.ll.x) && (q.x < bb.ll.x))|| ((p.y < bb.ll.y) &&
                                                    (q.y < bb.ll.y)))
    return TRUE;
  if (((p.x > bb.ur.x) && (q.x > bb.ur.x))|| ((p.y > bb.ur.y) &&
                                                    (q.y > bb.ur.y)))
    return TRUE;
  return same_side(p, q, bb);
}
```

Defines:
  disjoint, used in chunk 232a.
Uses same_side 233a.

The routine `same_side` calculates if the box bb is completely located on the same side of the straight line $\overline{pq}$.

233a   ⟨*same side* 233a⟩≡

```
static int same_side(Vector3 p, Vector3 q, Box3d bb)
{
  Vector3 l = v3_cross(v3_make(p.x,p.y,1),v3_make(q.x,q.y,1));
  Real d0 = v3_dot(l,v3_make(bb.ll.x, bb.ll.y, 1));
  Real d1 = v3_dot(l,v3_make(bb.ll.x, bb.ur.y, 1));
  Real d2 = v3_dot(l,v3_make(bb.ur.x, bb.ur.y, 1));
  Real d3 = v3_dot(l,v3_make(bb.ur.x, bb.ll.y, 1));

  return ((d0 < 0 && d1 < 0 && d2 < 0 && d3 < 0)
          || (d0 > 0 && d1 > 0 && d2 > 0 && d3 > 0));

}
```

Defines:
  `same_side`, used in chunk 232b.

The routine `b_split` performs a quaternary subdivision of the rectangle b.

233b   ⟨*bsplit* 233b⟩≡

```
static Box3d b_split(Box3d b, int quadrant)
{
  switch (quadrant) {
  case 1: b.ll= v3_scale(0.5, v3_add(b.ll,b.ur)); break;
  case 2: b.ll.x = (b.ll.x + b.ur.x) * 0.5; b.ur.y
                 = (b.ll.y + b.ur.y) * 0.5; break;
  case 3: b.ur= v3_scale(0.5, v3_add(b.ll,b.ur)); break;
  case 4: b.ll.y = (b.ll.y + b.ur.y) * 0.5; b.ur.x
                 = (b.ll.x + b.ur.x) * 0.5; break;
  }
  return b;
}
```

Defines:
  `b_split`, used in chunk 232a.

Algorithms of this type can be used for both the rasterization and visibility calculations of scenes made up of models with heterogeneous description. In this case, all the scene objects are tested in relation to v rectangles. This strategy is the same used in the classic Warnock viewing algorithm [Warnock 69b].

13.4 Comments and References

In this chapter we presented the rasterization algorithms for straight line segments, polygons, and implicit primitives. Figure 13.2 shows an example of the programs performing the rasterization of polygons using the intrinsic incremental method.

Figure 13.2. Polygon rasterization.

The API of the RASTER library is made up of the following routines:

```
void scan_obj(Poly *p, void (*paint)(), void *rc);
Vector3 seg_bilerp(Poly *p, Real t, int lv, Real lt, int rv, Real rt);

void scan_space(Prim *p, void (*paint)());

void rsubdiv_obj(Vector3 p, Vector3 q, void (*paint)());

void rsubdiv_space(Box3d bb, Vector3 p, Vector3 q, void (*paint)());
```

Exercises

1. Write a program to rasterize a straight line segment using intrinsic subdivision.

2. Write a program to rasterize a straight line segment using extrinsic subdivision.

3. Write a program to rasterize a polygon using intrinsic incremental rasterization.

4. Write a program to rasterize a sphere using extrinsic incremental rasterization.

5. Transform the programs of the previous exercises into interactive programs where the user can specify the objects being rasterized.

6. Use the programs of straight line rasterization to draw the objects of a 3D scene in wireframe.

7. Write a program to draw the silhouette of an implicit primitive. Hint: use a variation of the method of extrinsic incremental rasterization.

8.   Extend the program of the previous exercise for CSG objects.

9.   Include color attributes in the objects for rasterization.

10.   Develop a rasterization method for triangles using intrinsic subdivision.

14 | Visible Surface Calculation

The surfaces of a 3D scene are projected on the plane of the image for the viewing process. As this projection is not bijective, it is necessary to solve the conflicts that happen when several surfaces are mapped to the same pixel. For this problem, we use the visibility concept. In this chapter, we will study the problem of calculating the visible surfaces of a 3D scene.

14.1 Foundations

The visibility problem consists essentially of determining the closest surfaces within the visual field of the camera, which, consequently, will be visible. This can be seen as a sorting problem. Notice that we are interested in a partial order, that is, up to the first opaque surface along a viewing ray.

The visible surface calculation is strongly related to all other operations of the viewing process. This central role is justified, as the visibility algorithms need to structure the viewing operations to reach their solution. Within the context of this structuring, we can mention the following relations:

- □ The viewing transformations must be performed in a way to take the objects to the most appropriate coordinate system for each of the computations in the pipeline.

- □ The rasterization can be combined in several ways with the visibility algorithm being used.

- □ Once the visible surfaces are determined, the illumination calculation should be executed, producing the color of the image elements.

14.1.1 Scene Properties and Coherence

The various existing scene properties constitute one of the starting points for elaborating visibility algorithms. In this sense, the structure of the scene should be analyzed to explore the internal coherence and discussed in relation to a complexity measure.

To evaluate a 3D scene quantitatively, we can use several criteria. Among them, we have the number, complexity, and homogeneity (relative size) of the objects; the distribution of groups of objects in the scene; the interference among objects; and the complexity in scene depth.

The coherence is associated with intrinsic aspects of the scene objects, or the relations among them, that determine the degree of variation of the image. The types of coherence most explored in visibility algorithms are based on the:

□ Object,

□ Faces and edges,

□ Image,

□ Scene depth,

□ Temporal variation.

Note that in scenes with a high degree of complexity, the use of spatial coherence tends to decrease its importance as an efficiency factor of the algorithms. With the increase in complexity, the usual situation is inverted: instead of having an object occupying several pixels, we begin to have several objects contained in a single pixel.

14.1.2 Representation and Coordinate Systems

An important point being considered in the visibility calculation is related to the geometry of the objects. Visibility algorithms can be either general or specific, accepting either homogeneous or heterogeneous geometric descriptions of the scene objects.

The types of geometric descriptions most used in visibility algorithms include:

□ Polygonal meshes.

□ Bicubic parametric surfaces (spline, Bézier, etc.).

□ Algebraic implicit surfaces (quadrics, superquadrics, etc.).

□ Implicit constructive solid geometry models (CSG).

□ Procedural models (fractals, etc.).

Another issue related to the geometry is the internal representation adopted by the viewing system. The generality makes the algorithm more complex, with impact also in its performance. To simplify this problem, some viewing systems combine several specific procedures to perform some of the operations individually; in addition, they produce a common representation that can be combined in a subsequent integration stage. An extreme case of this strategy consists of converting, from the start, the geometry of all the objects to a common type (e.g., to a polygonal approximation). The other extreme case consists of combining, at the last instant, the images of groups of objects (e.g., using image composition).

Visibility algorithms can be divided into those operating in world space and those operating in image space. The first category works directly with the object representation. They calculate the exact solution, giving an orderly list of the faces projected on the plane of the virtual screen. In this case, the visibility is the first operation being performed. This type of algorithm generally uses a parametric description.

The algorithms working in the image space solve for a certain resolution level (that is not necessarily the same as that of the image). In this case, the algorithm tries to solve the problem for each pixel, analyzing the relative depths along the viewing ray. In this case, visibility is usually postponed until the last moment. This type of algorithm generally uses an implicit description.

14.1.3   Classification

Visibility algorithms can also be classified according to the ordering method used to determine the visible surfaces from the camera's point of view.

The ordering structure of the visibility algorithms is closely related to the rasterization operation, which determines the region of the image corresponding to the scene objects. Objects occupying disjunct areas of the image are independent in terms of visibility. The rasterization can be seen as a ordering process in which we make a spatial enumeration of the pixels occupied by each object.

Essentially, the rasterization process results in ordering along directions x and y (horizontal and vertical), while the visibility process results in ordering along z (depth), in the camera coordinate system.

The computational structures of the visibility algorithms use the following ordering sequences: (YXZ), (XY)Z, and Z(XY), where the parentheses indicate the combined ordering operation. These three ordering structures correspond to three types of algorithms that solve visibility along with rasterization, visibility after rasterization, and visibility before rasterization.

Algorithms of the type (YXZ) and (XY)Z calculate visibility in image precision, reducing the ordering problem to a neighborhood of the image elements (pixels). Algorithms of type (YXZ) solve visibility while processing the scene objects. As examples we have the *Z-buffer* and *Scanline* algorithms. Algorithms of type (XY)Z completely solve the visibility for each pixel. As an example we have the *ray tracing* and *recursive subdivision* algorithms. Algorithms of type Z(XY) precisely calculate the visibility, processing the ordering in Z globally, to the level of objects or the object faces. As an example we have the *Z-sort*, *space partition* and *recursive clipping* algorithms.

14.2   Z-Buffer

The Z-buffer algorithm stores, for each pixel, the distance up to the closest surface in that point of the image, which is the actual visible surface. This algorithm essentially corresponds to an ordering by cells (bucket sort).

The internal data structure zbuf stores the depth information for each pixel.

```
static Real *zbuf = NULL;
static int zb_h = 0, zb_w = 0;
```

Access to the structure is made by the macro ZBUF.

```
#define ZBUF(U,V) zbuf[U + V * zb_w]
```

The routine zbuf_init allocates a Z-buffer with resolution $(w \times h)$.

240a   ⟨*zbuff init* 240a⟩≡
```
void zbuf_init(int w, int h)
{
  zbuf = (Real *) erealloc(zbuf, w * h * sizeof(Real));
  zb_w = w; zb_h = h;
  zbuf_clear(MAX_FLOAT);
}
```
Defines:
  zbuf_init, never used.
Uses zb_h, zbuf, and zbuf_clear 240b.

The routine zbuf_clear initializes the Z-buffer with the real value *val*.

240b   ⟨*zbuff clear* 240b⟩≡
```
void zbuf_clear(Real val)
{
  int x, y;
  for (y = 0; y < zb_h; y++)
    for (x = 0; x < zb_w; x++)
      ZBUF(x,y) = val;
}
```
Defines:
  zbuf_clear, used in chunk 240a.
Uses zb_h and ZBUF.

The routine zbuf_store determines the visibility of a point $p = (x, y, z)$. The point is visible if its z-coordinate is smaller than the distance stored in the Z-buffer for pixel (x, y).

240c   ⟨*zbuff store* 240c⟩≡
```
int zbuf_store(Vector3 p)
{
  int x = p.x, y = p.y;
```

```
   if ((x > 0 && y > 0 && x < zb_w && y < zb_h) && p.z < ZBUF(x,y)) {
     ZBUF(x,y) = p.z;
     return TRUE;
   } else {
     return FALSE;
   }
 }
```

Defines:
  zbuf_store, never used.
Uses zb_h and ZBUF.

The routine zbuf_peek allows access to the Z-buffer and returns the distance stored at pixel (x, y).

241a   ⟨*zbuff peek* 241a⟩≡
```
 Real zbuf_peek(Vector3 p)
 {
   int x = p.x, y = p.y;
   return (x > 0 && y > 0 && x < zb_w && y < zb_h)? ZBUF(x,y) : MAX_FLOAT;
 }
```

Defines:
  zbuf_peek, never used.
Uses zb_h and ZBUF.

14.3   Ray Tracing

The ray tracing algorithm calculates the intersection between the viewing ray and all the objects of the 3D scene, selecting the intersection point with the closest surface. This process is performed for each pixel of the image, using the ray leaving from the center of projection of the camera and passing through the pixel.

14.3.1   Intersection with the 3D Scene Objects

The ray tracing method consists of calculating the intersection of the ray with each scene object. The visible surface corresponds to intersection with smaller positive parameter t along the ray. This process corresponds to the ordering by selection.

The routine ray_intersect calculates the closest intersection of ray r with the list of objects olist.

241b   ⟨*ray intersect* 241b⟩≡
```
 Inode *ray_intersect(Object *olist, Ray r)
 {
   Object *o; Poly *p;
   Inode *l = NULL, *i = NULL;
   for (o = olist; o != NULL; o = o->next ) {
     p  = (o->type == V_POLYLIST)? o->u.pols : NULL;
```

```
do {
  switch (o->type) {
  case V_CSG_NODE:
    l = csg_intersect(o->u.tcsg, r); break;
  case V_PRIM:
    l = prim_intersect(o->u.prim, r); break;
  case V_POLYLIST:
    if (p != NULL) {
      l = poly_intersect(p, poly3_plane(p), r);
      p = p->next;
    } break;
  }
  if ((l != NULL) && (i == NULL|| l->t < i->t)) {
    inode_free(i);
    i = l; i->m = o->mat;
    inode_free(i->next); i->next = NULL;
  }
} while (p != NULL);
}
return i;
}
```

Defines:
  `ray_intersect`, never used.
Uses `csg_intersect` 242.

14.3.2   Intersection with CSG Models

The ray tracing method for CSG models calculates the intersection with each primitive and it combines the intersections based on the boolean operation. This process corresponds to an ordering with merging (merge sort).

The routine `csg_intersect` calculates the intersection of a ray with a CSG solid.

242   ⟨*csg intersect* 242⟩≡
```
Inode *csg_intersect(CsgNode *n, Ray r)
{
  if (n->type == CSG_COMP)
    return csg_ray_combine(n->u.c.op, csg_intersect(n->u.c.lft, r)
                         , csg_intersect(n->u.c.rgt, r));
  else
    return prim_intersect(n->u.p, r);
}
```

Defines:
  `csg_intersect`, used in chunk 241b.
Uses `csg_ray_combine` 243a.

The routine `csg_ray_combine` combines, according to the boolean operation op, the intersections of two elements of a CSG composition given by the lists a and b.

The intersection is given by a list of points where the ray crosses the surface that delimits the solid. Starting from this list, intervals can be determined along the ray, corresponding to interior and exterior points of the solid. These intervals are combined by the CSG operation, thus creating a new list.

243a   ⟨*csg ray combine* 243a⟩≡
```
Inode *csg_ray_combine(char op, Inode *a, Inode *b)
{
  Inode in = {NULL, 0, {0,0,0}, 0, NULL}, *t, *head = *c = &in;
  int as = R_OUT, bs = R_OUT, cs = csg_op(op, as, bs);

  while (a|| b) {
    if ((a && b && a->t < b->t)|| (a && !b))
      CSG_MERGE(as, a)
    else
      CSG_MERGE(bs, b)
  }
  c->next = (Inode *)0;
  return head->next;
}
```
Defines:
  csg_ray_combine, used in chunk 242.
Uses CSG_MERGE 243b and csg_op 243c.

The macro CSG_MERGE merges two intervals according to the CSG operation.

243b   ⟨*csg merge* 243b⟩≡
```
#define CSG_MERGE(S, A) { int ts = cs;\
  S = !S;\
  if ((cs = csg_op(op, as, bs)) != ts) {\
    if (op == '-' && !S) \
      A->n = v3_scale(-1., A->n); \
    c->next = A; c = A; A = A->next;\
  } else {\
    t = A; A = A->next; free(t);\
  }\
}
```
Defines:
  CSG_MERGE, used in chunk 243a.
Uses csg_op 243c.

The routine csg_op determines the result of the CSG operation.

243c   ⟨*csg op* 243c⟩≡
```
int csg_op(char op, int l, int r)
{
  switch (op) {
  case '+': return l| r;
  case '*': return l & r;
```

```
      case '-': return l & (!r);
      }
   }
}
```
Defines:
  csg_op, used in chunk 243.

Extensions of the ray tracing method include stochastic sampling, use of rays to calculate the illumination (ray tracing), and optimizations.

14.4   The Painter's Algorithm

The painter's algorithm, also known as Z-sort, is essentially divided into two stages: in the first stage, the scene components are sorted in relation to the virtual camera; in the second stage, objects are rasterized in order, from most distant to closest.

Two possible implementations exist for the painter's algorithm: the approximated Z-sort method and the complete Z-sort method.

14.4.1   Approximated Z-Sort

In the approximated Z-sort method, polygons are sorted based on a distance value of the triangle to the observer. This value can be estimated starting from the centroid, or even from one of the polygon vertices. This method of using only a distance value for each polygon does not guarantee that the order of the polygons will always be correct from the point of view of the visible surface calculation. However, the method is simple to implement, works for most cases, and constitutes the initial stage of the complete Z-sort method.

The data structure Zdatum stores, in z, the representative value of the polygon of an object.

244a   ⟨*zdatum* 244a⟩≡
```
   typedef struct Zdatum {
      Real        zval;
      Poly        *l;
      IObject     *o;
   } Zdatum;
```
Defines:
  Zdatum, used in chunk 245.

The routine z_sort uses the ordering insertion method to construct a list of the polygons of the scene according to distances in z.

244b   ⟨*zsort* 244b⟩≡
```
   List *z_sort(List *p)
   {
      List *q = new_list();
```

```
    while (!is_empty(p)) {
      Item *i = z_largest(p);
      remove_item(p, i);
      append_item(q, i);
    }
    return q;
  }
```

Defines:
  z_sort, never used.
Uses z_largest 245.

The routine z_largest returns the list element p with larger z coordinate.

245 ⟨*zlargest* 245⟩≡
```
    Item *z_largest(List *p)
    {
      Item *i, *s;

      for (s = i = p->head; i != NULL; i=i->next)
        if (((Zdatum *)(i->d))->zval > ((Zdatum *)(s->d))->zval)
          s = i;
      return s;
    }
```

Defines:
  z_largest, used in chunk 244b.
Uses Zdatum 244a.

14.4.2 Complete Z-Sort

The complete Z-sort method begins with an orderly list of polygons produced by the approximated Z-sort. After that, the algorithm traverses this list, verifying whether the order of the polygons is correct from the point of view of the visible surface calculation. If two polygons P and Q are not in the correct order, their position in the list is changed.

To determine whether the painting order is correct, the method requires that polygon Q, to be painted after polygon P, cannot occlude it. This determination is performed by a series of tests of growing complexity which involve, for instance, testing the bounding boxes of P and Q, splitting a polygon by the support plane of the other, and intersecting the projections of P and Q on the screen.

Situations exist in which a sequence of polygons form a cycle in relation to the painting criterion. In those cases, it is not possible to determine a solid order and thus it is necessary to break the cycle by subdividing one of the polygons.

The pseudocode of the complete Z-sort algorithm is shown in Algorithm 14.1.

```
sort l by the centroid in z (approximated Z-sort);
while l ≠ ∅ do
    select P and Q;
    if P does not occlude Q then
        continue;
    else if Q flagged then
        resolve cycle;
    else if Q does not occlude P then
        swap P with Q;
        flag Q;
    end if
end while
paint l in order;
```

Algorithm 14.1. full_zsort(*l*).

14.5   Other Visibility Methods

In this section we will present other visibility algorithms that will not be used in the system.

14.5.1   Space Subdivision

The algorithms of space partitioning classify the scene objects independently from the parameters of the virtual camera, creating a data structure that, once the camera position is specified, can be traversed in a way to indicate the correct visibility order of the objects.

The structure most used for this goal is the binary space partition, or BSP-tree. The method consists of two steps:

1. **Preprocessing.** Constructs the BSP structure.

2. **Visibility.** Traverses the structure based on the camera.

Algorithm 14.2 describes the construction routine make_bsp. Algorithm 14.3 describes the routine bsp_traverse that calculates the visibility using BSP.

```
if plist == NULL then
    return NULL;
end if
root = select(plist);
for all p ∈ plist do
    if p on '+' side of the root then
        add(p, frontlist);
    else if p on '-' side of the root then
        add(p, backlist);
    else
        split_poly(p, root, fp, bp);
        add(fp, frontlist);
        add(bp, backlist);
    end if
end for
return combine(make_bsp(frontlist),make_bsp(backlist));
```

Algorithm 14.2. BSP make_bsp(plist).

```
if t == NULL then
    return;
end if
if c in front of t.root then
    bsp_traverse(c, t->back);
    render(t->root);
    bsp_traverse(c, t->front);
else
    bsp_traverse(c, (t->front);
    if backfaces then
        render(c, t->root);
    end if
    bsp_traverse(c, t->back);
end if
```

Algorithm 14.3. bsp_traverse(c, t).

```
for p in plist do
   if P in r then
      classify P;
   else
      remove P from plist;
   end if
end for
if configuration == SIMPLE then
   render r;
else
   divide r into 4;
   recursive_subdivision(plist, quadrant 1);
   recursive_subdivision(plist, quadrant 2);
   recursive_subdivision(plist, quadrant 3);
   recursive_subdivision(plist, quadrant 4);
end if
```

Algorithm 14.4. recursive_subdivision(plist, r).

14.5.2 Recursive Subdivision

The algorithm of recursive subdivision decomposes the image recursively into quadrants until the scene configuration in that area has a trivial visibility solution, or the area is of the size of a pixel. This algorithm is also known as a *Warnock algorithm* [Warnock 69b]. Algorithm 14.4 describes the routine recursive_subdivision.

14.5.3 Recursive Clipping

The recursive clipping algorithm determines a set of visible areas of the objects, which do not overlap on the image plane. With some modifications, this method can be applied for shadows and is also used in the beam tracing algorithm. Algorithm 14.5 describes the routine recursive_clipping.

```
if list == empty then
   return;
end if
sort approximately in Z;
select front poloygon P;
divide list into inside e outside clipping in relation to P;
while inside != empty do
   select Q;
   if P in front of Q then
      remove Q;
   else
      swap P and Q;
   end if
end while
render P;
recursive_clipping(outside);
```

Algorithm 14.5. recursive_clipping(lista).

14.6   Comments and References

The first systematic analysis of the algorithms for calculating the visible surfaces was made by [Sutherland et al. 74], which proposes a characterization of the visibility issue according to the ordering criterion.

There are several proposals for solving the visibility problem for scenes with heterogeneous geometry. [Crow 82] suggests the visibility calculation for groups of objects that would be combined in postprocessing by image composition. [Cook et al. 87] proposes preprocessing to convert all the scene surfaces into micropolygons, allowing an efficient visibility calculation.

The Z-sort algorithm is described in [Newell et al. 72a] and [Newell et al. 72b].

The space partition algorithm was initially introduced by [Shumacker et al. 69] for flight simulation applications, and later adapted for more general applications by [Fuchs et al. 83].

The recursive clipping algorithm was developed by Weiler and Atherton for calculating visible surfaces [Weiler and Atherton 77] and shadows [Atherton et al. 78]. A variation of this method was used in the beam tracing algorithm by [Heckbert and Hanrahan 84].

The ray tracing method to solve the visibility problem was firstly applied by [MAGI 68]. A complete description of this method can be found in [Roth 82].

The A-buffer method [Carpenter 84] extends the Z-buffer algorithm, allowing a more precise calculation of the visible surfaces at subpixel level.

The recursive image subdivision algorithm was introduced by [Warnock 69a]. The visibility algorithm by Scanline was independently developed by [Watkins 70] and [Bouknight and Kelly 70].

Figure 14.1 shows an example of the program that performs the visible surface calculation using the painter's algorithm. Figure 14.2 shows an image with the values of Z of the same scene.

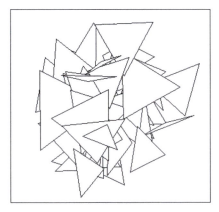

Figure 14.1. Visible surface calculation using the painter's algorithm.

Figure 14.2. Depth values (Z-buffer).

14.6.1   Routines

The API of the library for visible surface calculation consists of the routines below.

```
void zbuf_init(int w, int h);
void zbuf_clear(Real val);
int zbuf_store(Vector3 p);

Inode *ray_cast(Object *olist, Ray r);

Inode *csg_intersect(CsgNode *n, Ray r);
Inode *csg_ray_combine(char op, Inode *a, Inode *b);
int csg_op(char op, int l, int r);

List *z_sort(List *p);
Item *z_largest(List *p);

Item *new_item(void *d);
List *new_list();
int is_empty(List *q);
void append_item(List *q, Item *i);
void remove_item(List *q, Item* i);
void free_list(List *q);
```

Exercises

1.   Write a program to generate a set of triangles. Use the following parameters as input: number of triangles, size, orientation, aspect ratio, distribution with respect to the main (x, y, z) directions, and color. The output should be a list of triangles in the SDL language.

2.   Write a program to generate a set of spheres. The input should be constituted by parameters similar to those in the previous exercise. The output should be a set of primitive spheres in the SDL language.

3.   Write a program for scanning an SDL primitive and create a polygonal mesh approximating it. The output should be a list of triangles in the SDL language.

4.   Write a program to calculate visibility using Z-buffer. The input should be a list of triangles generated by the previous exercises. The output should be (1) an image with the visible surfaces and (2) an image with the values of Z.

5.   Write a program to calculate visibility using ray tracing. The input should be a set of primitives generated by the Exercise 14.2. The output should be (1) an image with the visible surfaces and (2) an image with the values of Z.

6.   Write a program to calculate the visibility using the painter's algorithm. The input should be a list of triangles generated by the previous exercises. The output should be (1) an image with the visible surfaces and (2) an image with the values of Z.

7.   Compare the results of the two previous exercises for the same set of spheres. First case: spheres that do not have intersections. Second case: spheres that can have intersections.

8.   Repeat the comparison of the previous exercise for a set of triangles.

15 Local Illumination Models

The viewing process is complete after color information is attributed to the objects represented in the image. In the case of 3D scenes, this correspondence can be established through the illumination calculation. This is a natural choice because it simulates our visual perception of the physical world. In this chapter, and in the subsequent ones, we will study the illumination and shading processes required for visualizing 3D scenes.

15.1 Foundations

Illumination and shading can be understood using the paradigm of the four universes. In the physical universe, illumination is related to the interaction between light and matter. In the mathematical universe, we describe this phenomenon through illumination models. In the representation universe, we have methods allowing the simulation of the illumination models. In the implementation universe, we have computational schema to construct the shading function (see Figure 15.1).

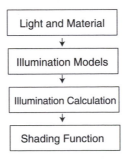

Figure 15.1. Abstraction levels for illumination.

15.1.1   Illumination

A 3D scene is composed of objects either emitting or transmitting luminous energy. In the viewing process we used a virtual camera, which we consider as a device sensitive to light.

The light has a dual nature: it behaves as a beam of particles and as a wave. The particle model of light assumes that the flow of energy along a ray is quantized by particles in motion called *photons*. This model is studied in *geometric optics*. On the other hand, the wave model of light describes the luminous energy by the combination of two fields: one electric and the other magnetic. This model is governed by the *Maxwell equations* of electromagnetism. Thus some illumination phenomena are explained by the particle model while others by the wave model.

In computer graphics, the particle model of light is the most useful because it allows us to simulate, in a simple way, most of the relevant phenomena for the illumination of 3D scenes. In this book we will use only this model. We will also consider only the problem of illuminating surfaces. This means the medium does not participate in the illumination model, as light propagates only in a vacuum. These choices considerably simplify the problem.

15.1.2   Light Propagation

Illumination is the study of the propagation of light in the environment space. To understand the concepts involved in the propagation of light, we should distinguish between *radiometric quantities* and *photometric quantities*. Radiometric quantities refer to the emission of radioactive energy and are used in the illumination calculation. Photometric quantities refer to the perception of radiant energy and are used in the shading function calculation.

Energy propagated in the form of electromagnetic waves is called *radiant energy*. A radiation beam is generally constituted by waves of several lengths within the visible spectrum. We call the function that associates the corresponding energy to each wavelength of this radiation *spectral distribution*.

We call the radiant energy that is emitted, transmitted, or received by a surface in a time unit *radiant flow*. Radiant flow is a scalar quantity. To study the propagation of radiant energy, we distinguish between the flow arriving (called *irradiance*) and leaving (called *radiant intensity* or *radiosity*) a surface in a certain direction.

Luminous flow is the quantity obtained by calculating the radiant energy as perceived by a standard observer. The sensibility of the standard receptor is measured by the *function of luminous efficiency*.

Radiant energy propagates along straight lines, and when it reaches the interface between two media, part of the energy is *reflected*—it returns to the original propagation medium—while another part is *transmitted*—it passes through the surface toward the other medium.

The laws of geometric optics determine the path of a ray reaching a surface. The reflection law states that the the incident ray, I, and the reflected ray, R, form equal angles $\theta_i = \theta_r$ with the normal N to the surface. The transmission follows *Snell's law*:

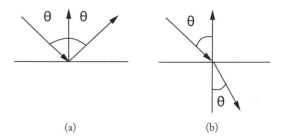

Figure 15.2. (a) Reflectance; (b) transmission.

$n_I \sin \theta_i = n_T \sin \theta_t$, where n_I and n_T are the refraction indices of the medium delimited by the surface and θ_I and θ_T are, respectively, the angles the incident ray I and the transmitted ray T form with the normal N to the surface (see Figure 15.2).

15.1.3   Surfaces and Materials

We are most interested in the interaction of light and material at the boundary between two media. The interaction here depends on both the geometry of the surfaces and the material of the objects, which determine the radiant energy and its path propagated at each interaction.

We can classify materials as dielectric, metallic, or composed. Dielectric materials are generally translucent and work as insulators of electricity. An example of this type of material is glass. Metallic materials are generally opaque and work as conductors of electricity. Copper, gold, and aluminum are examples of this type of material. Composed materials are formed by opaque pigments in suspension in a transparent substratum. Plastics and paints are examples of this type of material.

The geometry of a surface can be optically smooth or rough. A smooth surface is modeled locally by its tangent plane. In the case of smooth surfaces, light is propagated along the direction of reflection or transmission. A rough surface is approximated by a model of microfacets oriented in several directions. In the case of rough surfaces, light is propagated along several directions (see Figure 15.3).

A basic principle governing the propagation of light is the conservation of the energy, which states that energy arriving at a surface between two media is reflected, transmitted, or absorbed. In other words, the sum of the reflected, transmitted, and absorbed energies is the same as the incident energy.

At the boundary between air and a dielectric material, the most of the light is transmitted. At the boundary between air and a metallic material, most of the light is reflected. In addition, some of the luminous energy is absorbed in the interaction (for instance, transformed into heat). In general, the porportion of reflected and transmitted light depends on the angle between the incident ray and the normal to the surface.

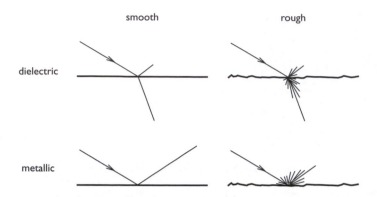

Figure 15.3. Light transmission and reflection on smooth and rough surfaces

15.1.4 Local Illumination Models

A local illumination model for surfaces describes the result of the interaction at the interface between two media. The model must be capable of predicting both the propagation path of radiant energy and the spectral distribution resulting from the incident light. This allows us to simulate the transport of luminous energy from one point to another on surfaces in the ambient space.

The bidirectional reflectance distribution function (*BRDF*) and the bidirectional transmittance distribution function (*BTDF*) are used to create a local illumination model. These functions depend on the direction and radiant energy of an incident luminous ray. They specify the resulting radiant energy along each direction of the hemisphere at the incidence point of the ray on the surface. Figure 15.4 illustrates the *BRDF* and *BTDF* functions for a determined incident direction.

The reflectance and transmittance functions can be calculated through radiometric measurements, but these functions are very complex. Therefore, we approximate them by simpler functions modeling the behavior of ideal surfaces. The two extreme cases are optically smooth and rough surfaces.

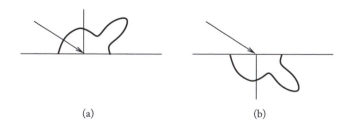

(a)   (b)

Figure 15.4. (a) BRDF and (b) BTDF.

Figure 15.5. (a) Diffuse and (b) specular reflections.

An ideal optically rough surface is called a *Lambertian surface*. This type of surface obeys the Lambert law: the radiant energy in any direction is proportional to the cosine of the angle between the direction of the incident ray and the normal; that is,

$$E_d = E_i \ \cos \theta.$$

In this case, we say that the reflection is *diffuse*, or the reflected energy is constant in all directions of the illumination hemisphere (see Figure 15.5(a)).

An ideal optically smooth surface is called *specular surface*. In this case, the light ray reaching the surface at a point p is reflected along direction R, so the incidence and reflection angles are the same (see Figure 15.2).

Given that the energy is uniquely reflected in direction R, it represents all the energy reaching the illumination hemisphere at p. In most materials, the specular reflection concentrates around the direction of reflection, gradually decreasing for directions away from it. An empirical illumination model for this type of specular reflection is the Phong model [Phong 75]. According to this model, the radiant energy reflected in a direction V is proportional to a power p of the cosine of the angle β between V and the reflection direction R (see Figure 15.5(b)):

$$E_s = E_i \ (\cos \beta)^p.$$

The local models of diffuse and specular illumination are combined to approximate the bidirectional reflectance function of a surface:

$$E_o = k_d E_d + k_s E_s,$$

where k_d and k_s are constants depending on the material.

Other more sophisticated illumination models exist. Among them we can mention the Blinn [Blinn and Newell 76], Cook-Torrance [Cook and Torrance 81], and Torrance-Sparrow [Torrance and Sparrow 76] models.

15.2   Light Sources

In this section we will describe the implementation of light sources and mechanisms for transporting luminous energy. These mechanisms are the basis for implementing the local illumination equation.

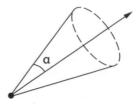

Figure 15.6. Cone of light.

15.2.1   Light Transport

To implement the light transport, we will define a new geometric element: a *cone* of light (see Figure 15.6). The structure Cone describes a light cone. It stores the source o, the direction d, and the cosine of the spread angle α of the cone.

256a
⟨*cone* 256a⟩≡

```
typedef struct Cone {
  Vector3 o, d;
  Real cosa;
} Cone;
```

Defines:
  Cone, used in chunks 256–61.

The routine cone_make implements the Cone constructor.

256b
⟨*cone make* 256b⟩≡

```
Cone cone_make(Vector3 o, Vector3 d, Real angle)
{
  Cone c;
  c.o = o; c.d = d; c.cosa = cos(angle);
  return c;
}
```

Defines:
  cone_make, used in chunks 260b and 261.
Uses Cone 256a.

The routines dir_coupling and point_coupling implement the visibility in relation to a cone and are used in the geometric calculation of the light transport (see Figure 15.7).

The routine dir_coupling determines whether a propagation direction is visible for a cone c.

256c
⟨*dir coupling* 256c⟩≡

```
int dir_coupling(Cone a, Vector3 v)
{
  if (v3_dot(a.d, v3_scale(-1, v)) > a.cosa)
    return TRUE;
  else
```

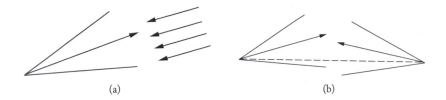

Figure 15.7. Visibility relations: (a) visibility between a cone and a direction; (b) visibility between two cones.

```
    return FALSE;
}
```
Defines:
  dir_coupling, used in chunks 257–59.
Uses Cone 256a.

The routine `point_coupling` determines whether two cones are mutually visible.

257 ⟨*point coupling* 257⟩≡
```
int point_coupling(Cone a, Cone b)
{
  Vector3 d = v3_unit(v3_sub(a.o, b.o));
  return dir_coupling(a, d) && dir_coupling(b, v3_scale(-1, d));
}
```
Defines:
  point_coupling, never used.
Uses Cone 256a and dir_coupling 256c.

15.2.2 Light Source Representations

There are several types of light sources. The most common are directional lights, point lights, and focused lights (spotlights). A *directional light* represents a light source that is very distant, such as the sun. Its energy propagates in a single direction and is not attenuated with distance. A *point light* represents a local light source, such as a candle or an incandescent lamp. Its energy propagates from a point in all directions and is attenuated with distance. A *focused light (spotlight)* represents a local concentrated light, such as a table lamp or a theater reflector.

We will use the structure Light to represent a light source. This structure serves as an element of a single linked list, and it stores the parameters of all types of light sources. Next, we will describe the common elements to all light sources: type indicates the type of light source; color specifies the spectral distribution of the light; intensity defines the intensity of the light; transport points to a function implementing the light transport; outdir is the direction of light emission calculated for each interaction with a surface; and outcol is the distribution of energy emitted in the interaction.

258a   ⟨*light struct* 258a⟩≡
```
typedef struct Light {
  struct Light *next;
  int          type;
  Color        color;
  Real         ambient;
  Real         intensity;
  Vector3      loc;
  Vector3      dir;
  Real         cutoff;
  Real         distr;
  Real         att0, att1, att2;
  Vector3      outdir;
  Color        outcol;
  int          (*transport)();
  void         *tinfo;
} Light;
```
Defines:
  Light, used in chunks 258–61, 263a, and 310c.
Uses ambient 260a.

The routine ambientlight implements the transport of an ambient light.

258b   ⟨*ambient light* 258b⟩≡
```
int ambientlight(Light *l, Cone recv, RContext *rc)
{
  return FALSE;
}
```
Defines:
  ambientlight, never used.
Uses Cone 256a, Light 258a, and RContext 259b.

The routine distantlight implements the transport of a directional light.

258c   ⟨*distant light* 258c⟩≡
```
int distantlight(Light *l, Cone recv, RContext *rc)
{
  if (dir_coupling(recv, l->dir) == FALSE)
    return FALSE;
  l->outdir = v3_scale(-1, l->dir);
  l->outcol = c_scale(l->intensity, l->color);
  return TRUE;
}
```
Defines:
  distantlight, used in chunk 263a.
Uses Cone 256a, dir_coupling 256c, Light 258a, and RContext 259b.

The routine pointlight implements the transport of a point light.

259a   ⟨*point light* 259a⟩≡

```
int pointlight(Light *l, Cone recv, RContext *rc)
{
  Real d, dist, atten;
  Vector3 v = v3_sub(rc->p, l->loc);
  dist = v3_norm(v);
  l->dir = v3_scale(1/dist, v);
  if (dir_coupling(recv, l->dir) == FALSE)
    return FALSE;
  atten = ((d = l->att0 + l->att1*dist + l->att2*SQR(dist))) > 0)? 1/d : 1;
  l->outdir = v3_scale(-1, l->dir);
  l->outcol = c_scale(l->intensity * atten, l->color);
  return TRUE;
}
```

Defines:
  `pointlight`, never used.
Uses `Cone` 256a, `dir_coupling` 256c, `Light` 258a, and `RContext` 259b.

15.3   Local Illumination

In this section we will present the implementation of the local illumination models.

15.3.1   Context of Illumination

Calculation of local illumination is performed in relation to a point p of a surface in the scene. The illumination functions are defined in the illumination hemisphere at that point, which is the set of rays on the tangent plane of the surface at p (see Figure 15.8).

    The structure `RContext` stores the data used in the local illumination.

259b   ⟨*render context* 259b⟩≡

```
typedef struct RContext {
  Vector3  v, p, n;
  Vector3  du, dv;
```

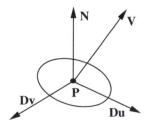

Figure 15.8. Geometry of local illumination.

```
    Vector3  t;
    Material *m;
    Light    *l;
    View     *c;
    Image    *img;
  } RContext;
```

Defines:
  RContext, used in chunks 258–62, 304–6, and 310.
Uses Light 258a and Material 262a.

15.3.2 Illumination Functions

We will use a simple local illumination model based on the ambient, diffuse, and specular components. Notice that all calculations are performed on the illumination hemisphere represented in the routines by the cone receiver, with spread angle $\alpha = \pi/2$.

The ambient component, implemented by the routine ambient, computes the constant illumination of the environment.

260a   ⟨*ambient* 260a⟩≡

```
    Color ambient(RContext *rc)
    {
      Light *l; Color c = C_BLACK;

      for (l = rc->l; l != NULL; l = l->next)
          c = c_add(c, c_scale(l->ambient, l->color));
      return c;
    }
```

Defines:
  ambient, used in chunks 258a and 262b.
Uses Light 258a and RContext 259b.

The diffuse component, implemented by the routine diffuse, follows Lambert's law. The contribution of each light source is given by $c_i < N, L_i >$, where N is the normal to the surface and L_i and c_i are, respectively, the incident direction and the distribution of energy of the light i (in the routine diffuse, L_i and c_i are given by l - > outdir and l - > outcol).

260b   ⟨*diffuse* 260b⟩≡

```
    Color diffuse(RContext *rc)
    {
      Light *l; Color c = C_BLACK;
      Cone receiver = cone_make(rc->p, rc->n, PI/2);

      for (l = rc->l; l != NULL; l = l->next)
        if ((*l->transport)(l, receiver, rc))
          c = c_add(c, c_scale(v3_dot(l->outdir, rc->n), l->outcol));
      return c;
```

```
}
```

Defines:
diffuse, used in chunk 262b.
Uses Cone 256a, cone_make 256b, Light 258a, and RContext 259b.

The specular component, implemented by the routine specular, uses the Blinn model, which is similar to the Phong model. This model avoids the calculation of the reflection vector R and, therefore, is more efficient. The calculation is performed as a function of the vector $H = (L + V)/2$, the bisector between the vectors L, in the direction of the light source, and V, in the direction of the observer. The specular term is given by $c_i < H_i, N >^{s_e}$, where N is the normal to the surface, and c_i, H_i, and s_e are, respectively, the distribution of energy, the bisecting vector of the light source i, and the exponent of specular reflection.

261 $\langle specular\ 261 \rangle \equiv$

```
  Color specular(RContext *rc)
  {
    Light *l; Vector3 h; Color c = C_BLACK;
    Cone receiver = cone_make(rc->p, rc->n, PI/2);

    for (l = rc->l; l != NULL; l = l->next) {
      if ((*l->transport)(l, receiver, rc)) {
        h = v3_unit(v3_scale(0.5, v3_add(l->outdir, rc->v)));
        c = c_add(c, c_scale(pow(MAX(0, v3_dot(h, rc->n)),rc->m->se),
                  l->outcol));
      }
    }
    return c;
  }
```

Defines:
specular, used in chunk 262b.
Uses Cone 256a, cone_make 256b, Light 258a, and RContext 259b.

15.4 Materials

In this section we will present the implementation of materials in the illumination calculation.

15.4.1 Describing Materials

The structure Material describes a material. It stores the parameters of the material that are used in the calculation of the local illumination. The colors C and S specify the spectral distribution for the diffuse and specular reflections of the material. The constants k_a, k_d, and k_s are the coefficients of ambient, diffuse, and specular reflections. The constant s_e is the exponent of specular reflection. The constant k_t is the transmittance coefficient, and i_r is the index of refraction of the material. The pointer `luminance` points to a routine implementing the behavior of the material. This routine is typically based on a local illumination model and uses the routines described in the previous section.

262a   ⟨*material struct* 262a⟩≡

```
typedef struct Material {
  Color c, s;
  Real  ka, kd, ks, se, kt, ir;
  Color (*luminance)();
  void  *tinfo;
} Material;
```

Defines:
    `Material`, used in chunks 259b, 263b, 304–6, and 310c.

15.4.2   Types of Materials

As we previously saw, materials are classified as dielectric, metallic, and composed. Here we will present the implementation of a single material type: plastic, which is a composed material and, for this reason, uses an illumination model involving the diffuse and specular components.

The routine `plastic` implements a plastic material. The illumination equation for this type of material is

$$C\ (k_a\ \text{amb}(p) + k_d\ \text{diff}(p)) + S(\ k_s\ \text{spec}(p)),$$

where amb, diff, and spec, are, respectively, the terms of the ambient, diffuse, and specular illumination, calculated for the illumination context `rc` at point p.

262b   ⟨*plastic* 262b⟩≡

```
Color plastic(RContext *rc)
{
  return c_add(c_mult(rc->m->c, c_add(c_scale(rc->m->ka, ambient(rc)),
                                      c_scale(rc->m->kd, diffuse(rc)))),
               c_mult(rc->m->s, c_scale(rc->m->ks, specular(rc))));
}
```

Defines:
    `plastic`, never used.
Uses `ambient` 260a, `diffuse` 260b, `RContext` 259b, and `specular` 261.

15.5   Specification in the Language

An example specifying a light source of directional type in the SDL language is given by the routine `distlight_parse`.

263a   ⟨*parse distlight* 263a⟩≡

```
Val distlight_parse(int pass, Pval *pl)
{
  Val v;
  if (pass == T_EXEC) {
    Light *l = NEWSTRUCT(Light);
    l->type = LIGHT_DISTANT;
    l->color = C_WHITE;
    l->intensity = pvl_get_num(pl, "intensity", 1);
    l->dir = v3_unit(pvl_get_v3(pl, "direction", v3_make(1,1,1)));
    l->transport = distantlight;
    v.type = LIGHT;
    v.u.v = l;
  }
  return v;
}
```

Defines:
  distlight_parse, never used.
Uses distantlight 258c and Light 258a.

An example specifying a material of metallic type in the SDL language is given by the routine metal_parse.

263b   ⟨*parse metal* 263b⟩≡

```
Val metal_parse(int pass, Pval *pl)
{
  Val v;
  if (pass == T_EXEC) {
    Material *m = NEWSTRUCT(Material);
    m->c = pvl_get_v3(pl, "d_col", C_WHITE);
    m->ka = pvl_get_num(pl, "ka", .1);
    m->ks = pvl_get_num(pl, "ks", .9);
    m->se = pvl_get_num(pl, "se", 10);
    m->luminance = metal;
    v.type = MATERIAL;
    v.u.v = m;
  }
  return v;
}
```

Defines:
  metal_parse, never used.
Uses Material 262a.

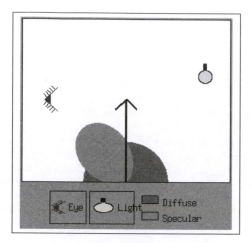

Figure 15.9. Local illumination model.

15.6   Comments and References

Figure 15.9 shows an example of the interactive programs that performs the illumination calculation.

The API of the library SHADE consists of the routines below.

```
Cone cone_make(Vector3 o, Vector3 d, Real angle);
int point_coupling(Cone a, Cone b);
int dir_coupling(Cone a, Vector3 v);

Vector3 faceforward(Vector3 a, Vector3 b);
RContext *rc_set(RContext *rc, Vector3 p, Vector3 n, Vector3 v);

Color ambient(RContext *rc, Light *l, Material *m, Vector3 d);
Color diffuse(RContext *rc, Light *l, Material *m, Vector3 d);
Color specular(RContext *rc, Light *l, Material *m, Vector3 d);

int ambientlight(Light *l, Cone recv, RContext *rc);
int distantlight(Light *l, Cone recv, RContext *rc);
int pointlight(Light *l, Cone recv, RContext *rc);
int spotlight(Light *l, Cone recv, RContext *rc);

Color constant(RContext *rc, Light *l, Material *m);
Color matte(RContext *rc,  Light *l, Material *m);
Color metal(RContext *rc,  Light *l, Material *m);
Color plastic(RContext *rc,  Light *l, Material *m);
```

Exercises

1. Write a program to calculate the diffuse illumination at a point on a surface for variable positions of a light source.

2. Write a program to calculate the specular illumination at a point on a surface for variable positions of a light source and of the observer.

3. Combine the two previous exercises in an interactive graphics program, in which the user can vary the position of the light and of the observer. The program should visually indicate the result of the illumination calculation.

16 | Global Illumination

Illumination of a 3D scene is the result of the global interaction between the light sources and surfaces of the environment. In this chapter we will study the illumination equation describing such phenomena, as well as computational methods to numerically solve that equation.

16.1 Illumination Model

The illumination equation describes the propagation of radiant energy in the ambient space. As we saw in the previous chapter, according to the particle light model, each photon carries a certain amount of radiant energy. At a certain instant in time, a photon can be characterized by its position and by the direction of its movement. In this way, the state of a photon is given by (s, ω), where $s \in \mathbb{R}^3$ and $\omega \in S^2$. The space $R^3 \times S^2$ is called *phase space*.

Illumination is the result of photon motion. Therefore, we want to measure the flow of radiant energy by unit of time, or *radiant power*. The radiant flow, $\Phi(s, \omega, t)$, is a function defined in phase space, such that

$$\Phi(s, \omega, t) dA d\omega$$

is the number of photons passing through a differential area dA in the neighborhood of a point s, under a differential solid angle $d\omega$ in the neighborhood of a direction ω, at an instant of time t (see Figure 16.1).

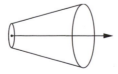

Figure 16.1. Geometry of the flow of radiant energy.

The illumination equation is part of *transport theory*, which studies the distribution of abstract particles in space and time. This theory takes two assumptions, which are appropriate for studying the illumination of surfaces and simplify the illumination problem considerably.

The first assumption is that the system is in *equilibrium*. In other words, the conditions of light propagation in the environment do not change during the simulated time interval. This condition means that flow is constant at every point in the scene. Consequently, we have

$$\frac{\partial \Phi}{\partial t} = 0.$$

The second assumption is that the transmission happens in a *nonparticipative* medium. We assume the simulation is performed in a vacuum, and therefore the only important phenomena happen on the surfaces of the scene objects.

16.1.1 Transport

The transport of radiant energy between two points in a vacuum is given by the following equation:

$$\Phi(r, \omega) = \Phi(s, \omega), \tag{16.1}$$

where r, s are points mutually visible along the direction ω. Notice the equation is valid for any pair of points of the ambient space satisfying the visibility condition. We are interested only in the surface points $r, s \in M = \cup M_i$ of the scene.

Given a point r, we find the point $s \in M$ using the *surface visibility function*, $\nu :$ $\mathbb{R}^3 \times S^2 \to \mathbb{R}$, which returns the distance of the closest visible point on a surface of the scene

$$\nu(r, \omega) = \inf \{\alpha > 0 : (r - \alpha\omega) \in M\}.$$

The point s, is then given by $s = r - \nu(r, \omega)\,\omega$.

The illumination function at point p on a surface potentially depends on the flow of radiant energy arriving from every direction. For this reason, we use the concept of an *illumination hemisphere*, Θ at point p, that is defined by an imaginary sphere of radius 1 whose center is at p. Figure 16.2 illustrates the geometry of the transport of radiant energy between visible points of two surfaces.

Figure 16.2. Transport of radiant energy between points on two surfaces.

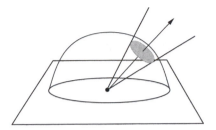

Figure 16.3. The illumination hemisphere.

The luminous energy irradiating from point p along direction ω defines a solid angle in the hemisphere Θ_o, and, reciprocally, the luminous energy arriving at a point p defines a solid angle in the illumination hemisphere Θ_i. In this way the illumination hemisphere controls every exchange of energy between a surface point p and the environment (see Figure 16.3).

16.1.2 Boundary Conditions

Equation (16.1) describes the transport conditions of radiant energy in a vacuum. To formulate the illumination problem completely, we need to specify the boundary conditions. In other words, what happens when luminous rays reach surfaces in the scene? Two boundary conditions exist:

☐ **Explicit.** The flow leaving point s on the surface in direction ω is independent of the incident flow. This is the case of light sources. The illumination function is given by

$$\Phi(s,\omega) = \mathcal{E}(s,\omega), \tag{16.2}$$

where $\mathcal{E}$ specifies the *emissivity function* of the surface.

☐ **Implicit.** The flow leaving point s on the surface in direction ω depends on the incident flow in the illumination hemisphere:

$$\Phi(s,\omega) = \int_{\Theta_i} k(s,\omega' \to \omega)\Phi(s,\omega')d\omega', \tag{16.3}$$

where $\omega \in \Theta_o$ and $\omega' \in \Theta_i$, and the function k is the bidirectional reflectance function of the surface. Notice that due to the law of conservation of energy, the radiant energy leaving Θ_o has to be smaller than the incident radiant energy in Θ_i.

16.1.3 Radiance Equation

We will formulate the illumination equation defining the boundary conditions in the transport equation.

At each point $r \in M$, we want to obtain the contribution of radiant energy coming from every point $s \in M$ that is visible inside the illumination hemisphere Θ_i in r.

We partition the transport equation between two points r and s:

$$\Phi(r, \omega) = \Phi(s \to r, \omega) \tag{16.4}$$

and replace, on the right side of the equality, the two boundary conditions (16.2) and (16.3):

$$\Phi(r, \omega) = \mathcal{E}(s, \omega) + \int_{\Theta_i} k(s, \omega' \to \omega) \Phi(s, \omega') d\omega', \tag{16.5}$$

where $r, s \in M$, $\omega \in \Theta_o$, $\omega' \in \Theta_i$, and s is determined by the visibility function ν. Equation (16.5) is a *Fredholm integral equation of the second kind*, which has been the subject of much study [Polyanin and Manzhirov 98].

The transport equation describes the flow of radiant energy in terms of the number of photons (irradiance). However, we want to obtain the total amount of radiant energy, or *radiance*, which is the flow Φ multiplied by the energy E of the transported photons $L = E\Phi$, where $E = h\, c/\lambda$, is related to the wavelength λ through the *Planck constant h* [Barrow 02], and c it is the speed of the light in the vacuum.

Radiance L is the radiant flow on a surface by unit of solid angle and by projected area:

$$L(r, \omega) = \frac{d^2 \Phi(r, \omega)}{d\omega\, dS \cos \theta_s}, \tag{16.6}$$

where θ_s is the angle between ω and the normal to the surface in dS. The factor $\cos \theta_s$ means that the flow by solid angle is independent of the surface angulation.

The *radiance equation* is given by

$$L(r, \omega) = L_E(r, \omega) + \int_{\Theta_i} k(s, \omega' \to \omega) L(s, \omega') \cos \theta_s\, d\omega'. \tag{16.7}$$

This equation is also known as the *rendering equation*, or the temporal invariant equation of monochrome radiance in the vacuum. Its geometry is illustrated in Figure 16.4(a).

A modified version of Equation (16.7) describes the energy irradiated from a point r along a direction ω^o in terms of the incident energy in the illumination hemisphere in r:

$$L(r, \omega^o) = L_E(r, \omega^o) + \int_{\Theta_i} k(r, \omega \to \omega^o) L(s, \omega) \cos \theta_r\, d\omega, \tag{16.8}$$

where $\omega^o \in \Theta_o$, and θ_r is the angle between the normal to the surface in r and $\omega \in \Theta_i$. The geometry of the equation is illustrated in Figure 16.4(b). This form of the radiance equation will be used to elaborate several methods for calculating illumination.

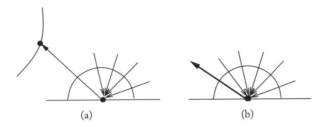

Figure 16.4. (a) Geometry of Equation (16.7); (b) geometry of Equation (16.8).

16.1.4 Numerical Approximation

The illumination equation should generally be solved in a numerical and approximate way. We will use operator notation to study the solution of this integral equation.

We define the integral operator $\mathcal{K}$ as

$$(\mathcal{K}f)(x) = \int k(x,y)f(y)dy,$$

where the function k is called the *kernel* of the operator. We indicate that the operator $\mathcal{K}$ is applied in a function $f(x)$ by $(\mathcal{K}f)(x)$.

Using the notation of operators, the illumination equation is written in the form

$$L(r,\omega) = L_E(s,\omega) + (\mathcal{K}L)(s,\omega), \tag{16.9}$$

or $L = L_E + KL$.

Part of the difficulty in solving Equation (16.9) comes from the fact that the unknown function L appears on both sides of the equality, inside and outside the integral.

A strategy for an approximate solution to the problem is to use the method of successive substitution. Notice that function L is defined in a reflexive way and, consequently, Equation (16.9) provides an expression for L.

The basic idea consists of substituting L by its expression on the right side of the equality, obtaining

$$L = L_E + K(L_E + KL)$$
$$= L_E + KL_E + K^2L,$$

where the exponent indicates the successive application of the operator K to a function f, i.e., $(\mathcal{K}^2 f)(x) = (\mathcal{K}(\mathcal{K}f))(x)$. Repeating the substitution process $n+1$ times,

$$L = L_E + KL_E + \ldots + K^nL_E + K^{n+1}L$$
$$= \sum_{i=0}^{n} K^iL_E + K^{n+1}L.$$

This recurrence relation provides a way to approximately calculate L. Ignoring the residual term of order $n + 1$, $K^{n+1}L$, we have

$$L \approx L_n = \sum_{i=0}^{n} K^i L_E.$$

The substitution method applied to the illumination function calculation has a quite intuitive physical interpretation. Notice the term L_E, which is known, corresponds to the radiant energy emitted by the light sources. The integral operator K models the propagation of the reflected light on the surfaces. Therefore, KL_E corresponds to the illumination of the light sources that is reflected directly by the surfaces. Its successive application models the propagation of the reflected light n times in the scene.

16.1.5 Methods for Calculating Illumination

We have developed a methodology to approximately calculate the illumination function. In practice, this strategy translates itself in two classes of methods for calculating illumination:

□ **Local methods.** The approximation given by $L_1 = L_E + KL_E$ corresponds to the direct contribution of the light sources. This class of methods uses only the local illumination model we studied in Chapter 15.

□ **Global methods.** The approximation given by $L_n = \sum_{i=0}^{n} K^i L_E$ corresponds to the direct contribution of the light sources and indirect contribution from the reflection of the surfaces. This class of methods uses the global illumination model studied in this chapter. The two most important implementation forms are the ray tracing and radiosity methods. In the next sections we will present them in detail.

16.2   Ray Tracing Method

The ray tracing method provides a solution for calculating global illumination by sampling the path of light rays in the scene. The basic idea consists of following the existing rays from the scene arriving on the virtual screen. For this reason, the most appropriate name for this method would be *reverse ray tracing*.

Ray tracing is appropriate for modeling specular reflection (and transmission) phenomena, which are dependents on the virtual camera. In this method, the illumination integral is calculated by probabilistic sampling, using Monte Carlo integration. In this section we will see that, in the case of perfect specular surfaces, the integration is not necessary.

16.2.1   Photon Transport

To solve the illumination equation by the ray tracing method, we calculate the photon transport in the scene using the geometric optics model. The goal is to follow the path of those particles carrying radiant energy.

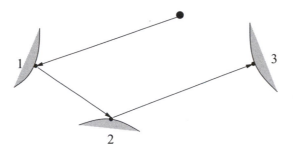

Figure 16.5. Ray path.

We will concentrate on a particle p. The path of this particle in the scene corresponds to a series of states $\{s_0, s_1, \ldots s_n\}$, where we associate to each state, at a stage t of the simulation, attributes of p, such as its position, direction, and energy.

A particle has an existence interval, or life span. This interval is determined by events associated with p: its creation in the initial state s_0 and its extinction in the final state s_n. The illumination equation describes the transport of radiant energy, which is equivalent to the propagation of photons (light particles) in the environment. Therefore, in the context of ray tracing, it is convenient to formulate the problem through an stochastic transport equation describing the change of state of these particles:

$$\ell(t) = g(t) + \int k(s \to t)\ell(s)ds. \qquad (16.10)$$

In this equation, ℓ, g, and k are interpreted as probability distributions. More precisely, $\ell(s_i)$ is the probable number of particles *existent* in the state s_i; $g(s_i)$ is the probable number of particles *created* in the state s_i; and $k(s_i \to s_j)$ is the probability a particle will pass from the state s_i to the state s_j.

We want to calculate the illumination function on the surfaces of the scene. Therefore, it is convenient to associate the states of the particles with events related to decomposition of the surfaces $M = \cup M_i$. We therefore say that a particle is in the state s_i when its path arrives at the surface M_i (see Figure 16.5).

We want to estimate ℓ, given g and k in Equation (16.10). To do so we will use Monte Carlo methods to calculate the value of the integral.

Notice we can follow the history of the particles moving forward or retreating along a path. In the viewing context, it is convenient to begin with particles on the image plane and to register the path traced from their creation (when they are emitted by the light sources) until that point.

Leaving state t_n and returning in the history of the particle, we have

$$\ell(t_n) \approx g(t_n) + \int k(s \to t_n)\ell(s)ds.$$

We know $g(t_n)$, and we need to estimate the value of the integral

$$\int k_n(s)\ell(s)ds,$$

where $k_n(s)$ indicates the probability of a particle arriving at state t_n coming from a previous state s.

Using the Monte Carlo method we can estimate $\ell(t_{n-1})$, performing a random sampling:

$$\ell(t_n) \approx g(t_n) + \int k_n(s)\ell(s)ds$$
$$= g(t_n) + \ell(t_{n-1})$$
$$= g(t_n) + g(t_{n-1}) + \int k(t_{n-1} \to r)\ell(r)dr.$$

Continuing the process we obtain an approximate estimate of the probability distribution $\ell(t_n)$:

$$\ell(t_n) \approx g(t_n) + g(t_{n-1}) + \dots.$$

Notice this result is according to the methodology of calculating the illumination equation developed in the previous section.

The stochastic transport equation has the same structure as the radiance equation:

$$L(r, \omega^o) = L_E(r, \omega^o) + \int_\Theta k(r, \omega \to \omega^o)L(s, \omega)\cos\theta_r \ d\omega.$$

To solve this equation using a probabilistic approach, we use two techniques, allowing us to efficiently estimate the value of the integral by the Monte Carlo method:

- □ **Stratification.** Decomposition of the illumination hemisphere $\Theta = \cup \ \Pi_m$ in *strata*

$$D_m = \{\omega; \omega \in \Pi_m\}$$

  so that the function $L(s, \omega)$ for $\omega \in \Pi_m$ presents small variation.

- □ **Importance sampling.** Sampling of $L(s, \omega)$ in each stratum to select more representative samples. This is done through the *importance function*:

$$g_m : R^3 \times S^2 \to [0, 1].$$

By incorporating these two techniques into the radiance equation, we obtain

$$L(r, \omega^o) = L_E(r, \omega^o) + \sum_{m=1}^{M} \int_{D_m} k(r, \omega \to \omega^o)\frac{L(s, \omega)\cos\theta_r}{g_m(r, \omega)}g_m(r, \omega) \ d\omega,$$

where each stratum D_i is given by a set of directions $\omega \in \Pi_i$. Notice we divided L by g_m, and later we multiplied the result by g_m to avoid introducing distortions into the equation.

We obtain the points of the visible surfaces in each stratum using the visibility function $N(r, \omega) = r - \nu(r, \omega) \, \omega$. In this way, we determine the contribution of each stratum D_i

$$\int_{D_i} = \int_{\omega \in \Pi_i} k(r, \omega \to \omega^o) L(N(r, \omega), \omega) \cos \theta d\omega.$$

In short, the general schema of the ray tracing method for calculating the illumination consists of the following steps:

1. Choose the strata $\{D_m\}$, with $\Theta = \cup \Pi_m$,

2. Determine the visibility $N(s, \omega)$ of the strata D_m,

3. Estimate the illumination integral in each stratum D_m.

The stratification and the importance function should be based on local information about the surface and global information about the scene. A good choice is to divide the information into two strata:

□ **Direct illumination.** In this case, the stratum is calculated based on knowledge of the light sources;

□ **Indirect illumination.** In this case the stratum is calculated based on the bidirectional reflectance function of the surface.

The classic ray tracing algorithm uses two assumptions that simplify the problem: point light sources and perfect specular surfaces. In this way, the reflectance function corresponds to a Dirac delta distribution [Strichartz 94], and the stratification is reduced to a discrete set of directions. The illumination equation is then reduced to

$$L(r, \omega) = \sum_{\omega^l} \left[k_l(r, \omega \to \omega^l) L_E(s_l, \omega^l) \right] + \left[k_r L(s_r, \omega^r) + k_t L(s_t, \omega^t) \right], \quad (16.11)$$

where $s_i = N(r, \omega^i) = r - \nu(r, \omega^i) \, \omega^i$ for $i = l, s, t$, given by the rays ω_l along the direction of the light sources, and by the the rays reflected ω^r and refracted ω^t. Notice the first part of the equation corresponds to the direct illumination of the light sources, while the second part corresponds to the specular indirect illumination. The second part is recursively calculated.

Next we will show the implementation of this algorithm.

The routine `ray_shade` calculates the illumination using ray tracing.

275   ⟨*ray shade* 275⟩ ≡
```
Color ray_shade(int level, Real w, Ray v, RContext *rc, Object *ol)
{
  Inode *i = ray_intersect(ol, v);
  if (i != NULL) { Light *l; Real wf;
```

```
        Material *m = i->m;
        Vector3 p = ray_point(v, i->t) ;
        Cone  recv = cone_make(p, i->n, PIOVER2);
        Color c = c_mult(m->c, c_scale(m->ka, ambient(rc)));

        for (l = rc->l; l != NULL; l = l->next)
          if ((*l->transport)(l, recv, rc) && (wf = shadow(l, p, ol))
                > RAY_WF_MIN)
            c = c_add(c, c_mult(m->c,
                      c_scale(wf * m->kd * v3_dot(l->outdir,i->n), l->outcol)));

        if (level++ < MAX_RAY_LEVEL) {
          if ((wf = w * m->ks) > RAY_WF_MIN) {
            Ray r = ray_make(p, reflect_dir(v.d, i->n));
            c = c_add(c, c_mult(m->s,
                        c_scale(m->ks, ray_shade(level, wf, r, rc, ol))));
          }
          if ((wf = w * m->kt) > RAY_WF_MIN) {
            Ray t = ray_make(p, refract_dir(v.d, i->n, (i->enter)?
                                            1/m->ir: m->ir));
            if (v3_sqrnorm(t.d) > 0) {
              c = c_add(c, c_mult(m->s,
                          c_scale(m->kt, ray_shade(level, wf, t, rc, ol))));
            }
          }
        }
        inode_free(i);
        return c;
      } else {
        return BG_COLOR;
      }
    }
```

Defines:
  ray_shade, never used.
Uses BG_COLOR, MAX_RAY_LEVEL, RAY_WF_MIN, reflect_dir 276, refract_dir 277a,
  and shadow 277b.

The recursive process halts when the ray path has more than MAX_RAY_LEVEL states, or when the contribution estimate wf of the rest of the path becomes smaller than MAX_WF_MIN.

The routine reflect_dir calculates the direction of the reflected ray.

276 ⟨*reflect dir* 276⟩≡

```
    Vector3 reflect_dir(Vector3 d, Vector3 n)
    {
      return v3_add(d, v3_scale(-2 * v3_dot(n, d), n));
    }
```

Defines:
  reflect_dir, used in chunk 275.

The routine `refract_dir` calculates the direction of the transmitted ray, using Snell's law.

277a   ⟨*refract dir* 277a⟩≡

```
Vector3 refract_dir(Vector3 d, Vector3 n, Real eta)
{
  Real c1, c2;

  if ((c1 = v3_dot(d, n)) < 0)
    c1 = -c1;
  else
    n = v3_scale(-1.0, n);

  if ((c2 = 1 - SQR(eta) * (1 - SQR(c1))) < 0)
    return v3_make(0,0,0);
  else
    return v3_add(v3_scale(eta, d), v3_scale(eta*c1 - sqrt(c2), n));
}
```

Defines:
  refract_dir, used in chunk 275.

The routine `shadow` determines whether the ray along the direction of the light source is in a shadow region.

277b   ⟨*shadow* 277b⟩≡

```
Real shadow(Light *l, Vector3 p, Object *ol)
{
  Real t, kt; Inode *i; Vector3 d;

  if (l->type != LIGHT_POINT)
    return 1.0;
  if ((i = ray_intersect(ol, ray_make(p, d))) == NULL)
    return 1.0;
  t = i->t; kt = i->m->kt; inode_free(i);

  if (t > RAY_EPS && t < 1)
    return 0.0;
  else
    return 1.0;
}
```

Defines:
  shadow, used in chunk 275.

Figure 16.6 illustrates the schema used in the ray tracing algorithm.

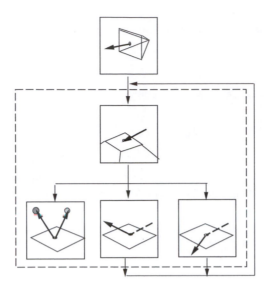

Figure 16.6. Schema of the ray tracing algorithm.

16.3   The Radiosity Method

The radiosity method provides a solution for calculating global illumination based on a discretization of the surfaces of the scene. The basic idea consists of decomposing the surfaces in polygonal elements and calculating the exchange of energy among all those elements. For this reason, the radiosity method is particularly suitable for modeling interactions of diffuse reflection, which are independent of the virtual camera.

In radiosity, the illumination integral is calculated using finite elements with the Galerkin method. We start from Equation (16.8), describing the radiance $L(r, \omega^o)$ propagated from a point r along the direction ω^o, as a function of the emitted and incident radiant energies in that point:

$$L(r, \omega^o) = L_E(r, \omega^o) + \int_{\Theta_i} k(r, \omega \to \omega^o) L(s, \omega) \cos \theta_r \; d\omega. \qquad (16.12)$$

We determine the energy transport arriving at r in direction ω using the visibility function ν such that $s = r + \nu(r, s)\omega$.

When $s \in dS$ is on a distant surface, the solid angle $d\omega$ can be written in the following way:

$$d\omega = \frac{dS \cos \theta_s}{\|r - s\|^2}, \qquad (16.13)$$

where θ_s is the angle between the normal to dS and the vector $(r - s)$.

To place this expression in the illumination equation, we have to guarantee that the integration will be performed only for the points on the visible surfaces. So we define the

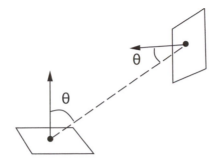

Figure 16.7. Geometry of point-to-point transport.

visibility function test:

$$V(r,s) = \begin{cases} 1 & \text{if } s = r - \nu(r, s - r)(s - r); \\ 0 & \text{otherwise.} \end{cases} \quad (16.14)$$

Substituting the expression for the solid angle in the equation and introducing the visibility function, we can change the integration domain of solid angles in the illumination hemisphere by areas on the visible surfaces. In this way, we have

$$L(r, \omega^o) = L_E(r, \omega^o) + \int_M k(r, \omega \to \omega^o) L(s, \omega) G(r, s) \, d\omega, \quad (16.15)$$

where the function

$$G(r, s) = \frac{\cos \theta_s \cos \theta_r}{\|r - s\|^2} V(r, s) \quad (16.16)$$

depends only on the geometry (see Figure 16.7).

The discretization method consists of dividing the surfaces by polygonal patches $M_i = \cup m_k$ (finite elements) and defining a basis of functions $\{b_j\}_{j \in J}$ that generates an approximation space on the surfaces of the scene. The projection of the solution $L(r, \omega)$ in that space can be written as a linear combination of the functions of the basis

$$\widehat{L}(r, \omega) = \sum_j L_j b_j(r, \omega). \quad (16.17)$$

Calculating the projection of the equation in that space of functions, we have

$$\langle \widehat{L}, \, b_i \rangle = \langle L_E, \, b_i \rangle + \left\langle \int_M k(r, \omega) G(r, s) \widehat{L}, \, b_i \right\rangle. \quad (16.18)$$

Substituting the expression of $\widehat{L}$ in the equation, we have

$$\left\langle \sum_j L_j b_j, \, b_i \right\rangle = \langle L_E, \, b_i \rangle + \left\langle \int_M k(r, \omega) G(r, s) \sum_j L_j b_j, \, b_i \right\rangle. \quad (16.19)$$

Rearranging the terms in L_j and removing the sum of the internal product,

$$\langle L_E,\ b_i \rangle = \left\langle \sum_j L_j b_j,\ b_i \right\rangle - \left\langle \int_M k(r,\omega)G(r,s)\sum_j L_j b_j,\ b_i \right\rangle,$$

$$\langle L_E,\ b_i \rangle = \sum_j L_j \left[\langle b_j,\ b_i \rangle - \left\langle \int_M k(r,\omega)G(r,s)b_j,\ b_i \right\rangle \right].$$

Notice we can write the above expression in matrix form $L_E = KL$.

The classic radiosity method makes the following assumptions to simplify the problem:

1. Surfaces are opaque: there is no propagation by transmission.

2. There is Lambertian reflectance, meaning we have perfectly diffuse surfaces.

3. Radiance and irradiance are constant in each element.

Diffuse reflection implies that the bidirectional reflectance function $k(s,\omega \to \omega')$ is constant in all directions and, therefore, does not depend on ω. Consequently we can replace it with a function $\rho(s)$ that is outside the integral:

$$\int_M k(s,\omega \to \omega')L(s,\omega)G(r,s)\ d\omega = \rho(s)\int_M L(s,\omega)G(r,s)\ d\omega. \tag{16.20}$$

In this way we can also make the following substitution to transform radiance into radiosity: $L\pi = B$.

The fact that we consider a piecewise constant illumination function implies that we adopt the Haar basis $\{b_i\}$ for the approximating space of the finite elements.

$$b_i(r) = \begin{cases} 1 & r \in M_i \\ 0 & \text{otherwise.} \end{cases} \tag{16.21}$$

As the functions of the Haar basis are disjunct, we have

$$\langle b_i,\ b_j \rangle = \delta_{ij} A_i. \tag{16.22}$$

Combining the above data, the illumination integral expressed in the Haar basis becomes

$$\left\langle \int_M k(r,\omega)G(r,s)b_j,\ b_i \right\rangle = \frac{\rho_i}{\pi} \int_{M_i} \int_{M_k} G(i,k)\ dk di = \rho_i A_i F_{i,k}, \tag{16.23}$$

where

$$F_{i,k} = \frac{1}{A_i} \int_{M_i} \int_{M_k} \frac{\cos\theta_i \cos\theta_k}{\pi \|i - k\|^2} V(i,k) dk di \tag{16.24}$$

is the *form factor*, which represents the percentage of radiant energy leaving element i and arriving at element j.

Using the fact that

$$\langle L_E, b_i \rangle = \int_{M_i} L_E(s)ds = E_i A_i,$$

and substituting $L \mapsto \frac{B}{\pi}$ into the equation, we have

$$E_i A_i = \sum_k B_k \left(\delta_{ik} A_i - \rho_i A_i F_{i,k} \right)$$

$$E_i A_i = B_i A_i - \rho_i \sum_k B_i A_i F_{i,k};$$

or, dividing both members by A_i and rearranging the terms,

$$B_i = E_i + \rho_i \sum_k B_i F_{i,k}. \tag{16.25}$$

This equation is called the *classic radiosity equation*. In reality, we have a system of n equations for the radiosities B of n elements of the discretization. In matrix form,

$$B = E + FB$$
$$(I - F)B = E,$$

or

$$\begin{pmatrix} 1 - \rho_1 F_{11} & \cdots & -\rho_1 F_{1n} \\ -\rho_2 F_{21} & \cdots & -\rho_2 F_{2n} \\ \vdots & & \\ -\rho_n F_{n1} & \cdots & 1 - \rho_n F_{nn} \end{pmatrix} \begin{pmatrix} B_1 \\ B_2 \\ \vdots \\ B_n \end{pmatrix} = \begin{pmatrix} E_1 \\ E_2 \\ \vdots \\ E_n \end{pmatrix},$$

as the discretization of the surfaces in finite elements is done by a polygonal mesh, we have that $F_{ii} = 0$ and the diagonal of the matrix is equal to 1.

We want to find the numerical solution of the system given by

$$B = (I - F)^{-1} E.$$

When the linear system is very large, inverting the matrix becomes impractical. In this case, the best solution is to use iterative methods based on successive refinements. In this type of method, given a linear system $Mx = y$, we generate a series of approximated solutions x^k that converge to the solution x when $k \to \infty$.

The approximation error in the stage k is given by

$$e^k = x - x^k, \tag{16.26}$$

and the residue r^k caused by the approximation $Mx^k = y + r^k$ is

$$r^k = y - Mx^k. \tag{16.27}$$

We want to minimize the residue r^k in each stage k. To express the residue in terms of the error, we subtract the equality $y - Mx = 0$ of r^k

$$
\begin{aligned}
r^k &= (y - Mx^k) - (y - Mx) \\
&= M(x - x^k) \\
&= Me^k.
\end{aligned}
$$

The basic idea of the iterative methods is to refine the approximation x^k, producing a better approximation x^{k+1}. We will describe the Southwell method here, which consists of seeking a transformation that makes the residue r_i^{k+1} of one of the elements x_i^{k+1} in the next stage equal to zero. In this way, we select the element x^i with the residue of larger magnitude and we calculate x_i^{k+1}, satisfying

$$
r_i^{k+1} = 0,
$$

$$
y_i + \sum_j M_{ij} x_j^{k+1} = 0.
$$

As only the component i of the vector x is altered, we have $x_j^{k+1} = x_j^k$ for $j \neq i$. The new value of x_i^{k+1} then is

$$
\begin{aligned}
x_i^{k+1} &= \frac{1}{M_{ii}} \left(y_i - \sum_{i \neq j} M_{ij} x_j^k \right) \\
&= x_i^k + \frac{r_i^k}{M_{ii}} \\
&= x_i^k + \Delta x_i^k.
\end{aligned}
$$

The new residue can be calculated

$$
\begin{aligned}
r^{k+1} &= y - Mx^{k+1} \\
&= y - M(x^k + \Delta x^k) \\
&= y - Mx^k - M\Delta x^k \\
&= r^k - M\Delta x^k.
\end{aligned}
$$

However, the vector $\Delta x^k = x^{k+1} - x^k$ has all the components equal to zero, except for Δx_i^k. Then

$$
r_j^{k+1} = r_j^k - \frac{K_{ji}}{K_{ii}} r_i^k. \tag{16.28}
$$

Notice that to update the vector of residues, we only used a column of the matrix. This is indicated below:

$$
\begin{pmatrix} x \\ x \\ x \\ x \end{pmatrix} = \begin{pmatrix} x \\ x \\ x \\ x \end{pmatrix} + \begin{pmatrix} \cdot \\ x \\ \cdot \\ \cdot \end{pmatrix} \begin{pmatrix} \cdot & x & \cdot & \cdot \\ \cdot & x & \cdot & \cdot \\ \cdot & x & \cdot & \cdot \\ \cdot & x & \cdot & \cdot \end{pmatrix}.
$$

The algorithm of progressive radiosity uses a variant of the Southwell method that results in good approximations to the solution with few iterations.

In the context of the illumination problem, we can interpret the residue R_i^k as being the radiant energy of the element M_i in the stage k that still was not spread in the scene.

With this physical interpretation, we can see that the Southwell method consists of updating the nondistributed radiant energy of an element M_i by all the the other elements M_j with $j \neq i$. On the other hand, these elements will spread the energy received at a subsequent stage.

In this case, $M = (I - F)$. We know that $M_{ii} = 1$ and that $M_{ij} = -\rho_j F_{ij}$. We therefore have the following rule for updating the vector of residues:

$$
R_j^{k+1} = R_j^k + (\rho_j F_{ij}) R_i^k,
$$

and $R_i^{k+1} = 0$. In progressive radiosity, we also update the vector of radiosities of the elements B_j, for $j \neq i$:

$$
B_j^{k+1} = B_j^k + (\rho_j F_{ij}) R_i^k.
$$

The routine `radiosity_prog` implements the progressive radiosity algorithm.

283   ⟨radiosity prog 283⟩≡
```
Color *radiosity_prog(int n, Poly **p, Color *e, Color *rho)
{
  int src, rcv, iter = 0;
  Real ff, mts, *a = NEWTARRAY(n, Real);
  Color d, *dm = NEWTARRAY(n, Color);
  Color ma, *m = NEWTARRAY(n, Color);

  initialize(n, m, dm, a, p, e);
  while (iter-- < max_iter) {
    src = select_shooter(n, dm, a);
    if (converged(src, dm))
      break;
    for (rcv = 0; rcv < n; rcv++) {
      if (rcv == src|| (ff = formfactor(src, rcv, n, p, a)) < REL_EPS)
        continue;
      d = c_scale(ff, c_mult(rho[rcv], dm[src]));

      m[rcv] = c_add(m[rcv], d);
```

```
        dm[rcv] = c_add(dm[rcv], d);
      }
      dm[src] = c_make(0,0,0);
    }
    ma = ambient_rad(n, dm, a);
    for (rcv = 0; rcv < n; rcv++)
      m[rcv] = c_add(m[rcv], ma);
    efree(a), efree(dm);
    return m;
  }
```

Defines:
  radiosity_prog, never used.
Uses ambient_rad 286, converged 285c, formfactor 285a, initialize 284a, max_iter,
  and select_shooter 284b.

The routine `initialize` performs the attribution of the initial values.

284a   ⟨*init radiosity* 284a⟩≡

```
    static void initialize(int n, Color *m, Color *dm, Real * a, Poly **p,
                           Color *e)
    {
      int i;
      for (i = 0; i < n; i++) {
        a[i] = poly3_area(p[i]);
        m[i] = dm[i] = e[i];
      }
    }
```

Defines:
  initialize, used in chunk 283.

The routine `select_shooter` chooses the element with larger nondistributed radiosity.

284b   ⟨*select shooter* 284b⟩≡

```
    static int select_shooter(int n, Color *dm, Real *a)
    {
      Real m, mmax; int i, imax;

      for (i = 0; i < n; i++) {
        m = c_sqrnorm(c_scale(a[i], dm[i]));
        if (i == 0|| m > mmax) {
          mmax = m; imax = i;
        }
      }
      return   imax;
    }
```

Defines:
  select_shooter, used in chunk 283.

The routine formfactor calculates the form factor F_{ij}.

285a   ⟨*form factor* 285a⟩≡

```
static Real formfactor(int i, int j, int n, Poly **p, Real *a)
{
  Real r2, ci, cj; Vector3 vi, vj, vji, d;
  vi = poly_centr(p[i]);
  vj = poly_centr(p[j]);
  vji = v3_sub(vi, vj);
  if ((r2 = v3_sqrnorm(vji)) < REL_EPS)
    return 0;
  d = v3_scale(1.0/sqrt(r2), vji);
  if ((cj =  v3_dot(poly_normal(p[j]), d)) < REL_EPS)
    return 0;
  if ((ci = -v3_dot(poly_normal(p[i]), d)) < REL_EPS)
    return 0;
  if (vis_flag  && visible(n, p, vj, vji) < REL_EPS)
    return 0;
  return a[i] * ((cj * ci) / (PI * r2 + a[i]));
}
```

Defines:
  formfactor, used in chunk 283.
Uses vis_flag and visible 285b.

The routine visible determines the visibility between two elements i, j.

285b   ⟨*visible* 285b⟩≡

```
static Real visible(int n, Poly **p, Vector3 v, Vector3 d)
{
  Ray r = ray_make(v, d);

  while (n--) {
    Real t = poly3_ray_inter(p[n], poly3_plane(p[n]), r);
    if (t > REL_EPS && t < 1)
      return 0.0;
  }
  return 1.0;
}
```

Defines:
  visible, used in chunk 285a.

The routine converged tests the convergence of the solution.

285c   ⟨*converged* 285c⟩≡

```
static int converged(int i, Color *dm)
{
  return (c_sqrnorm(dm[i]) < dm_eps);
}
```

Defines:
  converged, used in chunk 283.
Uses dm_eps.

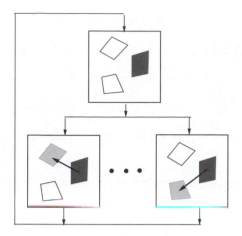

Figure 16.8. Progressive radiosity.

The routine `ambient_rad` calculates the ambient radiosity.

286   ⟨*ambient rad* 286⟩≡
```
static Color ambient_rad(int n, Color *dm, Real *a)
{
  int i; Real aa = 0;
  Color ma = c_make(0,0,0);
  for (i = 0; i < n; i++) {
    ma = c_add(ma, c_scale(a[i], dm[i]));
    aa += a[i];
  }
  return c_scale(1.0/aa, ma);
}
```
Defines:
   `ambient_rad`, used in chunk 283.

Figure 16.8 shows the processing schema of the progressive radiosity algorithm.

16.4 Comments and References

Figure 16.9 shows a scene calculated using ray tracing. Figure 16.10 shows the display screen of the program calculating illumination using radiosity.

The API of the GLOBAL library is made up of the routines below:

```
Color ray_shade(int level, Ray v, Inode *i, RContext *rc);
Ray ray_reflect(Ray r, Inode *i);
Ray ray_refract(Ray r, Inode *i);
```

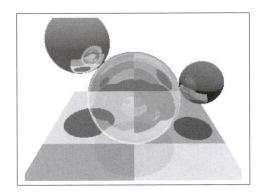

Figure 16.9. Ray tracing. (See Plate V.)

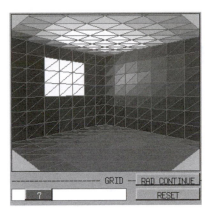

Figure 16.10. Radiosity. (See Plate VI.)

```
Inode *ray_intersect(Ray r, RContext *rc);

Color *progress_rad(int n, Poly **p, Color *e, Color *rho, Real eps);

void initialize(int n, Color *m, Color *dm, Real * a, Poly **p, Color *e);
int converged(int n, Color *dm, Real *a, Real eps);
int select_shooter(int n, Color *dm, Real *a);
Real formfactor(int i, int j, int n, Poly **p, Real *a);
Real visible(int n, Poly **p, Vector3 v, Vector3 d);
Color ambient_rad(int n, Color *dm, Real *a);
```

Exercises

1. Create a simple scene composed of two spheres and a light source. Write a program to calculate the illumination using ray tracing.

2. Create a simple scene consisting of a closed box. Associate a light source to a region of one of the box's walls. Write a program to calculate the illumination using radiosity.

17 | Mapping Techniques

In this chapter we will study mapping techniques, which specify the attribute functions of graphics objects.

17.1 Foundations

Mappings are a powerful technique for specifying attribute functions. In this section, we will see that all existng mapping techniques are part of a single mathematical model. That model can be used to study several texture applications in the viewing process.

17.1.1 The Concept of Mapping

A *texture* is an application $t : U \subset \mathbb{R}^m \to \mathbb{R}^k$, of a subset U of the Euclidean space $\mathbb{R}^m$, to the Euclidean space $\mathbb{R}^k$. The name "texture" comes from the particular case in which $m = 2$, $k = 3$, and the Euclidean space $\mathbb{R}^k$ is identified with a color space. In this case, t represents a digital image.

Given a function $g : V \to U \subset \mathbb{R}^m$, of a subset $V \subset \mathbb{R}^n$ of the object space, we call *texture mapping* the composition of applications

$$\tau = g \circ t : V \to \mathbb{R}^k$$

that associates, to each point (x, y, z) of the object space, an element $t(g(x, y, z))$ of the vector space $\mathbb{R}^k$.

This schema is represented in the diagram below.

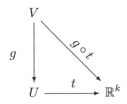

Texture mapping involves the following spaces:

□ **Object space.** $V \subset \mathbb{R}^n$.

□ **Texture space.** $U \subset \mathbb{R}^m$.

□ **Attribute space.** $\mathbb{R}^k$.

These spaces are related to the

□ **Texture function.** $t : U \subset \mathbb{R}^m \to \mathbb{R}^k$,

□ **Mapping function.** $g : V \subset \mathbb{R}^n \to U$.

The texture function establishes the association between the geometric texture domain and its attribute values. The mapping function establishes the correspondence between points of the object and points of the texture domain.

17.1.2 Types of Mapping

The texture function depends on the dimension m of the texture space $\mathbb{R}^m$ and on the nature of the attribute space $\mathbb{R}^k$. According to the dimension of the texture domain, we have three types of texture mapping:

□ **1D mapping.** When $m = 1$; in this case t is a *color map*,

□ **2D mapping.** When $m = 2$; in this case t is a digital image,

□ **3D mapping.** When $m = 3$; in this case t is called a *solid texture*.

The mapping function depends on the geometric description of the support V of the graphics object and on the dimension of the texture space. There are two basic ways to define the mapping function: the first is based on a *parameterization* associated with the object, and the second is based on some type of *projection*.

The parameterization provides a natural solution when the texture space has dimension 2 and V is a parametric surface. In this case, we have the surface equation $f : \mathbb{R}^2 \to V$, which is invertible, and whose inverse f^{-1} can be taken as being the mapping function g.

Projection is the recommended solution when the texture space has dimension 2, and V is an implicit surface. In this case, we are looking for a projection that would naturally adapt to the shape of the object. The spherical and cylindrical projections are mostly used for this purpose.

When the texture space has dimension 3, we can use as mapping function a constraint of the $\mathbb{R}^3$ to the points of $U \subset \mathbb{R}^3$. This solution serves equally well for surfaces defined in parametric and implicit ways.

17.1.3   Mapping Applications

Applications of texture mapping are closely related to the nature of the attributes. The most important applications are

- **Appearance.** This is a property of the surface of the object. For instance, color, reflectance, etc.

- **Geometry.** This is used to model the geometry of the object. For instance, specifying the roughness on the surface.

- **Illumination.** This represents data from the illumination calculation. In this case, the mapping works as a cache engine for the viewing algorithms. Examples of such use include mapping reflections and shadows.

In the next sections we will discuss the implementation of these mapping applications.

17.2   Texture Function

In this section we will present the implementation of 2D texture functions. We will describe a generic representation and two types of definition: by samples and procedural.

17.2.1   Representation

A generic 2D texture is represented by the data structure `TextureSrc`, which includes an access function and the texture data.

291a   ⟨*texture source* 291a⟩≡
```
typedef struct TextureSrc {
  Color (*texfunc)();
  void *texdata;
} TextureSrc;
```
Defines:
  TextureSrc, used in chunks 291b, 292b, 294b, 297b, and 299.

A texture can be described by an image (type `TEX_IMG`) or by a function (type `TEX_FUNC`). The routine `parse_texsource` performs the encapsulation of a generic texture in the scene description language.

291b   ⟨*parse texture source* 291b⟩≡
```
TextureSrc *parse_texsource(Pval *pl)
{
  Pval *p = pl;
  while (p != NULL) {
    if (p->name && strcmp(p->name,"tex_src") == 0) {
      if (p->val.type == TEX_IMG|| p->val.type == TEX_FUNC)
        return (TextureSrc *)(p->val.u.v);
```

```
      }
      p = p->next;
    }
    return default_tsrc();
  }
```

Defines:
  parse_texsource, used in chunks 295b and 301.
Uses default_tsrc and TextureSrc 291a.

17.2.2   Definition by Image

When the texture is defined by an image, the field texdata of the structure TextureSrc is of type Image. The access function is the routine image_texture.

292a ⟨*image texture* 292a⟩≡

```
      Color image_texture(Image *i, Vector3 t)
      {
        Color c00, c01, c10, c11, c;
        Real ru, rv, tu, tv; int u, v;
        ru = t.x * i->w;
        rv = (1 - t.y) * i->h;
        u = floor(ru); tu = ru - u;
        v = floor(rv); tv = rv - v;
        c00 = img_getc(i, u, v);
        c01 = img_getc(i, u, v+1);
        c10 = img_getc(i, u+1, v);
        c11 = img_getc(i, u+1, v+1);
        c = v3_bilerp(tu, tv, c00, c01, tv, c10, c11);
        return c_scale(1./255.);
      }
```

Defines:
  image_texture, used in chunk 292b.

The routine imagemap_parse implements a texture map defined by an image stored in the raster format.

292b ⟨*parse image map* 292b⟩≡

```
      Val imagemap_parse(int pass, Pval *pl)
      {
        Val v;
        if (pass == T_EXEC) {
          Pval *p = pl;
          TextureSrc *i = NEWSTRUCT(TextureSrc);
          i->texfunc = texture_default;
          while (p != NULL) {
            if (p->name && strcmp(p->name,"fname") == 0 && p->val.type == V_STR) {
              i->texfunc = image_texture;
              i->texdata = img_read(p->val.u.v);
```

```
        }
        p = p->next;
      }
      v.type = TEX_IMG;
      v.u.v = i;
    }
    return v;
  }
```

Defines:
  imagemap_parse, never used.
Uses image_texture 292a, texture_default, and TextureSrc 291a.

The routine `imagemap_parse` is associated with the following construction of the scene description language:

```
tex_src = imagemap { fname = "name.ras"}}
```

17.2.3 Procedural Definition

When the texture is defined in a procedural way, the access function is a routine to generate the attribute values using parameters stored in the field `texdata`.

We will give an example of a procedural texture that consists of a chess pattern. The routine `chequer_texture` implements a chess texture defining its parameters in the routine API.

293a   ⟨*chequer texture* 293a⟩≡
```
      Color chequer_texture(ChequerInfo *c,  Vector3 t)
      {
        return chequer(c->xfreq, c->yfreq,  c->fg, c->bg, t);
      }
```

Defines:
  chequer_texture, never used.
Uses chequer 293b and ChequerInfo.

The routine `chequer` calculates the color of chess pattern.

293b   ⟨*chequer* 293b⟩≡
```
      Color chequer(Real freq, Color a, Color b, Vector3 t)
      {
        Real sm = mod(t.x * freq, 1);
        Real tm = mod(t.y * freq, 1);

        return ((sm < .5) ? ((tm < .5)? a : b) : ((tm < .5)? b : a));
      }
```

Defines:
  chequer, used in chunk 293a.
Uses mod 294a.

The routine `mod` is used as an auxiliary function to generate the chess texture.

294a   ⟨*mod* 294a⟩≡
```
Real mod(Real a, Real b)
{
  int n = (int)(a/b);
  a -= n * b;
  if (a < 0)
    a += b;
  return a;
}
```
Defines:
  mod, used in chunks 293b and 294c.

17.3   Texture Mapping

The texture mapping associates, to each point (x, y, z) of the support V of the object, an attribute value $t(g(x, y, z))$ that is used to calculate the illumination function at the given point. The attribute can be the color of the surface, or some other property of the material of the object. When the texture space has dimension 2, we the effect is an elastic wrap that is stretched over the surface of the object.

The structure `TmapInfo` stores the data for the texture mapping.

294b   ⟨*tmap info* 294b⟩≡
```
typedef struct TmapInfo {
  TextureSrc *src;
  int code;
  Color bg;
} TmapInfo;
```
Defines:
  TmapInfo, used in chunks 294c and 295b.
Uses TextureSrc 291a.

The routine `texture_map` performs the texture mapping. The texture application can be of type `TMAP_TILE` or `TMAP_CLAMP`.

294c   ⟨*texture map* 294c⟩≡
```
Color texture_map(void *info, Vector3 t)
{
  TmapInfo *i = info;

  switch (i->code) {
  case TMAP_TILE:
    t.x = mod(t.x, 1); t.y = mod(t.y, 1);
    break;
  case TMAP_CLAMP:
```

```
      if (t.x < 0|| t.x > 1|| t.y < 0|| t.y > 1)
        return i->bg;
      break;
    }
    return (*i->src->texfunc)(i->src->texdata, t);
  }
```

Defines:
 texture_map, used in chunk 295a.
Uses mod 294a, TMAP_CLAMP, TMAP_TILE, and TmapInfo 294b.

The routine `textured_plastic` implements a plastic material whose color is given by a texture.

295a ⟨*textured plastic* 295a⟩≡

```
  Color textured_plastic(RContext *rc)
  {
    Color ct = texture_map(rc->m->tinfo, rc->t);

    return c_add(c_mult(ct, c_add(c_scale(rc->m->ka, ambient(rc)),
                                  c_scale(rc->m->kd, diffuse(rc)))),
                 c_mult(rc->m->s, c_scale(rc->m->ks, specular(rc))));
  }
```

Defines:
 textured_plastic, used in chunk 295b.
Uses texture_map 294c.

The routine `textured_parse` defines a plastic material textured in the scene description language.

295b ⟨*parse textured* 295b⟩≡

```
  Val textured_parse(int pass, Pval *pl)
  {
    Val v;
    if (pass == T_EXEC) {
      Material *m = NEWSTRUCT(Material);
      TmapInfo *ti = NEWSTRUCT(TmapInfo);
      ti->src = parse_texsource(pl);
      ti->bg = pvl_get_v3(pl, "bg_col", C_WHITE);
      ti->code = parse_code(pl);
      m->tinfo = ti; m->luminance = textured_plastic;
      v.u.v = m; v.type = MATERIAL;
    }
    return v;
  }
```

Defines:
 textured_parse, never used.
Uses parse_code 296, parse_texsource 291b, textured_plastic 295a, and TmapInfo 294b.

Figure 17.1. Texture mapping.

The routine `parse_code` interprets the code on the application type for the texture on the surface.

296 ⟨*parse code* 296⟩≡
```
int parse_code(Pval *pl)
{
  Pval *p = pl;
  while (p != NULL) {
    if (p->name && strcmp(p->name,"code") == 0 && p->val.type) {
      if (strcmp(p->val.u.v, "tile") == 0)
        return TMAP_TILE;
      else if (strcmp(p->val.u.v, "clamp") == 0)
        return TMAP_CLAMP;
    }
    p = p->next;
  }
  return TMAP_CLAMP;
}
```
Defines:
  parse_code, used in chunk 295b.
Uses TMAP_CLAMP and TMAP_TILE.

Figure 17.1 shows an example of texture mapping. In one of the spheres, a procedural texture has been applied; in the other, an image.

17.4   Bump Mapping

Roughness mapping, also known as bump mapping, performs a perturbation of the surface normal to simulate irregularities in its geometry.

The routine `rough_surface` implements the material of an irregular surface using bump mapping.

297a ⟨*rough surface* 297a⟩≡
```
Color rough_surface(RContext *rc)
{
    Vector3 d = bump_map(rc->m->tinfo, rc->t, rc->n, rc->du, rc->dv);
    rc->n = v3_unit(v3_add(rc->n, d));
    return matte(rc);
}
```
Defines:
  `rough_surface`, never used.
Uses `bump_map` 297b.

The routine `bump_map` calculates a perturbation to be applied to the normal vector.

297b ⟨*bump map* 297b⟩≡
```
Color bump_map(void *info, Vector3 t, Vector3 n, Vector3 ds, Vector3 dt)
{
    TextureSrc *src = info;
    Real h = 0.0005;
    Real fo = texture_c1((*src->texfunc)(src->texdata, t));
    Real fu = texture_c1((*src->texfunc)(src->texdata,
                                v3_add(t,v3_make(h,0,0))));
    Real fv = texture_c1((*src->texfunc)(src->texdata,
                                v3_add(t,v3_make(0,h,0))));
    Real du = fderiv(fo, fu, h);
    Real dv = fderiv(fo, fv, h);
    Vector3 u = v3_scale(du, v3_cross(n, dt));
    Vector3 v = v3_scale(-dv, v3_cross(n, ds));

    return v3_add(u, v);
}
```
Defines:
  `bump_map`, used in chunk 297a.
Uses `fderiv` 298a, `texture_c1` 297c, and `TextureSrc` 291a.

The routine `texture_c1` returns the first component of a color vector.

297c ⟨*texture c1* 297c⟩≡
```
Real texture_c1(Color c)
{
    return c.x;
}
```
Defines:
  `texture_c1`, used in chunk 297b.

The routine `fderiv` calculates the derivative by finite differences.

Figure 17.2. Bump mapping.

298a   ⟨*fderiv* 298a⟩≡

```
Real fderiv(Real f0, Real f1, Real h)
{
  return (f1 - f0)/h;
}
```

Defines:
  fderiv, used in chunk 297b.

Figure 17.2 shows an example of bump mapping.

17.5   Reflection Mapping

In reflection mapping, the object reflects texture t. The projection p at each point (x, y, z) of the object is determined by the reflection vector at that point. The value $g \circ t$ resulting from the mapping is then used to modulate the color intensity function. Reflection mapping depends on the camera position.

Several techniques are used to perform the mapping in the texture space from the reflection vector. The Blinn and Newell method considers the point where the reflection vector intersects a sphere containing the environment and uses the parametric equations of the sphere to define the projection p. A cube can also be used instead of a sphere.

Reflection mapping is an approximation of the ray tracing method; however, it has the advantage that it simulates diffuse illumination by incorporating reflection mapping in the texture space.

The routine `shiny_surface` implements a material that reflects the environment.

298b   ⟨*shiny surface* 298b⟩≡

```
Color shiny_surface(RContext *rc)
{
  Color ce = environment_map(rc->m->tinfo, reflect_dir(rc->v, rc->n));
```

```
    return c_add(c_scale(rc->m->ka, ambient(rc)),
                 c_scale(rc->m->ks, c_add(ce, specular(rc))));
}
```
Defines:
  shiny_surface, never used.
Uses environment_map 299a.

The routine environment_map implements reflection mapping using polar coordinates.

299a   ⟨environment map 299a⟩≡
```
Color environment_map(void *info, Vector3 r)
{
    TextureSrc *src = info;

    Vector3 t = sph_coord(r);
    t.x = (t.x / PITIMES2) + 0.5; t.y = (t.y / PI) + 0.5;

    return (*src->texfunc)(src->texdata, t);
}
```
Defines:
  environment_map, used in chunk 298b.
Uses sph_coord 299b and TextureSrc 291a.

The routine sph_coord performs the conversion from rectangular to polar coordinates.

299b   ⟨sph coord 299b⟩≡
```
Vector3 sph_coord(Vector3 r)
{
    Real len = v3_norm(r);
    Real theta = atan2(r.y/len, r.x/len);
    Real phi = asin(r.z/len);

    return v3_make(theta, phi, len);
}
```
Defines:
  sph_coord, used in chunk 299a.

Figure 17.3 shows an example of environment (or reflection) mapping.

17.6 Light Sources Mapping

In this section we will give an example of a light source that simulates a slide projector.
    The structure TslideInfo stores the mapping information.

299c   ⟨tslide info 299c⟩≡
```
typedef struct TslideInfo {
    TextureSrc *src;
```

Figure 17.3. Environment (or reflection) mapping.

```
    Vector3 u, v;
  } TslideInfo;
```
Defines:
  TslideInfo, used in chunks 300 and 301.
Uses TextureSrc 291a.

The routine slide_projector implements the light source.

300   ⟨*slide projector* 300⟩≡
```
    int slide_projector(Light *l, Cone recv, RContext *rc)
    {
      Vector3 c, v, t, m;
      TslideInfo *ti = l->tinfo;

      if (point_coupling(recv, cone_make(l->loc, l->dir, l->cutoff)) == FALSE)
        return FALSE;

      v = v3_sub(rc->p, l->loc);
      m = v3_make(v3_dot(v, ti->u), v3_dot(v, ti->v), v3_dot(v, l->dir));
      t = v3_make(m.x / m.z * l->distr, m.y / m.z * l->distr, m.z);
      t.x = t.x * 0.5 + 0.5; t.y = t.y * 0.5 + 0.5;
      c = (*ti->src->texfunc)(ti->src->texdata, t);

      l->outdir = v3_scale(-1, v3_unit(v));
      l->outcol = c_scale(l->intensity, c);
      return TRUE;
    }
```
Defines:
  slide_projector, used in chunk 301.
Uses TslideInfo 299c.

The routine slideproj_parse defines the light source in the scene description language.

Figure 17.4. Mapping light sources by projection.

301 ⟨*parse slide projector* 301⟩≡

```
    Val slideproj_parse(int pass, Pval *pl)
    { Val v;
      if (pass == T_EXEC) {
        Light *l = NEWSTRUCT(Light); TslideInfo *ti = NEWSTRUCT(TslideInfo);
        l->type = LIGHT_DISTANT; l->color = C_WHITE; l->ambient = 0.1;
        l->intensity = pvl_get_num(pl, "intensity", 1);
        l->cutoff = (DTOR * pvl_get_num(pl, "fov", 90))/2.0;
        l->distr = 1/tan(l->cutoff);
        l->loc = pvl_get_v3(pl, "from", v3_make(0,0,-1));
        l->dir = pvl_get_v3(pl, "at", v3_make(0,0,0));
        l->dir = v3_unit(v3_sub(l->dir, l->loc));
        l->transport = slide_projector; l->tinfo = ti;
        ti->src = parse_texsource(pl);
        ti->v = v3_unit(v3_cross(l->dir, v3_cross(l->dir, v3_make(0,1,0))));
        ti->u = v3_cross(l->dir, ti->v);
        v.u.v = l; v.type = LIGHT;
      } return v;
    }
```

Defines:
  slideproj_parse, never used.
Uses parse_texsource 291b, slide_projector 300, and TslideInfo 299c.

Figure 17.4 shows an example of light source mapping by projection.

17.7 Comments and References

The API of the MAP library is composed of the following routines:

```
Val textured_parse(int pass, Pval *pl);
Val imagemap_parse(int pass, Pval *pl);
TextureSrc *parse_texsource(Pval *pl);
```

```
Color textured_plastic(RContext *rc);

Color texture_default();
Color image_texture(Image *i, Vector3 t);

Color texture_map(void *info, Vector3 t);
Color bump_map(void *info, Vector3 t, Vector3 n, Vector3 ds, Vector3 dt);
Color environment_map(void *info, Vector3 r);

Color rough_surface(RContext *rc);
Val rough_parse(int pass, Pval *pl);

Color shiny_surface(RContext *rc);
Val shiny_parse(int pass, Pval *pl);

Real mod(Real a, Real b);
Color chequer(Real freq, Color a, Color b, Vector3 t);

int slide_projector(Light *l, Cone recv, RContext *rc);
Val slideproj_parse(int pass, Pval *pl);
```

18 | Shading

In this chapter we will present the implementation of the shading (coloring) function calculation.

18.1 Shading Function Sampling and Reconstruction

The shading function is defined on the image plane. It is given by the projection of the illumination function on the visible surfaces of the scene. The shading function calculation is a process of *sampling* and *reconstruction*. The sampling consists of evaluating the illumination function at points on the visible surfaces that correspond to pixels in the image. The reconstruction consists of the interpolation of known values of the function at some pixels for other pixels of the image.

First the image is partitioned into regions, allowing us to separate the process: we perform sampling of the shading function for the pixels at the boundary of the regions, and we perform interpolation of the function for the pixels in the interior of each region. The type of partition depends on the geometric description of the scene objects and also on the rasterization method. Notice that interpolation is accomplished by the rasterization routine. In the case of objects described in a parametric way by a polygonal mesh, the image is decomposed into polygonal regions.

18.2 Sampling Methods

Sampling of the shading function can be done by point or area sampling. In this book we will only discuss point sampling. Area sampling is used with *anti-aliasing* methods.

18.2.1 Point Shading

The routine `point_shade` performs the sampling of the shading function at point p.

304a ⟨*point shade* 304a⟩≡
```
Color point_shade(Vector3 p, Vector3 n, Vector3 v, RContext *rc,
                  Material *m)
{
  return (*m->luminance)(rc_set(rc, v3_unit(v3_sub(v, p)), p, n, m));
}
```
Defines:
 point_shade, used in chunks 304b and 306c.
Uses Material 262a, rc_set, and RContext 259b.

18.3   Basic Reconstruction Methods

The reconstruction methods most used for shading include

□ **Bouknight shading.** Piecewise constant,

□ **Gouraud shading.** Linear interpolation of the color,

□ **Phong shading.** Linear interpolation of the normal.

18.3.1   Bouknight Shading

The routine flat_shade samples the shading function at the centroid of a polygon. This calculation is used as the constant color of the polygonal region on the image.

304b ⟨*flat shade* 304b⟩≡
```
Color flat_shade(Poly *p, Vector3 v, RContext *rc, Material *m)
{
  Vector3 c = poly_centr(p);
  Vector3 n = poly_normal(p);
  return point_shade(c, n, v, rc, m);
}
```
Defines:
 flat_shade, never used.
Uses Material 262a, point_shade 304a, and RContext 259b.

18.3.2   Gouraud Method

The structure GouraudData stores the data for the Gouraud shading method.

304c ⟨*gouraud data* 304c⟩≡
```
typedef struct GouraudData {
  Image *img;
  Poly *cols;
} GouraudData;
```
Defines:
 GouraudData, used in chunk 305.

The routine `gouraud_set` initializes the structure `GouraudData`.

305a

⟨*gouraud set* 305a⟩≡
```
void *gouraud_set(GouraudData *g, Poly *c, Image *i)
{
  g->img = i; g->cols = c;
  return (void *)g;
}
```
Defines:
  gouraud_set, never used.
Uses GouraudData 304c.

The routine `gouraud_shade` evaluates the illumination function at each polygon vertex. The color at each vertex is stored in the polygon c. This routine should be used before rasterization. The data calculated by this routine, which is the polygon c, can be stored using the routine `gouraud_set`.

305b

⟨*gouraud shade* 305b⟩≡
```
void gouraud_shade(Poly *c, Poly *p, Poly *n, Vector3 v,
                   RContext *rc, Material *m)
{
  int i;
  for (i = 0; i < p->n; i++)
    c->v[i]=(*m->luminance)(rc_set(rc,v3_unit(v3_sub(v,p->v[i]))),p->v[i],
                            n->v[i],m));
}
```
Defines:
  gouraud_shade, never used.
Uses Material 262a, rc_set, and RContext 259b.

The routine `gouraud_paint` reconstructs the shading function, starting from the colors at the vertices of a polygonal region on the image. This routine uses bilinear interpolation for doing this. Notice that `gouraud_paint` is called by the rasterization routine at each pixel of the polygonal region.

305c

⟨*gouraud paint* 305c⟩≡
```
void gouraud_paint(Vector3 p, int lv, Real lt, int rv, Real rt, Real st
                   , void *data)
{
  GouraudData *d = data;
  Vector3 c = seg_bilerp(d->cols, st, lv, lt, rv, rt);
  img_puti(d->img, p.x, p.y, col_dpymap(c));
}
```
Defines:
  gouraud_paint, never used.
Uses col_dpymap 312 and GouraudData 304c.

18.3.3   Phong Method

The structure PhongData stores the data for the Phong shading method.

306a   ⟨*phong data* 306a⟩≡
```
typedef struct PhongData {
  Poly *pnts;
  Poly *norms;
  Vector3 v;
  RContext *rc;
} PhongData;
```
Defines:
  PhongData, used in chunk 306.
Uses RContext 259b.

The routine phong_set initializes the structure PhongData.

306b   ⟨*phong set* 306b⟩≡
```
void *phong_set(PhongData *d, Poly *p, Poly *n, Vector3 v,
                RContext *rc, Material *m)
{
  d->pnts = p;
  d->norms = n;
  d->v = v;
  d->rc = rc;
  d->rc->m = m;
  return (void *)d;
}
```
Defines:
  phong_set, never used.
Uses Material 262a, PhongData 306a, and RContext 259b.

The routine phong_shadepaint interpolates the normal at the vertices of a polygon and evaluates the illumination function.

306c   ⟨*phong shadepaint* 306c⟩≡
```
void phong_shadepaint(Vector3 p, int n, int lv, Real lt,
                      int rv, Real rt, Real st, void * data)
{
  PhongData *d = data;
  Vector3 pv = seg_bilerp(d->pnts, n, st, lv, lt, rv, rt);
  Vector3 pn = v3_unit(seg_bilerp(d->norms, n, st, lv, lt, rv, rt));
  Color c = point_shade(pv, pn, d->v, d->rc, d->rc->m);
  img_putc(d->rc->img, p.x, p.y, col_dpymap(c));
}
```
Defines:
  phong_shadepaint, never used.
Uses col_dpymap 312, PhongData 306a, and point_shade 304a.

18.4   Reconstruction of Texture Attributes

In the previous sections we presented the Gouraud and Phong methods to reconstruct the shading function. These methods use linear interpolation to reconstruct, at each pixel, the values of attributes associated with the vertices of the scene polygons.

Linear interpolation only produces a correct reconstruction for the camera transformation by orthogonal projection. In the case of the projective camera transformation (perspective projection), the linear interpolation produces incorrect results. Despite this problem, linear interpolation is widely used. This is because the error is not significant, from a perceptual point of view, when the attribute function has little variation, such as in the color and the normal.

However, for attribute functions with high frequencies, such as the texture, the errors are obvious and it is necessary to use projective reconstruction methods, which are discussed next.

18.4.1   Interpolation and Projective Transformation

We will begin by reviewing the concepts related to projective transformations. To map a point $p \in \mathbb{R}^3$ of a scene surface in its projection $s \in \mathbb{R}^2$ on the image plane, we use the projective transformation

$$s = Mp$$

or, in matrix form,

$$\begin{pmatrix} uw \\ vw \\ \vdots \\ w \end{pmatrix} = \begin{pmatrix} e_1 & e_2 & \cdots & e_n \\ f_1 & f_2 & \cdots & f_n \\ \vdots & & & \\ g_1 & g_2 & \cdots & g_n \end{pmatrix} \cdot \begin{pmatrix} x \\ y \\ \vdots \\ 1 \end{pmatrix},$$

where M is the projective transformation matrix, and both p and s are represented in homogeneous coordinates.

The point $p = (x, y, \ldots, 1)$ belongs to the affine hyperplane embedded in the projective space $\mathbb{RP}^3$. To transform the point $s = (uw, vw, \ldots, w)$ in the normalized affine point $\bar{s} = (u, v, \ldots, 1)$, it is necessary to perform the homogeneous division by w. We then have

$$u = \frac{e_1 x + e_2 y + \ldots + e_n}{g_1 x + g_2 y + \ldots + g_n},$$

and similar results for the other coordinates $(, v, \ldots)$.

The inverse transformation from the screen plane to the world space is given by

$$p = M^{-1}s,$$

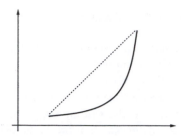

Figure 18.1. Linear (dotted line) and rational (solid line) interpolation.

or

$$\begin{pmatrix} x \\ y \\ \vdots \\ 1 \end{pmatrix} = \begin{pmatrix} a_1 & a_2 & \dots & A \\ b_1 & b_2 & \dots & B \\ & \vdots & & \\ c_1 & c_2 & \dots & C \end{pmatrix} \cdot \begin{pmatrix} uw \\ vw \\ \vdots \\ w \end{pmatrix},$$

where the coordinate x of p can be calculated as

$$x = \frac{(a_1 u + b_1 v + \dots + c_1)w}{(A + B + \dots + C)w} = \frac{a_1 u + b_1 v + \dots + c_1}{A + B + \dots + C},$$

and similarly for the other coordinates.

Notice the attribute values in the world space can be expressed by a reconstruction function that is parameterized by the screen coordinates $s = (u, v, \dots, w)$. For instance, x is given by

$$x(s) = \frac{a_1 u + \dots + c_1}{A + \dots + C}.$$

In other words, this shows that the correct reconstruction function for the projective camera transformation should use linear rational interpolation.

Figure 18.1 shows the difference between linear and rational interpolation.

We saw that the Gouraud and Phong methods use linear interpolation of the attributes, and it has the following structure:

1. Evaluate $x(s_0)$ and $x(s_k)$,

2. Linearly interpolate: $x(s) = (1 - t)x(s_0) + tx(s_k)$.

We know this schema produces wrong results, which are perceptually questionable if $x(s)$ contains high frequencies.

One way to solve this problem is to interpolate the parameter s and calculate the attribute values for each pixel using inverse mapping:

1. Linearly interpolate: $s = s_0, \dots s_k$,

2. Evaluate $x(s) = M^{-1}s$.

This method, although correct, is inefficient because it requires a matrix multiplication by a vector at each pixel.

An efficient solution consists of using rational linear interpolation as the reconstruction function:

1. Calculate $x_w = \frac{x}{w}$ and $d_w = \frac{1}{w}$ in s_0 and s_k,

2. Linearly interpolate both $x_w(s)$ and $d_w(s)$; then obtain $x(s) = \frac{x_w(s)}{d_w(s)}$.

Notice the value of w is already calculated by the direct projective transformation $s = (u \dots w)^T = Mp$.

To prove the result is correct, observe that the interpolated values

$$\frac{x(s)}{w(s)} = a_1 u + \dots + c_1 \quad \text{and} \quad \frac{1}{w(s)} = A + \dots + C$$

are linear expressions.

When the division is performed for each pixel s, we obtain

$$x(s) = \frac{x(s)/w(s)}{1/w(s)} = \frac{a_1 u + \dots + c_1}{A + \dots + C},$$

which is what we were looking for.

18.4.2 Rational Linear Interpolation of Texture

To reconstruct by rational linear interpolation we first separate the homogeneous coordinate w associated with each vertex of the scene polygons. Then all the attributes to be interpolated are divided by w. Finally, those attributes are passed to the rasterization routine that will perform the interpolation and the final division to each pixel.

The routine `poly_wz_hpoly` calculates the coordinate w for each polygon vertex and places the values $1/w$ in an attribute polygon.

309   ⟨*poly wz hpoly* 309⟩≡

```
Poly  *poly_wz_hpoly(Poly *q, Hpoly *s)
{
  Poly *w; int i;
  for (i = 0; i < s->n; i++) {
    q->v[i] = v3_make(s->v[i].x, s->v[i].y, s->v[i].z);
    if (w = q->v->next) {
      Real rw = 1./s->v[i].w;
      w->v[i] = v3_make(rw, rw, rw);
    }
  }
  return q;
}
```

Defines:
  `poly_wz_hpoly`, never used.

The routine `texture_wscale` multiplies all the texture attributes by $1/w$.

310a   ⟨*texture wscale* 310a⟩≡
```
Poly *texture_wscale(Poly *w, Poly *p)
{
  Poly *l; int i;
  for (i = 0; i < w->n; i++)
    for (l = p; l != NULL; l = l->next) {
      l->v[i] = v3_scale(w->v[i].z, l->v[i]);
    }
  return w;
}
```
Defines:
  texture_wscale, never used.

The data structure `TextureData` contains the interpolated attributes `vpar`.

310b   ⟨*texture data* 310b⟩≡
```
typedef struct TextureData {
  Image *img;
  Vector3 eye;
  Poly *vpar;
  RContext *rc;
} TextureData;
```
Defines:
  TextureData, used in chunks 310c and 311.
Uses RContext 259b.

The routine `texture_set` initializes the structure `TextureData`, storing the attributes and other data.

310c   ⟨*texture set* 310c⟩≡
```
void *texture_set(TextureData *d, Poly *param, Vector3 eye,
                  RContext *rc, Light *l, Material *m, Image *i)
{ int n;
  if ((n = plist_lenght(param)) < 1|| n > TEX_MAXPAR)
    fprintf(stderr, "Texture: not enough parameters\n");
  d->img = i;
  d->vpar = param;
  d->eye = eye;
  d->rc = rc;
  d->rc->l = l;
  d->rc->m = m;
  return (void *)d;
}
```
Defines:
  texture_set, never used.
Uses Light 258a, Material 262a, RContext 259b, and TextureData 310b.

The routine `texture_shadepaint` performs the rational linear interpolation and calls the illumination function, which can use the texture coordinates.

311   ⟨*texture shadepaint* 311⟩≡

```
void texture_shadepaint(Vector3 s, int lv, Real lt, int rv, Real rt, Real st,
                        void *data)
{
  Vector3 a[TEX_MAXPAR+1];
  Poly *l; Color c; int i;
  TextureData *d = data;

  a[TEX_W] = seg_bilerp(d->vpar, st, lv, lt, rv, rt);
  for (l = d->vpar->next, i = 1; l != NULL; l = l->next, i++)
    a[i] = v3_scale(1/a[TEX_W].z, seg_bilerp(l, st, lv, lt, rv, rt));
  a[TEX_N] = v3_unit(a[TEX_N]);
  a[TEX_E] = v3_unit(v3_sub(d->eye, a[TEX_P]));
  c = (*d->rc->m->luminance)(rc_tset(d->rc, a[TEX_E], a[TEX_P], a[TEX_N],
                                     a[TEX_T], a[TEX_U] ,a[TEX_V]));
  img_puti(d->img, s.x, s.y, col_dpymap(c));
}
```

Defines:
  `texture_shadepaint`, never used.
Uses `col_dpymap` 312, `rc_tset`, and `TextureData` 310b.

The following attributes are established in this implementation:

```
#define TEX_W 0          // 1/w
#define TEX_T 1          // texture coordinates
#define TEX_P 2          // position on surface
#define TEX_N 3          // normal to P
#define TEX_U 4          // partial derivative df/du
#define TEX_V 5          // partial derivative df/dv
#define TEX_E 6          // vector towards observer
```

18.5 Imaging

Once the shading function is calculated, it is necessary to map the calculated values to the color space of the image. The color representation used for calculating the illumination is given by the structure `Color`. This structure is defined from the structure `Vector3` and incorporates the vector operations. The operation `c_mult` is implemented separately.

```
#define Color Vector3

#define c_add(a, b) v3_add(a,b)
#define c_sub(a, b) v3_sub(a,b)
#define c_scale(a, b) v3_scale(a, b)
#define c_sqrnorm(a) v3_sqrnorm(a)
```

```
Color c_mult(Color a, Color b);
```

We define macros for the construction of basic colors: white , and black .

```
#define C_WHITE v3_make(1,1,1)
#define C_BLACK v3_make(0,0,0)
```

The routine `col_dpymap` transforms a normalized color, with components varying between 0 and 1, to a color where the components vary between 0 and 255.

312   ⟨*color dpy map* 312⟩≡
```
    Pixel col_dpymap(Color c)
    {
      double gain = 255.0;
#ifdef RGB_IMAGE
      return rgb_to_index(c_scale(gain, c));
#else
      return rgb_to_y(c_scale(gain, c));
#endif
    }
```
Defines:
   col_dpymap, used in chunks 305c, 306c, and 311.

18.6   Comments and References

The API of the SHADE library consists of the following routines:

```
Color point_shade(Vector3 p,Vector3 n,Vector3 v, RContext *rc, Light *l,
                  Material *m);
Color flat_shade(Poly *p, Vector3 v, RContext *rc, Light *l, Material *m);
Color gouraud_paint(Vector3 p, int lv, Real lt, int rv, Real rt, Real st,
                    void *data);

void gouraud_shade(Poly *p, Poly *n, Poly *c, Vector3 v, RContext *rc,
                   Light *l, Material *m);

Color phong_shade(Vector3 p, int lv, Real lt, int rv, Real rt, Real st,
                  void *data);

Poly *texture_wscale(Poly *w, Poly *p);
Poly  *poly_wz_hpoly(Poly *q, Poly *w, Hpoly *s);

void *texture_set(TextureData *d, Poly *param, Vector3 eye,
                  RContext *rc, Light *l, Material *m, Image *i);
void texture_shadepaint(Vector3 p, int lv, Real lt, int rv, Real rt, Real st,
                        void *data);

Pixel col_dpymap(Color c);
```

19 3D Graphics Systems

In this final chapter, we will show how to integrate all the computer graphics algorithms studied in the book to build 3D graphic systems. Two subsystems make up a 3D graphics system: modeling and rendering. We now present three 3D system architectures that combine, in the most natural way, the various techniques of these two areas. The systems are as follows:

- **System A.** Generative modeling + rendering with Z-buffer.

- **System B.** CSG modeling + rendering by ray tracing.

- **System C.** Modeling with primitives + rendering with the painter's algorithm.

We next present an implementation of these three systems. In this basic version, the systems operate in noninteractive mode through the command line. The interactive system version will be specified as part of the implementation projects at the end of this chapter.

19.1 System A

System A is based on generative modeling and Z-buffer rendering.

19.1.1 Generative Modeling

The modeling subsystem `rotsurf` generates surfaces of revolution approximated by polygonal meshes. The geometry description is parametric, the representation schema is by boundary decomposition, and the modeling technique used is generative. The modeler receives as input a polygonal curve and produces as output a triangle mesh.

The main program reads the input data and calls the routines `rotsurf` and `trilist_write` to construct the revolution surface and to write the polygonal mesh.

313   ⟨*rotsurf* 313⟩ ≡
```
#define MAXPTS 2048
Vector3 g[MAXPTS];
```

```
main(int argc, char **argv)
{
  int nu, nv = NVPTS;
  Poly *tl;
  if (argc == 2)
    nv = atoi(argv[1]);
  nu = read_curve();

  tl = rotsurf(nu, g, nv);
  trilist_write(tl, stdout);
  exit(0);
}
```

Defines:
  g, used in chunks 314, 321b, and 322b.
  MAXPTS, used in chunk 314.
Uses main 47 187b 315 321b and read_curve 314.

The routine `read_curve` reads the vertices of the polygonal curve, storing them in the global array g.

314   ⟨*read curve* 314⟩≡
```
int read_curve(void)
{
  int  k = 0;
  while (scanf("%lf %lf %lf\n" ,&(g[k].x),&(g[k].y),&(g[k].z)) != EOF)
    if (k++ > MAXPTS)
      break;
  return k;
}
```

Defines:
  read_curve, used in chunk 313.
Uses g 313 and MAXPTS 313.

For example, the command `rotsurf 12 < ln.pts > cyl.scn`, constructs the polygonal mesh of a cylindrical surface with 12 sides.

The input file `ln.pts` specifies a line on the plane $z = 0$.

```
1 1 0
1 -1 0
```

The output file `cyl.out` contains the list of surface polygons (notice that a part of the list was omitted to save space).

```
trilist {
{{0.186494, -1, 0.0722484}, {0.2, -1, 0}, {1, -1, 0}},
{{0.932472, -1, 0.361242},  {0.186494, -1, 0.0722484},  {1, -1, 0}},
{{0.932472, -1, 0.361242},  {1, -1, 0},  {1, 1, 0}},
{{0.932472, 1, 0.361242},  {0.932472, -1, 0.361242},  {1, 1, 0}},
{{0.932472, 1, 0.361242},  {1, 1, 0},  {0.2, 1, 0}},
```

```
{{0.186494, 1, 0.0722484}, {0.932472, 1, 0.361242}, {0.2, 1, 0}},
{{0.147802, -1, 0.134739}, {0.186494, -1, 0.07224}, {0.93247, -1, 0.361}},
{{0.739009, -1, 0.673696}, {0.147802, -1, 0.13473}, {0.93247, -1, 0.361}},
....
{{0.2, 1, 0}, {1, 1, 0}, {0.186494, 1, -0.0722483}}}}
}
```

19.1.2 Rendering with Z-buffer

The renderer `zbuff` uses incremental ratserization, performing the visibility calculation using the Z-buffer. The illumination is based on the diffuse Lambert model with faceted shading.

The global data structures, `s`, `rc`, `mclip`, and `mdpy` store, respectively, the list of scene objects, the rendering context, and the two camera transformations:

```
static Scene *s;
static RContext *rc;
static Matrix4 mclip, mdpy;
```

The main program reads the scene data, initializes the global structures, and processes the list of objects. For each polygon facing the camera, the illumination function is calculated at the centroid of the polygon. Next the polygon is transformed, and clipping and rasterization are applied with the Z-buffer. At the end of the process, the image produced is written to the output file.

315   ⟨zbuff 315⟩≡
```
   int main(int argc, char **argv)
   {
     Object *o;  Poly *p;  Color c;

     init_sdl();
     s = scene_read();
     init_render();
     for (o = s->objs; o != NULL; o = o->next) {
       for (p = o->u.pols; p != NULL; p = p->next) {
         if (is_backfacing(p, v3_sub(poly_centr(p), s->view->center)))
           continue;
         c = flat_shade(p, s->view->center, rc, o->mat);
         if (poly_clip(VIEW_ZMIN(s->view), poly_transform(p, mclip), 0))
           scan_poly(poly_homoxform(p, mdpy), pix_paint, &c);
       }
     }
     img_write(s->img, "stdout", 0);
     exit(0);
   }
```
Defines:
  main, used in chunks 313, 317, and 318c.
Uses **init_render** 316c 319b 322b, **init_sdl** 316b 319c 322a, and **pix_paint** 316a.

The routine `pix_paint` paints the image using the Z-buffer.

316a   ⟨*pix paint* 316a⟩ ≡

```
void pix_paint(Vector3 v,int n,int lv,Real lt,int rv,Real rt,Real st,
               void *c)
{
  if (zbuf_store(v))
     img_putc(s->img, v.x, v.y, col_dpymap(*((Color *)(c))));
}
```

Defines:
    pix_paint, used in chunk 315.

The routine `init_sdl` registers the operators of the scene description language.

316b   ⟨*sdl zbuff* 316b⟩ ≡

```
void init_sdl(void)
{
  lang_defun("scene", scene_parse);
  lang_defun("view", view_parse);
  lang_defun("dist_light", distlight_parse);
  lang_defun("plastic", plastic_parse);
  lang_defun("polyobj", obj_parse);
  lang_defun("trilist", trilist_parse);
}
```

Defines:
    init_sdl, used in chunks 315, 318c, and 321b.

The routine `init_render` initializes the transformation matrices, the Z-buffer, and the rendering context.

316c   ⟨*init zbuff* 316c⟩ ≡

```
void init_render(void)
{
  mclip = m4_m4prod(s->view->C, s->view->V);
  mdpy = m4_m4prod(s->view->S, s->view->P);
  zbuf_init(s->img->w, s->img->h);
  rc_sset(rc = NEWSTRUCT(RContext), s->view, s->lights, s->img);
}
```

Defines:
    init_render, used in chunks 315, 318c, and 321b.

The command `zbuff < cyl.scn > cyl.ras` generates an image from the scene description file below (notice that part of the polygon list was omitted).

316d   ⟨*cyl scn* 316d⟩ ≡

```
scene {
    camera = view { from = {0, 0, -2.5}, up = {0, 1, 0}},
    light = dist_light {direction = {0, 0, -1} },
    object = polyobj { shape = trilist {
```

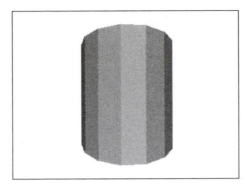

Figure 19.1. Rendering of a polygonal model.

```
       {{0.186494, -1, 0.0722484}, {0.2, -1, 0}, {1, -1, 0}}
   ...

       {{0.2, 1, 0},  {1, 1, 0},  {0.186494, 1, -0.0722483}}}
     }
};
```

Figure 19.1 shows the rendering of a surface: image `cyl.ras`.

19.2   System B

System B is based on CSG modeling and visualization using ray tracing.

19.2.1   CSG Modeling

The modeler `csg` interprets constructive solid models. The primitives are spheres, the representation is a CSG expression, and the modeling technique is language-based.

The main program reads a CSG expression and writes the corresponding construction in the scene description language.

317   ⟨csg 317⟩≡
```c
main(int argc, char **argv)
{
  CsgNode *t;
  if((t = csg_parse()) == NULL)
    exit(-1);
  else
    csg_write(t, stdout);
  exit(0);
}
```
Uses **main** 47 187b 315 321b.

For example, the command csg < s.csg > s.scn translates the CSG expression in s.csg for s.scn. The object in the file s.csg is made up of the difference between two spheres.

318a   ⟨*spheres csg* 318a⟩≡
```
(s{ 0 0 0 1} \ s{ 1 1 -1 1}
```

The file s.scn contains the corresponding commands in the scene description language.

318b   ⟨*sphere scn* 318b⟩≡
```
csgobj = csg_diff {
                     csg_prim{ sphere { center = {0, 0,  0}}},
                     csg_prim{ sphere { center = {1, 1, -1}}} }
```

This program serves as a basis for the development of a more complete modeler with operations for editing CSG objects.

19.2.2 Rendering by Ray Tracing

The renderer rt uses extrinsic rasterization and performs the visibility calculation by ray tracing. The illumination is based on the Phong specular model model, with shading by point sampling.

The main program reads the scene data, initializes the global structures, and generates the image. For each pixel on the image a ray is shot in the scene, and the intersection between the ray with the CSG objects is calculated. The value of the illumination function is determined for the intersection with the closest surface. In the end, the image is written to an output file.

318c   ⟨*rt* 318c⟩≡
```
main(int argc, char **argv)
{
  Color c; int u, v;
  Ray r; Inode *l;
  init_sdl();
  s = scene_read();
  init_render();
  for (v = s->view->sc.ll.y; v < s->view->sc.ur.y; v += 1) {
    for (u = s->view->sc.ll.x; u < s->view->sc.ur.x; u += 1) {
      r = ray_unit(ray_transform(ray_view(u, v), mclip));
      if ((l = ray_intersect(s->objs, r)) != NULL)
        c = point_shade(ray_point(r, l->t), l->n, s->view->center, rc,
                        l->m);
      else
        c = bgcolor;
      inode_free(l);
      img_putc(s->img, u, v, col_dpymap(c));
    }
```

```
        }
        img_write(s->img,"stdout",0);
        exit(0);
    }
```

Uses init_render 316c 319b 322b, init_sdl 316b 319c 322a, main 47 187b 315 321b,
and ray_view 319a.

The routine `ray_view` constructs a ray leaving the virtual camera and passing through
the pixel of coordinates (u, v) on the image plane.

319a   ⟨*ray view* 319a⟩≡

```
    Ray ray_view(int u, int v)
    {
        Vector4 w = v4_m4mult(v4_make(u, v, s->view->sc.ur.z, 1), mdpy);
        return ray_make(v3_v4conv(v4_m4mult(v4_make(0, 0, 1, 0), mdpy)),
                        v3_make(w.x, w.y, w.z));
    }
```

Defines:
    ray_view, used in chunk 318c.

The routine `init_render` initializes the camera transformations.

319b   ⟨*init rt* 319b⟩≡

```
    void init_render(void)
    {
        mclip = m4_m4prod(s->view->Vinv, s->view->Cinv);
        mdpy = m4_m4prod(s->view->Pinv, s->view->Sinv);
        rc_sset(rc = NEWSTRUCT(RContext), s->view, s->lights, s->img);
    }
```

Defines:
    init_render, used in chunks 315, 318c, and 321b.

The routine `init_sdl` registers the operators of the scene description language.

319c   ⟨*sdl rt* 319c⟩≡

```
    void init_sdl(void)
    {
        lang_defun("scene", scene_parse);
        lang_defun("view", view_parse);
        lang_defun("dist_light", distlight_parse);
        lang_defun("plastic", plastic_parse);
        lang_defun("csgobj", obj_parse);
        lang_defun("csg_union", csg_union_parse);
        lang_defun("csg_inter", csg_inter_parse);
        lang_defun("csg_diff", csg_diff_parse);
        lang_defun("csg_prim", csg_prim_parse);
        lang_defun("sphere", sphere_parse);
    }
```

Defines:
    init_sdl, used in chunks 315, 318c, and 321b.

Figure 19.2. Rendering of a CSG scene.

As an example of using the renderer, the command `rt < s.scn > s.ras` generates an image of the CSG scene described in the file `s.scn` below.

320　　⟨*csg2 scn* 320⟩ ≡
```
scene{
    camera = view {
        from = {0, 0, -4}, at = {0, 0, 0}, up = {0,1,0}, fov = 60},
    light = dist_light {direction = {0, 1, -1} },
    object = csgobj{
        material = plastic {  ka = .2, kd = 0.8, ks = 0.0 },
        shape = csg_diff {
                csg_prim{ sphere { center = {0, 0,  0}}},
                csg_prim{ sphere { center = {1, 1, -1}}}
            }
        }
    }
}
```

Figure 19.2 shows the rendering of the scene: image `s.ras`.

19.3   System C

System C is based on modeling by primitives and rendering by the painter's method.

19.3.1   Modeling by Hierarchy of Primitive

The modeler uses geometric primitives described in two forms—parametric and implicit—and grouped in a hierarchical way by groups of affine transformations. An example of a primitive hierarchy, in the scene description language, can be seen next.

321a   ⟨*hier scn* 321a⟩≡
```
    hier {
            transform { translate = { .5, .5, 0}},
            group {
                    transform { zrotate = .4 },
                    obj = sphere{ },
                    transform { translate = {.2, 0, 1}},
                    group {
                            transform{ scale = {2, 0.4, 1}},
                            obj = sphere{ radius = .1} } }
    };
```

19.3.2   Rendering by the Painter's Method

The renderer zsort uses the painter's method to determine the visible surfaces. The illumination uses the diffuse model with Gouraud interpolation. The global data structures
z and g store, respectively, a sorted list of scene polygons and the data for the Gouraud
interpolation of the current polygon.

```
static Scene *s;
static Object *o;
static Matrix4 mclip, mdpy;
static RContext *rc;
static List *z = NULL;
static GouraudData *g;
```

The main program reads the scene data, initializes the structures, and performs polygon
clipping and elimination. The polygons in the field of view of the camera are sorted in Z
and rasterized.

321b   ⟨*zsort* 321b⟩≡
```
    int main(int argc, char **argv)
    {
      Poly *l, *p, *c = poly_alloc(3);
      Item *i;
      init_sdl();
      s = scene_read();
      init_render();
      for (o = s->objs; o != NULL; o = o->next) {
        for (l = prim_uv_decomp(o->u.prim, 1.); l != NULL; l = l->next) {
          p = poly_transform(prim_polys(o->u.prim, l), mclip);
          if (!is_backfacing(p, v3_unit(v3_scale(-1, poly_centr(p)))))
            hither_clip(VIEW_ZMIN(s->view), p, z_store, plist_free);
        }
      }
      z = z_sort(z);
```

```
  for (i = z->head; i != NULL; i = i->next) {
    gouraud_shade(c, P(i), N(i), s->view->center, rc, M(i));
    p = poly_homoxform(S(i),mdpy);
    scan_poly(p, gouraud_paint, gouraud_set(g,s->img));
  }
  img_write(s->img, "stdout", 0);
  exit(0);
}
```

Defines:
    main, used in chunks 313, 317, and 318c.
Uses **g** 313, **init_render** 316c 319b 322b, **init_sdl** 316b 319c 322a, **prim_polys** 323a, and **z_store** 322c.

The routine `init_sdl` registers the operators of the scene description language.

322a   ⟨*sdl zsort* 322a⟩≡

```
  void init_sdl(void)
  {
    lang_defun("scene", scene_parse);
    lang_defun("view", view_parse);
    lang_defun("dist_light", distlight_parse);
    lang_defun("plastic", plastic_parse);
    lang_defun("primobj", obj_parse);
    lang_defun("sphere", sphere_parse);
  }
```

Defines:
    init_sdl, used in chunks 315, 318c, and 321b.

The routine `init_render` initializes the global data structures.

322b   ⟨*init zsort* 322b⟩≡

```
  void init_render(void)
  {
    mclip = m4_m4prod(s->view->C, s->view->V);
    mdpy = m4_m4prod(s->view->S, s->view->P);
    z = new_list();
    g = NEWSTRUCT(GouraudData);
    rc_sset(rc = NEWSTRUCT(RContext), s->view, s->lights, s->img);
  }
```

Defines:
    init_render, used in chunks 315, 318c, and 321b.
Uses **g** 313.

The routine `z_store` stores a polygon in the z list.

322c   ⟨*zstore* 322c⟩≡

```
  void z_store(Poly *l)
  {
    Zdatum *d = NEWSTRUCT(Zdatum);
    d->zmax = MIN(l->v[0].z, MIN(l->v[1].z, l->v[2].z));
```

```
    d->l = 1;   d->o = o;
    append_item(z, new_item(d));
  }
```
Defines:
z_store, used in chunk 321b.

The macros below are used to access the list of the polygon attributes:

```
#define S(I)  (((Zdatum *)(I->d))->l)
#define P(I)  (((Zdatum *)(I->d))->l->next)
#define N(I)  (((Zdatum *)(I->d))->l->next->next)
#define M(I)  (((Zdatum *)(I->d))->o->mat)
#define SL(L) (l)
#define PL(L) (l->next)
#define NL(L) (l->next->next)
```

The routine prim_polys creates triangles with the position and the normal of the surface points of the primitive.

323a ⟨prim polys 323a⟩≡
```
    Poly *prim_polys(Prim *s, Poly *p)
    {
      int i; Poly *l = plist_alloc(3, p->n);
      for (i = 0; i < p->n; i++) {
        PL(l)->v[i] = SL(l)->v[i] = prim_point(s, p->v[i].x, p->v[i].y);
        NL(l)->v[i] = prim_normal(s, p->v[i].x, p->v[i].y);
      }
      return l;
    }
```
Defines:
prim_polys, used in chunk 321b.

For example, the command zsort < pr.scn > pr.ras generates an image of the scene with two spheres, described in the file prim.scn (shown below).

323b ⟨prim scn 323b⟩≡
```
    scene{
            camera = view {
                    from = {0, 0, -2.5}, at = {0, .5, 0}, up = {0,1,0}, fov = 90},
            light = dist_light {direction = {0, 1, -1} },
            object = primobj{
                    material = plastic {  ka = .2, kd = 0.8, ks = 0.0 },
                    shape = sphere { center = {0, 0, 0}}},
            object = primobj{
                    material = plastic {  ka = .2, kd = 0.8, ks = 0.0 },
                    shape = sphere { center = {2, 2, 2}}},
    };
```

Figure 19.3 shows the rendering of the scene: image prim.ras.

Figure 19.3. Rendering spheres by Z-sort.

19.4   Projects

In this section we will specify several projects that integrate the libraries developed throughout the book. The modeling and rendering programs are based in the architecture of Systems A, B, and C discussed in the previous section.

19.4.1   Programs for Rendering Images

Develop a program for rendering images using the libraries GP, COLOR, and IMAGE. The program should accept files in the rasterfile format of the following types:

- Raw gray scale,

- Raw true color (RGB),

- Raw indexed color,

- RLE compressed gray scale,

- RLE compressed indexed color.

The program should still be capable of displaying both the image and the associated color map.

The following windowing system events should be managed by the program: *Window Exposure Event* and *Window Resize*. The test images, "Mandrill" and "Lenna," are shown in Figure 19.4.

Figure 19.4. Test images "Mandrill" (left) and "Lenna" (right). (See Plate VII.)

19.4.2 Modeling System

Develop one of the basic modeling systems and implement at least one of the options from the lists of possible extensions. The basic systems described in the previous sections are

- Generative modeling,

- CSG modeling,

- Modeling by primitives.

In every system, an engine should be included for the specification of object attributes (e.g., name, color, material, etc.).

The system should be tested with a nontrivial example. To do so,

1. Construct a reasonably complex object with the modeler,

2. Explain how the object was produced,

3. Discuss the difficulties you found.

Generative modeling.

1. Include rendering of three orthogonal (XYZ) views.

2. Include interactive capabilities. The user should be able to draw a curve on the screen and generate a revolution surface from this curve.

3. Include the possibility of editing the curve, with the following operations: move a vertex, and append and eliminate vertices. These changes should appear on the current surface.

4. Include other types of generative models, besides surfaces of revolution. For instance, extrusion, twist, bend, and taper.

5. Include support for a command language integrated with the interactive options.

GSG modeling.

1. Include rendering of three orthogonal (XYZ) views.

2. Include transformations ("csg_transform" operator). The user should be able to group the primitives and transform them;

3. Include interactive capability. The user should be able to select and move primitives or groups of primitives.

4. Include the rendering of the CSG tree and the possibility of manipulating its structure. The user should be able to create and to edit the CSG structure in the interactive graphics mode.

5. Include capability of calculating object properties (e.g., volume, etc.).

6. Include support for a command language integrated with the interactive options.

Primitive-based modeling.

1. Include rendering of three orthogonal (XYZ) views and an auxiliary view.

2. Include editing commands, such as create, delete, rename, undo, select, etc.

3. Include the following primitives: box, cone, cylinder, torus, and superquadrics. Primitive instances should be identified by a symbolic name and have a transformation associated with them. The user should be able to modify all the parameters of an object after it is created.

4. Include groups of objects. Groups should be also identified by a name. The group hierarchy should be rendered in an auxiliary window.

Modeling of articulated objects.

1. Include the primitive cylinder.

2. Include support for articulated joints (ball-pivot type).

3. Include cinematic sequences.

19.4.3 Rendering System

Develop one of the basic rendering systems and implement at least one of the options of the list of extensions. The basic systems described in the previous sections are:

☐ Rendering by scanline,

☐ Rendering by ray tracing,

☐ Rendering by the painter's method.

The system should be tested with a nontrivial example. Produce images to demonstrate the particular characteristics of the renderer.

Write a technical report with an analysis of the program operation. The work should cover the following points: (1) based on the program execution profile (profiling), identify and explain the bottlenecks of the algorithm; (2) discuss options to accelerate the program.

Rendering by scan-line.

1. Include global illumination using radiosity for preprocessing.

2. Include acceleration for progressive radiosity: adaptive refinement.

3. Include implicit primitives and CSG models.

Rendering by ray tracing.

1. Include global illumination with recursive ray tracing.

2. Include a ray tracing acceleration method.

3. Include polygonal objects.

Rendering by the painter's method.

1. Include texture mapping.

2. Include illumination mapping.

3. Include 3D procedural textures.

4. Include level-of-detail (LOD) for acceleration.

5. Use reverse polygon painting for better efficiency.

Bibliography

[Aho and Ullman 79] A. Aho and J. Ullman. *Principles of Compiler Design*. Addison-Wesley, 1979.

[Atherton et al. 78] P. Atherton, K. Weiler, and D. Greenberg. "Polygon Shadow Generation." *Computer Graphics (SIGGRAPH '78 Proceedings)* 12:3 (1978), 275–281.

[Barrow 02] John D. Barrow. *The Constants of Nature: From Alpha to Omega—The Numbers that Encode the Deepest Secrets of the Universe*. New York: Pantheon Books, 2002.

[Blinn and Newell 76] James F. Blinn and Martin E. Newell. "Texture and Reflection in Computer Generated Images." *Communications of the ACM* 19:10 (1976), 542–547.

[Bouknight and Kelly 70] W. J. Bouknight and K. C. Kelly. "An Algorithm for Producing Half-Tone Computer Graphics Presentations with Shadows and Movable Light Sources." In *Proc. AFIPS JSCC*, 36, 36, pp. 1–10. New York: ACM, 1970.

[Carpenter 84] Loren Carpenter. "The A-buffer, an Antialiased Hidden Surface Method." *Computer Graphics (SIGGRAPH '84 Proceedings)* 18:3 (1984), 103–108.

[Clark 82] James H. Clark. "The Geometry Engine: A VLSI Geometry System for Graphics." *Computer Graphics (SIGGRAPH '82 Proceedings)* 16:3 (1982), 127–133.

[Cook and Torrance 81] R. L. Cook and K. E. Torrance. "A Reflectance Model for Computer Graphics." *Computer Graphics (SIGGRAPH '81 Proceedings)* 15:3 (1981), 307–316.

[Cook et al. 87] Robert L. Cook, Loren Carpenter, and Edwin Catmull. "The Reyes Image Rendering Architecture." *Computer Graphics (SIGGRAPH '87 Proceedings)*, pp. 95–102.

[Crow 82] F. C. Crow. "A More Flexible Image Generation Environment." *Computer Graphics (SIGGRAPH '82 Proceedings)* 16:3 (1982), 9–18.

[Fuchs et al. 83] H. Fuchs, G. D. Abram, and E. D. Grant. "Near Real-Time Shaded Display of Rigid Objects." *Computer Graphics (SIGGRAPH '83 Proceedings)* 17:3 (1983), 65–72.

[Gomes and Velho 95] Jonas Gomes and Luiz Velho. *Computação Gráfica: Imagem*. IMPA-SBM, 1995.

[Gomes and Velho 97] Jonas Gomes and Luiz Velho. *Image Processing for Computer Graphics*. New York: Springer-Verlarg, 1997.

[Gomes and Velho 98] Jonas Gomes and Luiz Velho. *Computação Gráfica: Volume 1*. IMPA-SBM, 1998.

[Gomes et al. 96] J. Gomes, L. Darsa, B. Costa, and L. Velho. "Graphical Objects." *The Visual Computer* 12 (1996), 269–282.

[Gomes et al. 12] Jonas Gomes, Luiz Velho, and Mario Costa Sousa. *Computer Graphics: Theory and Practice.* Boca Raton, FL: CRC Press, 2012.

[Heckbert and Hanrahan 84] Paul S. Heckbert and Pat Hanrahan. "Beam Tracing Polygonal Objects." *Computer Graphics (SIGGRAPH '84 Proceedings)* 18:3 (1984), 119–127.

[MAGI 68] MAGI. "3-D Simulated Graphics Offered by Service Bureau." *Datamation* 14 (1968), 69.

[Malacara-Hernandez 02] D. Malacara-Hernandez. *Color Vision and Colorimetry: Theory and Applications.* Bellingham, WA: SPIE Press, 2002.

[Newell et al. 72a] Martin E. Newell, R. G. Newell, and T. L. Sancha. "A New Approach to the Shaded Picture Problem." In *Proc. ACM Nat. Conf.*, p. 443, 1972.

[Newell et al. 72b] Martin E. Newell, R. G. Newell, and T. L. Sancha. "A Solution to the Hidden Surface Problem." In *Proceedings of the ACM annual conference - Volume 1, ACM '72*, pp. 443–450. New York: ACM, 1972. Available online (http://doi.acm.org/10.1145/800193.569954).

[Phong 75] B. T. Phong. "Illumination for Computer Generated Pictures." *Communications of the ACM* 18:6 (1975), 311–317.

[Polyanin and Manzhirov 98] A. D. Polyanin and A. V. Manzhirov. *Handbook of Integral Equations.* Boca Raton, FL: CRC Press, 1998.

[Requicha 80] A. A. G. Requicha. "Representations for Rigid Solids: Theory, Methods, and Systems." *ACM Computing Surveys* 12 (1980), 437–464.

[Roth 82] S. D. Roth. "Ray Casting for Modelling Solids." *Comput. Graphics and Image Process. (USA)* 18 (1982), 109–144.

[Shumacker et al. 69] R. A. Shumacker, R. Brand, M. Gilliland, and W. Sharp. "Study for Applying Computer-Generated Images to Visual Simulation." Report AFHRL-TR-69-14, U.S. Air Force Human Resources Lab., 1969.

[Smith and Lyons 96] Alvy Ray Smith and Eric Ray Lyons. "HWB: A More Intuitive Hue-Based Color Model." *Journal of Graphics Tools* 1:1 (1996), 3–17.

[Smith 81] Alvy Ray Smith. "Color Tutorial Notes." Technical Report No. 37 37, Lucasfilm, 1981.

[Strichartz 94] R. Strichartz. *A Guide to Distribution Theory anFourier Transforms.* Boca Raton, FL: CRC Press, 1994.

[Sutherland and Hodgman 74] Ivan Sutherland and Gary W. Hodgman. "Reentrant Polygon Clipping." *Communications of the ACM* 17 (1974), 32–42.

[Sutherland et al. 74] I. E. Sutherland, R. F. Sproull, and R. A. Shumacker. "A Characterization of Ten Hidden Surface Algorithms." *ACM Computing Surveys* 6 (1974), 1–55.

[Torrance and Sparrow 76] K. Torrance and E. Sparrow. "Theory for Off-Specular Reflection from Roughened Surfaces." *J. Optical Soc. America* 57 (1976), 1105–1114.

[Warnock 69a] J. Warnock. "A Hidden-Surface Algorithm for Computer Generated Half-Tone Pictures." Technical Report TR 4–15, NTIS AD-733 671, University of Utah, Computer Science Department, 1969.

[Warnock 69b] John Warnock. "A Hidden Surface Algorithm for Computer Generated Halftone Pictures." Ph.D. thesis, University of Utah, 1969.

[Watkins 70] G. S. Watkins. "A Real-Time Visible Surface Algorithm." Report UTEC-CS-70-101, Dept. Comput. Sci., Univ. Utah, Salt Lake City, UT, 1970.

[Weiler and Atherton 77] K. Weiler and K. Atherton. "Hidden Surface Removal Using Polygon Area Sorting." *Computer Graphics (SIGGRAPH '77 Proceedings)* 11:2 (1977), 214–222.

Index